ELIOT TO DERRIDA

Eliot to Derrida

The Poverty of Interpretation

John Harwood
Reader in English
Flinders University of South Australia

St. Martin's Press   New York

St. Martin's Press, Scholarly and Reference Division,
175 Fifth Avenue, New York, N.Y. 10010

First published in the United States of America in 1995

Printed in Great Britain

ISBN 0–312–12558–5 (cloth)
ISBN 0–312–12559–3 (pbk.)

Library of Congress Cataloging-in-Publication Data
Harwood, John, 1946–
Eliot to Derrida : the poverty of interpretation / John
Harwood.
p. cm.
Includes bibliographical references and index.
ISBN 0–312–12558–5 (cloth). — ISBN 0–312–12559–3 (pbk.)
1. Eliot, T. S. (Thomas Stearns), 1888–1965—Criticism and
interpretation—History. 2. Pound, Ezra, 1885–1972—Criticism
and interpretation—History. 3. American poetry—20th century—History
and criticism—Theory, etc. 4. Eliot, T. S. (Thomas Stearns),
1888–1965. Waste land. 5. Modernism (Literature)—United States.
6. Derrida, Jacques. I. Title.
PS3509.L43Z68165 1995
801′ .95′0904—dc20   94–41943
                                                            CIP

To Robin

Contents

Acknowledgements

Chapter 2 was first published, in a slightly different form, in *Ezra Pound in Multiple Perspective*, ed. Andrew Gibson (Macmillan, 1993), and some passages from the prologue appeared in an essay in *Island* magazine (Hobart, Spring 1992).

I thank the Flinders University of South Australia for granting me study leave and financial support towards this book, and the staff of Flinders University Library for their assistance.

I am indebted, on many points, to Louis Menand's work, both on T. S. Eliot and on the problems of institutionalised criticism, and am grateful to him for permission to quote from his chapter on Eliot in *Modernism and the New Criticism*, Volume 7 of the forthcoming *Cambridge History of Literary Criticism*.

Warm thanks to Murray Bramwell and Michael Meehan for their friendship and encouragement, and, once again, to Deirdre Toomey and Warwick Gould, who have lived with this project as long as I have. And, most of all, to Robin Haines; without her love, good judgement and constant companionship, I doubt that I would ever have begun this book, and I would certainly never have finished it.

Prologue

Because I have profess'd to be a most devoted Servant of all *Modern* Forms: I apprehend some curious *Wit* may object against me, for proceeding thus far in a Preface, without declaiming, according to the Custom, against the Multitude of Writers whereof the whole Multitude of Writers most reasonably complains.

Swift, A Tale of a Tub

'Modernism is not a meaningful category of literary history or art history. It's a feather bed for critics and professors, an endlessly renewable pretext for scholars to hold conferences, devise special numbers, and gloss one another's works into powder.... The time has come for a definitive polemic called "The Poverty of Modernism".'

Roger Shattuck[1]

I

The 'crisis in English studies', in its present form, is often said to have begun in the 1960s, with the rapid expansion of theory, cultural studies, Marxist and feminist criticism, and the associated challenges to the traditional canon. In *Professing Literature* (1987), Gerald Graff presents the history of academic literary studies in America from its inception as 'a tale ... of a series of conflicts that have been masked by their very failure to find visible institutional expression',[2] but there is, as he would acknowledge, nothing masked about the present furore. In the 1950s, it was still possible to talk about 'criticism' as a homogeneous activity, internal conflicts notwithstanding; by the mid-1970s, this was no longer possible. Though traditionalists sometimes portray theory as a virulent French disease invading the previously healthy organs of criticism, the 1960s mark, not the sudden disruption of a harmonious enterprise, but the point at which the lid finally blew off the institutional pressure-cooker.

Complaints about the bad state of academic criticism, and in particular interpretive criticism, had become increasingly vociferous from the late 1940s onwards, as the critical population entered a phase of rapid expansion. Too many critics interpreting too few texts, was the refrain: literature is being buried in a slag-heap of commentary. Randall Jarrell, in 'The Age of Criticism', the best-known anti-critical polemic of the 1950s, was convinced that the critical tail was already wagging the literary dog. Politics aside, the 1960s was the decade in which academic criticism reached critical mass, so to speak; the decade in which the problems of overcrowding became impossible to ignore. In the United States alone, there were, by the early 1960s, over ten thousand literary critics working in universities and colleges, many of them under pressure to publish on a few hundred canonical authors, with much of the publication devoted to a small subset of the canonical texts.

Something had to give; and so far as twentieth-century literature was concerned, the effects of overcrowding were felt first, and most acutely, in the field of Eliot criticism. They were felt, somewhat later but just as acutely, by me at Cambridge in the early 1970s, where I was writing a doctoral thesis on the history of Eliot criticism – an experience from which, in his own phrase, I have never quite recovered. As an undergraduate, I had already discovered that the mysterious 'core' of Eliot's poetry seemed to dissolve whenever I tried to write about it, and that nothing I had read about Eliot seemed to capture it either. Writing a history of Eliot criticism, I thought, would ensure that I had something to write about, while enabling me to insinuate my own views (if I could only work out what they were) by arbitrating between his interpreters.

I set out with the intention of ranking the critics but instead became absorbed in the literary wars of 1914–18: Georgians, Imagists, Vorticists, Amygists, members of the 'Western School', *vers librists*, and rugged individualists slugging it out in the pages of the little magazines – and in trying to understand how Eliot had contrived to remain both above and central to the controversies. When I presented my supervisor with a first chapter based on the reviews of the early poems, arguing that Eliot hadn't been as harshly treated by the literary establishment as was generally supposed, I was left in no doubt that this was heresy. The reviews appeared to support my case, but I was sternly advised to 'consider the *silence* of so many established journals'.

So I went away and rewrote my chapter, dwelling as best I could on the hostile silence surrounding the not-so-consistently-hostile reviews I had collected. We had a similar exchange over the reviews of *The Waste Land*. Never mind the praise; never mind the *Dial* prize; think of all the people who would have condemned the poem if *they* had reviewed it. In an earlier lapse, I had argued that Eliot's poetry seemed oddly Romantic in flavour. Another heresy. 'He edited Dryden, you know', was the steely reply. This was clearly unanswerable, and I slunk away confounded (though I restored some of the argument after reading Frank Kermode's *Romantic Image*).

Even at the time, I was aware that these difficulties had something to do with the Gospel According to Leavis, as recorded in *New Bearings in English Poetry* (1932) and the afterword to the edition of 1950: that he, more or less single-handed, had rescued Eliot from incomprehending admirers and detractors alike. I had, looking back, embarked on much the same quest, but by the time I completed the project, I no longer believed in the One True Meaning I had hoped to track down. My commentary was largely aimed at rescuing Eliot from his interpreters; among the heroines and heroes of the story were those who had refused to give him the full treatment, dwelling rather upon the limits of interpretation. When one stood well back from the hundreds of exegeses of *The Waste Land*, the apparent differences seemed to dissolve. From a distance, they were nearly all 'right' in a vague sort of way, and wrong in a more fundamental way that I could not define. I did, however, coin some rules of thumb. The criticism I found illuminating was always tentative, exploratory, and incomplete, proceeding by way of hints and guesses rather than systematic explication. The 'full treatment', no matter what the mode or content, was invariably reductive and unhelpful, and the fuller the treatment, the more unhelpful it became. I was inclined to agree with Eliot's late assertion that 'a good deal of the value of an interpretation is – that it should be my own interpretation',[3] but my own attempts at commentary seemed equally unsatisfactory.

Though the interpretive enterprise seemed futile, others had accumulated a vast amount of information – as opposed to the pseudo-information retailed in the guise of studies in 'sources and influences', for which I had acquired a deep distrust – about

Eliot and his works. Stephen Stepanchev's discovery of Prufrock-Littau, wholesale furniture merchants in St Louis, c. 1900,[4] or J. Isaacs' report that a furrier named Bleistein had set up in the City around 1918,[5] or Robert A. Day's discovery that a Mr Eugenides had been among the clients at Lloyds' Bank,[6] seemed more il-luminating than reams of quasi-philosophical analysis.

Much of the exegesis, as Randall Jarrell had said in 1952, 'might just as well have been written by a syndicate of encyclopedias for an audience of International Business Machines':

> It is not only bad or mediocre, it is *dull*; it is, often, an aston-ishingly graceless, joyless, humourless, long-winded, niggling, blinkered, methodical, self-important, cliché-ridden, prestige-obsessed, almost-autonomous criticism. Who *can* believe that either readers or writers are helped by most of the great leaden articles on Great or currently fashionable writers . . .?[7]

My three years' immersion in it had inspired a level of hostility which is still hard to convey; the phrase 'academic criticism' had become an imprecation rather than a description. Within the pro-fession, the style castigated by Jarrell seemed to pass almost un-noticed; to me it seemed an absolute disqualification for the task in hand. It was not just a matter of leaden prose; orthodox ex-egesis, leaden or not, was a travesty of what it claimed to illumi-nate. Surely no poet, no writer with a spark of imagination, ever sat down to encode platitudes in a complex symbolic language invented solely to ensure that only professional interpreters could recover them. Nor, I was convinced, did poets work with 'sources and influences' in ways remotely resembling those attributed to them by the exegetes who, in a kind of reverse alchemy, had reinvented their subject in their own image.

The source of my disillusion was not a particular gang of vil-lains, but an identikit portrait, drawn from several hundred books and articles, of the worst that had been thought and said about Eliot. Though the archetypal Bad Critic could indeed be encoun-tered in the journals, he (being almost invariably male) seemed more like an unusually severe case of an endemic disease than a man dedicated to crimes against literature. In order to deal with the vast mass of postwar Eliot criticism, I had divided the inter-preters into two categories, 'orthodox' and 'radical', which really meant conformist and non-conformist. The orthodox (some 95 per cent of the population) went in for Eliot-worship, close paraphrase, scholarship of the sources-and-influences variety, and the extraction of morally improving sentiments (or philosophical systems) from the poems. And the more orthodox they were, the more closely they resembled the archetypal Hack, whereas all that the radicals had in common was that they weren't orthodox. They all seemed to be mavericks, outsiders in spirit even if they worked within the academy. Their essays did not conform to the standard template. They did not go in for 'full treatments'. Most, if not as fiery as Jarrell, were evidently depressed by the output of many of their colleagues. And above all, they could write.

Traditionalist critics, especially those who entered the profession before 1960, often seem pained and bewildered by the hostility of theorists. What have we done to deserve this? Why is the new generation bent on tearing down everything we worked for – including literature itself? Theory could never have attracted so many if the *ancien régime* had not become intolerable. My anger at what a friend later called 'the betrayal of literature in the universities' was by no means atypical. Many of my fellow graduate students seemed equally discontented. Frank Kermode has described the Cambridge English Faculty as 'exceptionally hostile to any kind of thought at all';[8] which was, as he says elsewhere, by no means true of all its members, but 'insofar as they functioned as a corporate body, they were philistine'.[9]

The doctrinaire Cantabrians among them functioned, indeed, as a sort of Groucho Marx club, an embodiment of the malaise I was struggling to identify. We were summoned, one afternoon, to an audience with a senior member. A student had proposed a thesis on an area of popular culture which was thought altogether *too* popular by some members of the Faculty. Let him apply to Sociology if he wanted to study comic strips. The paralysing sneer with which 'sociology' was pronounced (accompanied by a dutiful laugh from the nervous audience) summed up the collective relations between Faculty and students. One could see that Superman was, perhaps, stretching the canon a bit far, but it felt more like a show trial than a reasoned defence of traditional English studies.

Cambridge was then caught in something of a time-warp; one was never quite sure whether the year was supposed to be 1972 or 1932. All the great questions, so far as the dominant faction was concerned, had been decided; their collective task was to uphold the verities, add a few grace-notes, and encourage (or intimidate) their students into doing likewise. Poststructuralism had not yet arrived; structuralism was still being digested, at least by the more adventurous of my contemporaries, some of whom went on to join Kermode's celebrated seminar at University College London. The sort of hostility towards new thinking that one encountered at Cambridge was evidently a propelling force behind it: 'there was nobody there', says Kermode, 'who was willing to say *a priori*, this is a lot of garbage, which is of course what happened in Cambridge'.[10]

That seminar was not without its ironies; two of its leading lights, Jonathan Culler and Christopher Norris, have figured prominently in Kermode's recent reaction against theory. Culler's *Framing the Sign* (1988) is one of his principal targets in the prologue to *An Appetite for Poetry* (1989); reviewing Norris's *Spinoza and the Origins of Modern Critical Theory* (1991), he notes

> that this extremely interesting book enlists Spinoza's aid in a task that now occupies so many willing hands, the deconstruction, or destruction, of literature.... The question ... what is to become of literary criticism? – is really a question of how it can survive in a time when its most influential exponents are doing their best to abolish it....[11]

And in response to a conference devoted to his own work, he comes as close as politeness allows to condemning 'high-powered academic literary criticism' as worthless, if not actively destructive:

> I regard it as essential to 'keep the road open' – to maintain, somehow, a style of talking about literature (in classrooms and in literary journalism as well) which will preserve the reading public, and – quite simply – literature (which we must presume to recognise) from destruction. I regard this as by far the most important single element in the task of university teachers of literature; it is nothing less than the preservation of what we give that name. In their own time they can read what they like and deconstruct or neo-historicise what they like, but in the classroom they should be on their honour to make people know books well enough to understand what it is to love them. If they fail in that, either because they despise the humbleness of the task or because they don't themselves love literature, they are failures and frauds.[12]

Between those who regard *Of Grammatology* or *The Postmodern Condition* as more important than anything which (as they would put it) used to be called literature, and those like Kermode who insist that 'there is a valid experience of poetry',[13] no dialogue is possible:

> I have no religious experience but I claim to be familiar with the experience of poetry, and from that knowledge I infer that Norris isn't, so that like all who dismiss literature as a mysti-fied concept he is simply, though very intelligently, wrong. My knowledge will of course be discounted on the score that it is merely an inherited and false set of presuppositions, the con-sequence of brainwashing by devious or deluded purveyors of 'tradition'. Yet it is as well founded as Norris's confidence in Spinozan reason, and his certainty that politics provides the only terminus of sound theoretical discourse about writing.[14]

Brainwashing by deluded purveyors of 'tradition' is, however, a good description of the worst that Cambridge had to offer in 1972. I dwell on that experience, not to settle old scores, but to evoke something of the anger and contempt inspired by the old regime – in print and in person, as it were – because I don't think the present impasse can be understood in purely ideologi-cal, or even institutional, terms. My sojourn in the waste land of Eliot exegesis had provoked a deep, though confused hostility to any form of systematic interpretation; I had arrived at the stand-ard outsider's view of interpretive criticism as a parasitic growth on literature:

> The True Criticks are known by their Talent of swarming about the noblest Writers, to which they are carried meerly by In-stinct, as a Rat to the best Cheese, or a Wasp to the fairest Fruit. So, when the King is a Horse-back, he is sure to be the *dirtiest* Person of the Company, and they that make their court best, are such as *bespatter* him most.

Those of my contemporaries who went in for theory obviously did not subscribe to anything like this venerable, and to them very conservative opposition between literature and criticism. The idea that literature spoke directly to cultivated readers was built into the old-guard view of criticism as an occupation for gentlemen,

in which the canonical authors were regarded as honorary members of the Senior Common Room. A caricature, perhaps, but one
which could be encountered more or less verbatim at Cambridge,
where 'the tradition' was, in the worst cases, narrowly identified
with a virulent provincial snobbery. So far as the emergent theorists
were concerned, to argue that criticism was parasitic, or literature
transparent, was to surrender the field to the enemy. What was
needed, in their view, was a revolution which would transform
'criticism' and 'literature', and the relations presumed to exist
between them, expose the ideological foundations of the old criticism, and make it impossible for defenders of the status quo to
claim that literature was transparent to their own – or anyone
else's – reading of it.

No one – least of all, by the sound of it, the contributors to
Kermode's seminar – then supposed that theory would become
an academic orthodoxy as oppressive and intolerant as the one it
set out to challenge:

> it didn't seem discontinuous with the ordinary practice of liter-
> ary criticism, somehow. It didn't seem – although Stephen [Heath],
> I daresay, didn't see it in this light – that we were doing some-
> thing absolutely new; it was our kind of thing, only given a
> new and rather exciting dress, as it were. And now I see that's
> no longer a tenable view of it. . . .[15]

It's now hard to find anyone interested in literature, but outside
the ranks of the theorists, who doesn't feel that the cure has been
worse than the disease. The battle between traditionalists and
theorists has revolved around control of the canon and its interpretation; to counter the rhetoric of transparency, the theorists
developed the argument that interpretation is always, and ines-
capably, politicised. This, coupled to the assertion that literature
does not exist apart from interpretations of it, led more or less
inevitably to the position that 'literature' is an ideologically constituted category – the ideology being, in the more simplistic versions, that of the oppressive white males who had done most of
the writing and interpreting prior to the advent of theory.

Deconstruction could, as it were, defer the consequences of this
stance by enabling theorists to argue that 'literature' *always* sub-
verted the intentions of its authors by reinstating that which the

author had sought to exclude. But this sort of oppositional reading made sense – at least to its exponents – only while theory
remained at the margin. As the leading theorists began to assume distinguished chairs, and control of departments, and as
deconstructive reading became routine, its subversive air was bound
to fade. The argument that canonical texts, though complicit with
every form of oppression, nevertheless managed to smuggle in
the point of view of the oppressed, was bound to seem an increasingly convoluted mode of attack on the oppressors, and literature an increasingly redundant vehicle for the purpose. Once it
was possible to assert, from a position of institutional strength,
that theory had superseded literature, the wheel had come full
circle; doctrinaire theorists were now in a position to do to their
students what the old guard had done to them.

None of this, however, seemed likely to happen in 1972. I was
aware that some sort of critical liberation movement was under
way, but, as Kermode remarked, it didn't seem discontinuous with
the existing forms of close analysis. And that, in a way, was my
reservation about it. *Why* was the full treatment, whatever the
mode, invariably worse than the brief, exploratory comment? Why
was so much academic criticism so bad? And if systematic interpretation invariably falsified the experience of reading, then what
was the point of interpretation?

Back in Australia, attempting to teach poetry to first-year undergraduates, I noticed that many of them arrived with strong
convictions about the subject. A poem never meant what it said,
but always something else, which could only be divined by oc-
cult means. A spade in a poem was never a spade, or a digging
implement, or even a bloody shovel, but always a Symbol: of
Death, or Lost Love, or the Search for Meaning, so that one was
constantly saying, well – er – yes, sort of – but why a *spade*?
Somehow the object was always getting lost in the fog of the
Human Condition:

> A fortnight later, sense a single man
> upon the trampled scene at 2 a.m.
> insomnia-plagued, with a shovel

digging like mad, Lazarus with a plan
to get his own back, a plan, a stratagem
no newsman will unravel.

John Berryman,
'Op. post. no. 14'

The scene, a typical student commentary might say, 'symbolises the despair of modern man trapped in a meaningless world'. Wrong? If Cleanth Brooks could 'take the Dog' in *The Waste Land* as 'Humanitarianism', why couldn't the student take the shovel as 'a symbol of despair'? He or she could point to reams of professional commentary in precisely this vein. My lectures were resolutely directed against this sort of thing, but I was less clear about what they were directed towards. The sort of response I was looking for was more evocative than explanatory, dwelling on the atmosphere surrounding the frenzied figure in the graveyard, the quirkiness of the voice, blackly comic, suicidally exuberant. But if one pursued this to its logical conclusion, didn't it follow that the best commentary on the poem was, in fact, the poem?

There was no method, no set of rules one could teach that would enable anyone to see in advance that the poem was not flatly declarative, not a lecture on the Human Condition; and the best way of showing it was simply to read the poem aloud. We were running, at this stage, a series of exercises modelled on I. A. Richards' *Practical Criticism*; or, as a student later put it, 'doing crossword puzzles in the tutor's head'. (We were also replicating Richards' original error; most of what we called 'an understanding of the text' was in fact knowledge of the context, which was why the mature-age students usually did so much better.) There was a lot of talk about 'tone' and 'tact' and 'respecting the literal level', but it all felt somehow beside the point. Some students arrived with a feel for what we were talking about; those who didn't seldom seemed to acquire it as a result of our instruction. One could, with luck, instil a greater respect for syntax, but not, it seemed, an ear for voices. Various experiments were being tried in schools, such as encouraging students to relate their reading more directly to their own experience. This could produce some very evocative writing; it could also produce something along the lines of: 'Macbeth's tragic fate was just like what happened

to me and my mate Kevin last Saturday night when we got full
and pinched the old man's car and wrapped it round a stobie
pole.' General rules, again, did not seem to be much use.

Academic exegesis, I had decided, was a form of translation
which annihilated what it claimed to illuminate. Art undermined
the normality of 'normal', but then along came the exegetes and
undid the undermining, converting radical insights into tired old
philosophies, and visionary artists into responsible citizens. Literature – in the selective tradition attained by voting the full late
Sixties ticket – was subversive, not so much politically as metaphysically: it revealed the strangeness of the world, the abnor-
mality of the normal, the contours of the buried life. Blake and
Dostoievsky and Kafka and early Eliot, blended with a heady
brew of R. D. Laing, Jung, Nerval, Hesse, Castenada, Dylan, Pink
Floyd, Californian mysticism and controlled substances could take
us into the heart of light – or darkness. What we would do when
we got there was never entirely clear. What portion in the world
could the artist have, who had awakened from the common dream
only to have his or her vision of reality flattened and denatured
by academic critics? Not a lot, given that Berryman, Plath and
Lowell figured prominently in the syllabus.

The visionary gleam, like the purple flares and the blue denim
jackets, faded rapidly, but the dilemma remained. Reading Robert
Pirsig's *Zen and the Art of Motorcycle Maintenance*, I felt that here
at last was someone who knew the problem from the inside: the
anger, the obsession with the limits of orthodox analytical method,
and in particular, Phaedrus's loathing for aesthetics.

It wasn't any particular esthetician who produced this reaction
in him. It was all of them. It wasn't any particular point of
view that outraged him so much as the idea that Quality should
be subordinated to *any* point of view. The intellectual process
was forcing Quality into servitude, prostituting it. I think that
was the source of his anger.

He wrote in one paper, 'These estheticians think their subject is some kind of peppermint bonbon they're entitled to smack
their fat lips on; something to be devoured; something to be
intellectually knifed, forked and spooned up bit by bit with
appropriate delicate remarks and I'm ready to throw up. What
they smack their lips on is the putrescence of something they
long ago killed.'

Now, as the first step of the crystallisation process, he saw
that when Quality is kept undefined by definition, the entire
field called esthetics is wiped out ... completely disenfran-
chised ... kaput. By refusing to define Quality he had placed
it entirely outside the analytical process. If you can't define
Quality, there's no way you can subordinate it to any intellectual rule. The estheticians can have nothing more to say. Their
whole field, definition of Quality, is gone.

The thought of this completely thrilled him. It was like discovering a cancer cure. No more explanations of what art is.
No more wonderful critical schools of experts to determine ra-
tionally where each composer had succeeded or failed. All of
them, every last one of those know-it-alls, would finally have
to shut up. This was no longer just an interesting idea. This
was a dream.[16]

Not being in a position to shut up, I set out to construct, along
similar lines, a systematic account of what was wrong with academic interpretation. But in order to define what was wrong with
it, one had to talk about what was being falsified. And that could
not be done, not at any rate satisfactorily, in the idiom of academic debate. Later, I realised that my essential response to Eliot
had always been 'I wish I had said that', rather than 'What does
this mean?'. As usual in such cases, I couldn't write the poems I
wanted to write until I had got him out of my system (or so I
believed) by way of the inevitably violent reaction. Perhaps in
consequence, the anti-critical project began to look more and more
cumbersome, and was gradually displaced by other interests.

II

Roger Shattuck's story, 'The Poverty of Modernism', begins with
a chance meeting between teacher and former student on the night-
train to New York. Edgar, chairman of the comparative literature
programme at the University of Pennsylvania, is on his way to
the Modern Language Association's annual convention to deliver
a paper, with which he is deeply dissatisfied, on modernism. Chuck,
the ex-student, has declined the offer of a place in the Ph.D. programme and joined a publishing firm, because he 'couldn't stand
the way literary works got lined up and systematised and left

behind in most graduate courses – sometimes just ignored in favour of criticism and critical theory'. In a Socratic reversal of roles,
Chuck draws Edgar into declaring what he has known all along:

> 'Modernism is not a period, like the Victorian Era. It's not a
> proper school or movement, like Surrealism. It has no geographi-
> cal character or associations, like *Der Blaue Reiter*. It serves no
> heuristic purpose, like the Enlightenment or Romanticism. It
> suggests no stylistic practice, like Baroque or Imagism. It's the
> weakest term we've had since Symbolism, which even Verlaine
> mocked by spelling it with a *c* and an *a*. But best of all . . .
> modernism embodies a disabling contradiction. It has cancer.
> The only general characteristic of the modern era is the cel-
> ebration of individual experience, of particular feelings in par-
> ticular circumstances, not repeatable. Every epiphany is *sui generis*.
> The term "modernism" tries to make a category of items that
> will not fit into a category . . .'

I began this book with the intention of writing a revisionist
history of 'the modernist movement in literature', much along
the lines indicated by Roger Shattuck. My themes were to be diversity and discontinuity; the aim, to demonstrate that 'modernism' is not a meaningful category of literary history. But it soon
became apparent that no history of the upheavals of 1909–22 (or
1870–1930, for that matter) would be adequate to the task. 'Modernism', in any of the reified versions now deployed in academic
debate, did not exist in 1909, or 1922; it is an academic invention
of the 1960s and after, retrospectively imposed on the works and
doctrines it supposedly illuminates.

The problem is straightforward: any 'modernism' broad enough
to embrace the variety of literary experiment in the first quarter
of this century turns out to be nothing more than a portmanteau
label, a synonymn for 'innovative or experimental writing'. Once
reified, it inevitably becomes a straitjacket: the diverse history of
the period has to be flattened and denatured in order to justify
the existence of the concept. Over the last three decades, so much
explanatory and evaluative power has been invested in 'modernism' and 'postmodernism' that, according to many academic critics
and theorists, twentieth-century literature amounts to a two-party
system in which all serious writing must belong in one or the
other category. Both terms have now been reified to the point

where literary works are frequently interpreted as products of cultural forces called 'modernism' and 'postmodernism'. In its most aggressive form, this style of explanation is founded on a myth of schismatic progress, from an undifferentiated 'tradition' to 'modernism' to 'postmodernism', in which criticism, reborn as 'theory', finally displaces literature as a primary source of insight into the human (or 'posthuman') condition.

The problem of 'modernism', therefore, cannot be understood apart from its institutional context, and in pursuing it I have ended up writing a partial and polemical history of interpretive criticism in the academy. Though the ground has been heavily trampled, much of the debate has been conducted in general theoretical terms, arguing the merits and demerits of competing theories and methodologies. I see no point in tackling the issues at that level: critical practice seldom conforms to the theories on which it is supposedly founded, and much of what passes for theory amounts, in practice, to dogma. This book is a study of what critics actually do, rather than what they claim to be doing. It is built around a hierarchy of related topics: the interpretation of Eliot's poetry, and in particular *The Waste Land*; the problems caused by the reification of 'modernism'; the conflicts between New Critical theory and interpretive practice; the emergence of poststructuralist 'theory' as a network of personality cults, and the role of institutional and professional imperatives in determining some of the key trends in mainstream interpretive criticism since the 1930s.

It is only a little over half a century since criticism was first established as an identifiable academic discipline, distinct from philology and literary history. But in order to qualify as 'research', the interpretation and evaluation of literary works had to be presented as a progressive, cumulative, and theoretically-grounded activity which, in its institutionalised form, could best be conducted by university-trained professionals. The best and most concise analysis of the consequences is Louis Menand's 'Lost Faculties' (1990). Criticism, as he observes, 'became academically respectable not because the university was persuaded to modify its notion of what counts as knowledge, but because criticism was modified to meet the institutional requirements of the university':

So long as the interpreter of a text could demonstrate that his or her reading was not a mere subjectivist appreciation by grounding that reading in a theory of literature or of criticism, then the interpretation could count as a contribution to knowledge. And since the era of the New Criticism, every new way of criticising literary texts has earned academic acceptance by exactly the same strategy: by presenting itself as a theory.

The modern university system has produced remarkable achievements in scholarly research, an activity for which it is spectacularly well equipped. But mainstream academic criticism, if we take criticism in something like Arnold's sense, has been, on the whole, inferior to the criticism of literary journalists, social and political commentators, other independent thinkers, and academic mavericks – writers whose work is generally more widely read, more timely and useful, better written, and intellectually braver than the criticism produced in the academy.

For most of the academic world is a vast sea of conformity, and every time a new wave of theory and methodology rolls through, all the fish try to swim in its direction.[17]

And for this conformity, the pseudo-scientific research model is principally to blame. The reification of 'modernism' is a paradigm case: the greater the explanatory power attributed to an 'ism', a critical theory, or a methodology, the more transparent literature must be made to appear to it. No theory or methodology can cope with the sheer variety of literature; therefore literature has to be straitjacketed to justify the existence of the methodology. Ostensibly, the aim is to reach a better understanding of literature, or some aspect of it, but the better understanding invariably turns out to be that which justifies the application of the theory. Gerald Graff describes mid-century explication as a 'protection racket' which 'subtly and unintentionally worked to protect literature from criticism':

Critical explication was, if anything, even more prone than the old scholarship had been to a kind of guild mentality where it is assumed as the natural course of things that any specialist in a writer or period will be a *promoter* of that writer or period. . . . Whereas scholarly accumulations of sources, influences, and other information had functioned as a silent endorsement, explication seemed to be an even more authentic endorsement, claiming as it did to lay bare the innermost structure of the work. Then, too, the very stockpiling of explications came to seem a prima facie proof of a work's complexity and therefore of its value.[18]

I would reverse the emphasis: explication had to be protected
from criticism in order to justify the stockpiling of explications.
There was, as Graff later acknowledges, nothing subtle about the
protectionism:

> Having established unprecedented levels of scholarly and critical
> productivity, departments did not want to hear that there might
> be no one uniquely literary mode of language, susceptible to
> infinite reexamination in text after text. An industry on the move,
> generating 'fruitful new approaches,' does not want to be told
> that its major successes may have been rigged.[19]

The same applies to every critical theory or methodology known
to me which has been adopted for the purposes of mass-produced
interpretation, from I. A. Richards to the present. Intellectual histories of academic criticism, in which one methodological or theoretical advance gives way to another, are invariably the work of
insiders more or less in thrall to the idea of progress. In the
poststructuralist version propounded by Jonathan Culler, J. Hillis
Miller, Paul de Man and others, literary history is subsumed, along
with that of criticism, into the eventual triumph of theory; in the
opposing version, espoused by traditionalists such as René Wellek
and M. H. Abrams, a Golden Age of Academic Criticism, from I.
A. Richards through to the 1960s, gives way to an age of theoretical brass. Both sides are intent on shoring up the authority of
their own professional factions while undermining that of their
opponents.

Gerald Graff's *Professing Literature*, to which I am indebted on
many points, is the best full-length institutional history to date,
but it still seems to me too much an inside view. His solution to
the problem of endemic conflict within the profession is to teach
the conflicts, but that amounts to saying that whatever mess the
profession happens to have got itself into at the moment should
determine the curriculum. No outsider, so far as I know, has ever
written a defence of institutionalised interpretation, whereas the
objections of non-professional readers would fill a large anthology. At many points in the writing of this book, I have found
myself imagining two incompatible readers: the one an amateur
in the true sense of the word, who reads for love, likes sentences,
as Annie Dillard says, and needs no persuading; the other a dedicated professional critic who *can't* be persuaded. It is impossible

to address them simultaneously, and that impossibility is, at least implicitly, one of my central themes.

Roger Shattuck's story concludes with Chuck commissioning Edgar to write a definitive polemic called 'The Poverty of Modernism', but neither of them asks, 'definitive for whom?' 'I can just see the programme of your panel', says Chuck:

> 'Modernism and the Strategies of Desire.' 'Tolstoy, or the Closet Modernist.' 'The Modern, Modernism, Post-Modernism, Modernismo, Modernisation, Modernité, Merdonité – a Trial Taxonomy'. . . . it's all make-work, an exercise in nomenclature with no grounding in compelling events or works.

That was written over a decade ago. Papers actually delivered at the 1993 MLA convention included: 'Star Power: or, how to (De)Flower the Rectal Brain: the Increments and Excrements of "Influence" in *Dorian Gray* and *Edward II*'; 'Teledildonics: Virtual Lesbians in the Fiction of Jeanette Winterson'; 'Autophagy and the Logic of the Absolute Fragment'; and 'Fuck Your Gender'.[20]

Imagine, for a moment, the definitive conference on literary modernism, convened by the MLA, with the usual twelve thousand members in attendance. Everyone, from the most eminent professor to the humblest graduate student, is there. The main conference-hall is packed; every available room in the building has been commandeered and wired into the audiovisual network for the opening address. The chairman approaches the microphone. He looks pale; his suit is rumpled; he has evidently not slept well. He has a book in his hand.

'My fellow scholars: I bring you bad – indeed the worst possible – news. This book was delivered to my suite yesterday morning. It is called *The Poverty of Modernism*. Immediately upon finishing it, I ordered a further hundred copies by express delivery. Every senior member of the panel has read the book; we have conferred all night; we are unanimous. Modernism is not a meaningful category of literary history. It is nothing more than a pretext for conferences. Our subject does not exist. We can see no honourable course but to present you all with complimentary copies of *The Poverty of Modernism*, and declare this conference closed. May I suggest, in conclusion, that in seeking a new field of scholarly endeavour you do *not* turn to postmodernism? I understand that *The Poverty of Postmodernism*, by the same author, will shortly be published. And now, if you will excuse me . . .'.

It is obviously inconceivable that a hundred distinguished professors could agree about anything beyond the need to keep the
show on the road. The audience would include linguists,
semioticians, literary and cultural historians old and new, feminists,
old-style New Critics, Afrocentrists, Derridareans, Foucaultians,
Lacanians, Marxists, Bakhtinians, Lyotardians, neo-Marxists, post-
Marxists, New Historicists, and devotees of numerous other persuasions that don't immediately spring to mind. Any polemic, on
any subject, that was judged definitive by one faction would necessarily be condemned by others as bourgeois totalisation, postmodernist trifling, or just plain incomprehensible.

Not present at the conference, however, would be a much larger
group of people, who read widely in literature and a great deal
else besides. Many of them are engaged in teaching literature at
secondary or tertiary level; many more are undergraduate or
postgraduate students, from teenagers to nonogenarians. Many
are also writers, amateur or professional, freelance or university-
based, journalists, diarists, poets, novelists, scriptwriters, docu-
mentary-makers, working in every imaginable form and publishing
in almost every imaginable outlet other than – with rare exceptions – specialist academic journals. They – along with the vast,
captive, student market – are the people who keep the quality
paperback publishers in business. They subscribe to, and sustain,
a great variety of quality periodicals – with the exception of the
specialist journals.

If a representative cross-section of this group were to attend
our hypothetical conference, they would find many of the papers
unintelligible, and the remainder, with rare exceptions, dull and
trivial. The process described as 'reading' by the participants would
be, for the most part, unrecognisable. One of the main items of
business would appear to be A's objections to B's critique of C's
hypothesis about what might happen if D's methodology were
applied to E's analysis of F's theory of interpretation, this being
the current 'state of the question'. Some of the participants could no
doubt be found talking about poems and novels in a familiar way,
but mostly after hours, in quiet corners, with a slightly furtive air.

The time, as Frank Kermode observes,

is long past when the Common Reader could expect to follow
the discourses of theoretical professors, and we have a rather

remarkable situation in which literary theorists would actually
be offended if it were suggested that they had any obvious
relation to common readers. They claim to be specialists, with
no more obligation to common readers than theoretical physi-
cists have. And so there is an ever-increasing supply of books
classified as literary criticism which few people interested in
literature, and not even all professionals, can read.[21]

An increasing proportion of the specialist output consists of disputes over the value and function of the industry, but whether
the disputant is a diehard traditionalist or a Foucaultian theorist,
one thing is clear: the future of civilisation is at stake. The traditionalist wants a return to sweetness and light; the Foucaultian
wants to sweep away the bourgeois hegemony; both are convinced
that their goal could be achieved by further publication if only
their opponents would desist.

One would hardly expect General Motors to condemn the internal combustion engine – not, at least, until the oil runs out.
General Motors would soon discover the virtues of renewable
energy if its customers refused to buy the current product, but
since academic critics and their apprentices are their own, and
frequently their only customers, the market analogy collapses. The
'oil' is fees and government subsidies, and it will run out, so far
as academic criticism is concerned, when the taxpayer is no longer
prepared to support it. Any disinterested defence will have to
come from outside the academy, and since the trend over the last
two decades has been to sever all links with the outside world,
the chances are not good. Northrop Frye, uneasily aware of the
problem in the mid-1950s, argued that

> [a] public that tries to do without criticism, and asserts that it
> knows what it wants or likes, brutalises the arts and loses its
> cultural memory.[22]

This is a civilisation-as-we-know-it argument, and the obvious
reply is that the vast bulk of the reading public have always done
without criticism, in anything like the sense intended, and now
have no choice but to do without it. The criticism which does
contribute to public interest in literature is precisely not the theory-
driven kind professionally valued by specialists and published in
books and referee journals which are read by no one outside the

profession, and only under protest by an increasing number within
it. Thus, when Stanley Fish insists that 'the profession' is the sole
arbiter of value in academic publication, he means, in fact, that
its only surviving *raison d'être* is personal and professional ad-
vancement.[23] His logic is indisputable: in so far as the product is
consumed only by other professionals, its value will be determined only by those with a direct interest in its survival.

Factional divisions are, in my view, trivial compared to the
differences between those who write only for other specialists and
those who seek a wider audience. Learning how not to write is a
strenuous business; it takes years of professional training to eliminate every trace of vitality, every spark of interest, from a style.
It begins in the graduate school, where the apprentice learns to
write dissertationese. Qualify this; tone down that; take account
of the following six possible objections; demonstrate your familiarity with the most recent theories and the associated jargon. Page
Smith describes the ethos:

> It was as a candidate for the Ph.D. at Harvard that I first en-
> countered the Cult of Dullness.... My professor ... warned
> me gently that, although he himself did not object to a well-
> written paper ... his colleagues might be put off. They might
> suspect that I was not really committed to dull writing (he didn't
> put it exactly that way) and thus not a suitable candidate for
> the Ph.D. I encountered the problem again when I sent my
> doctoral dissertation to a typist to have it typed up for presen-
> tation.... The typist called shortly to express her concern. It
> did not read like a Ph.D. Was I sure it would be acceptable?
> What was the problem? I asked. Well, she was enjoying read-
> ing it, and that made her uneasy on my account. She was con-
> cerned that it might not be accepted. It was not as dull as she
> felt it ought to be.[24]

Many supervisors enter into a similar conspiracy with the candidate: *I* don't want you to write like this, but the examiners....
The person who does want dissertationese is always somewhere
else, and always more powerful than those who don't want it.
Never mind, says the supervisor; when you turn it into a book
you can take all that out again. The examiners mark the thesis,
and *they* complain about the dissertationese. But now, it seems,
we must think of the specialist reviewers, upon whose judgement
that tenure application hangs.

The advisers' tune changes. The reviewers, it appears, will want even more jargon, more qualification, more caution, but never mind, when you've got tenure. . . . The reviewers, in due course, complain about the jargon and the qualification, but declare it a valuable contribution nonetheless. Our candidate now has tenure, but must keep publishing, and knows that only refereed publication counts. The referee journal editors, it seems, don't like a lot of the articles they print, but *they* have to reckon with what the other editors are doing. A reader for one such journal, some years back, told me that after wading through a heap of articles carefully tailored to the latest theoretical fashion, he complained that they were all – well – dreadful. 'I know,' replied the editor cheerfully, 'but if we wait for the good stuff, the boom will be over.'

The boom continues, but the good stuff has yet to arrive, so far as what Kermode calls 'the high-tech, jargoned, reader-alienating . . . modern product' is concerned.[25] The result is a situation in which many distinguished professional teachers of writing (which is, after all, what their students are examined on) are, in the eyes of everyone but themselves, among the worst professional writers in the business. Quality control, without anyone's having intended it to happen, is directed towards the *exclusion* of quality. The torrent of futile criticism in prestigious theoretical journals and university presses has not overwhelmed professional standards; it is propelled by them. Anyone who insists that the bulk of the output is high-quality product must ask: what does 'quality' mean if it is detectable only by the manufacturers? The same might be said of an old-style Soviet shoe factory: the occasional pair of decent shoes presumably slipped past the foreman, but that was hardly a tribute to the system.

These pressures are, obviously, endemic throughout the academy. But the effects on academic criticism are particularly striking, first because the pseudo-scientific research paradigm is uniquely inappropriate, and second because of the contrast with a long and continuing tradition of public criticism. Writing for other specialists seems to require something like a reversal of normal assumptions about one's audience. Of Stanley Fish's reader-response theory (Mark I), Frederick Crews remarks:

> Though Fish's theory was clever to a fault, the reader it invoked was a dunce – a Charlie Brown who, having had the syntactic football yanked away a hundred times, would keep

right on charging it with perfect innocence, never learning to
suspend judgement until he arrived at the poet's verb.[26]

The same applies to the incurably 'logocentric' (i.e. literal-minded,
unimaginative) reader invoked in deconstructive analysis. Orthodox academic interpretation, old- or new-style, generally requires
a straw person, or mug punter, to confirm the need for interpretive expertise. Few interpreters seem aware that anyone who can
get through a 200-page explication of *Four Quartets*, or a deconstructive analysis of 'The Purloined Letter', probably doesn't require their services in the first place.

III

In 1920, today's vast secondary literatures hardly existed; in Britain, the first critical Ph.D.s were rolling off the assembly line,
and to gain one, the candidate had only to choose a topic, read
some literature and write about it. The result was almost bound
to be 'an original contribution to knowledge', at least within the
meaning of the act. Fifty years later, a doctoral candidate reading
full-time for three years could not, in the case of some authors,
have read the entire secondary literature, let alone written anything. A few figures will illustrate the point. Alexander Nehamas
notes that by 1972, Kafka's *Metamorphosis* had already provoked
148 studies, which he describes as a 'flood of criticism'.[27] If this
(probable underestimate) is a flood, then Eliot criticism is a case
of *après moi, le déluge*. By 1965, some 2700 books and articles had
been devoted to Eliot and his works.[28] By the late 1970s, the esti-
mate had risen to 4319.[29] Rough extrapolation suggests that the
current total may exceed 10 000. Pound, in 1985, was towing at
least 5390 English-language books and articles in his wake.[30] By
the early 1970s, Yeats had already attracted at least 7500 contri-
butions,[31] with the current total approaching 15 000.[32] Alongside
lie other, equally vast accumulations of unpublished honours,
master's and doctoral theses.

The bulk of the output is the product of the last four decades,
following the rapid expansion of universities from the late 1940s
onwards. In the space of fifty years, the situation has changed
beyond recognition, from one in which the critic could sit down
and write with a fair certainty of saying something new, to one

apparently resembling that of Bertrand Russell's army of monkeys who, typing endlessly at random, eventually write all the books in the British Library (or Borges's Library) by chance. Yet, as any outsider, or maverick, who has tunnelled through a significant proportion of one of these print mountains will testify, the impression that everything must have been said is deceptive. The debates run as if on rails, rearranging the same points and deploying the same approaches over and over again, while all around lie unexplored areas.

This is not, however, the view from within. Northrop Frye argued in his 'Polemical Introduction' to *Anatomy of Criticism* that unless criticism was founded on 'a coherent and comprehensive theory of literature, logically and scientifically organised . . . the main principles of which are as yet unknown to us',

> the high percentage of sheer futility in all criticism should be honestly faced, for the percentage can only increase with its bulk, until criticising becomes, especially for university teachers, merely an automatic method of acquiring merit, like turning a prayer-wheel.[33]

Frank Kermode, reviewing a later book of Frye's in 1965, thought there was nothing for it but to acknowledge the futility:

> The one thing certain about modern criticism is that there is too much of it, and it is only rarely that one can say of a practitioner that he cannot safely be left unread.[34]

Randall Jarrell had reached a similar conclusion in 'The Age of Criticism'. Having no solution to offer, he dwelt bleakly upon the effects of overproduction. A torrent of bad criticism, he argued, was driving out not only the good, but literature itself.

> Criticism, which began by humbly and anomalously existing for the work of art, and was in part a mere by-product of philosophy and rhetoric, has now become, for a good many people, almost what the work of art exists for: the animals come up to Adam and Eve and are named – the end crowns the work.[35]

There is a certain amount of golden-age nostalgia here: many of his themes can be found in Pope and Swift; the essay could be

illustrated with a cartoon depicting two hairy characters peering
at the first rock drawing ('touchingly *primitive*, isn't it?'); and as
the most feared poetry-reviewer of his day, Jarrell was not well-
placed to condemn the excessive influence of criticism on mid-
century readers.[36] 'The Age of Criticism' is nevertheless prophetic
of later developments, as in his account of 'that strange sort of
Law French which the critic can now set up like a Chinese Wall
between himself and the lay (i.e. boreable) reader',[37] and above
all in his conviction that the relationship between artist and critic
was being inverted – at least in the eyes of the critics.

'Journals', said Pierre van den Burghe in 1970,

> are like proliferating repositories of academic night soil, which,
> far from fertilizing the ivory tower, slowly drown it in a stead-
> ily rising tide,[38]

an image redeployed by Page Smith twenty years later:

> If bad research (not technically 'bad' or methodologically bad
> but unimportant and largely irrelevant research) does not drive
> out good, it constantly threatens to bury the good in a vast
> pile of mediocrity.[39]

Iain McGilchrist made himself unpopular in 1982 by remarking
that the obvious solution to overcrowding was to do what the
motor registry does when it runs out of numbers:

> You simply begin again at the beginning, but *add a new letter*.
> In parallel fashion, all you need to give literary studies another
> ten years is to find a new methodology – let us call it Magnet-
> ism – and the Magnetic approach to Spenser, the Magnetic ap-
> proach to Dickens, are still to write. . . . The continual
> development of new methodologies will be a vital condition
> for the maintenance of a large number of academics – each con-
> demned to teach and publish something new – on a limited
> field of enquiry. The alternative, of genuinely original insights,
> is too unreliable, and is by definition an option confined to the
> creative few.[40]

This is more or less what happened in the ensuing decade (a
new methodology is now doing well if it lasts five years). 'By

definition' is, however, slippery: in so far as the definition is institutional, it is a tautology, whereas from the outsider's perspective, the 'creative few' may include persons apparently incapable of assembling a coherent paragraph.

Now that the shelves of the critical hypermarket are stocked with an ever-increasing variety of theories and methodologies, it is worth reconsidering the standard hierarchical model of literary studies: namely, the assumption that theory and interpretation are the *raison d'être* of the profession. The 1993 MLA convention programme, as John Sutherland remarks, provides

> no more telling statistic ... than the 70 sessions devoted to 'Literary Criticism and Theory' (by far the largest category) and the puny six devoted to 'Research and Bibliography', of which two take as their subject the chronically depressed status of bibliography in the profession.[41]

Though theorists and traditionalists disagree violently over the nature and purpose of interpretation, the hierarchy itself is not in dispute. Editing, biography, bibliography, and historical studies are still generally regarded as service industries. Yet, from literary studies in the 1940s and 1950s, almost nothing survives of the 'central' interpretive and theoretical output, whereas many of the products of the service industries are still in everyday use. Richard Ellmann's life of Joyce remains a standard reference; Yeats scholars still refer frequently to his pioneering *Yeats: The Man and the Masks*, whereas – with a handful of exceptions – purely interpretive studies of Joyce and Yeats from the period are gathering dust in library stores. A few years ago, a distinguished American scholar remarked to me that Ellmann, for all his achievements, remained in the second division of literary studies because he had devoted much of his life to biography rather than criticism. This was said without malice, and without any desire to disparage Ellmann's achievement. But there is something very odd about a business which declares that its finest product is one which is doomed to immediate obsolescence, while dismissing another, which has sold steadily for forty years, as a side-line.

Few in the field of literary studies question the value of a good biography, or a scholarly edition of a writer's works, letters, manuscripts or diaries. We are not constantly assailed by warnings that the demise of editing or bibliography will bring about the end of civilisation as we know it. In contrast, doubts about the value of theory and interpretation are endemic in the profession, and it is these activities which are characteristically scorned and satirised by sceptical outsiders. Despite the efforts of some theorists to problematise them, the 'service industries' seem remarkably crisis-free. (In the mid-1980s, theorists were talking about a 'return to history' as if no one had done any historical work since the advent of Derrida.) Literary works, manuscripts, letters and diaries are better edited than ever before; while theorists have been celebrating 'the death of the author', biographical and contextual investigation has become increasingly rigorous and wide-ranging; the relations between life and work, literature and society, are now being explored in ways that can no longer be dismissed as reductive.

As Peter Keating remarks in his preface to *The Haunted Study* (1989),

> [t]he main trend of twentieth-century literary criticism has been to establish itself as an autonomous discipline, cut off from and independent of other 'agencies': in that process literature's connections with social history have been particularly, and surprisingly neglected.[42]

Ironically, the New Critical effort to establish an autonomous criticism in the 1930s was fuelled by the shortcomings of the old, Gradgrindian historical 'scholarship', in which the opinions of the scholars were paraded as 'scientific fact'. The distinction is, in any case, spurious, as the best scholarship, like the best criticism, repeatedly demonstrates; the belief that the two are, or should be, distinct activities serves only to impoverish both. The old scholarship failed because it was so uncritical; the New Critical rebellion, despite the good intentions of the founding fathers, degenerated into uncritical explication. With the rise of post-structuralist theory came 'the death of the author', attacks on the validity of any form of empirical investigation, and the dissolution of contextual questions into the primordial soup of *textualité* – or ideology.

It is difficult to avoid the conclusion that theory and interpretation have received top billing because they can accommodate an immense volume of rapid publication. But prestige is also involved: theorising about literature generates the illusion of control over it. From Leavis to Lyotard, the emphasis characteristically falls on what 'we' must *not* do, read, think, investigate, or question. Each aspiring master-critic or theorist naturally tries to discredit lines of argument and investigation which threaten his authority. The cumulative effect, paradoxically, is the progressive removal of contextual constraints on interpretation: whenever the anti-contextual, anti-historical trend in interpretive theory begins to weaken, it tends to reappear in a more extreme form. The process runs in cycles – 'from rags to riches to routine', as Gerald Graff puts it – each new methodology tends to be more complex than the last, and the contextual constraints progressively fewer.

If critical expertise is not defined in terms of literary, historical and general knowledge, it must be defined in terms of theory and methodology. The less the professional critic is required to know, the more formidable the methodology must be made to appear; otherwise what distinguishes the professional from the well-read amateur who has not been trained to write academic prose, and may well come up with something which looks, to the unblinkered eye, superior to the professional product? Louis Menand, in an admirable account of the de Man furore, bleakly encapsulates the trend.

Academic criticism has become almost entirely professionalised: not literature, but what professors do with literature has become the subject of literary study. . . . No doubt the beguilements of French poststructuralist theory helped speed along this trend in the 1970s and 1980s; but I think that the principal cause was the terrible shrinkage, during the same period, of the job market for humanities Ph.D.s, and the fanatical careerism (and forced overproduction of professional publications) that shrinkage incited. It became virtually impossible to establish a serious academic career as a writer with general interests, or as a literary critic without a theoretical portfolio, and students whose interests did not fit the predominant mould went into other lines of work. . . . The Modern Language Association's image of the literature professor became, nearly everywhere, the defining image.

The consequence is that the academic interpretation and evaluation of literature have become almost completely predictable, driven by a set of theoretical and ideological assumptions that decide the results of critical inquiry in advance. This is no longer criticism; it is self-fulfilling prophecy, born of the belief (illustrated

by the deconstructionist handling of the de Man case) that critical
theory is a kind of magic bullet, which targets the important
issues and does the job of interpretation for you. Very little
variety or independence of mind is possible in these circumstances; and the recent emergence, in some places, of a grim
and reductive political orthodoxy has squeezed the sense of
personality, the sense of soul, out of academic criticism even
further.

The idea that each critical undertaking is a new try with doubtful equipment, that each object criticism addresses is a different object, and that the purpose of criticism is to say something
about literature that will seem new and interesting and, in the
end, true to other people, not just to other specialists – an idea
that has never been very welcome in the knowledge bureauc-
racy of the research university – is almost gone from literature
departments.[43]

There is – or ought to be – a Parkinson's Law of Criticism.
Like committee members who approve a million-dollar item in
five minutes, and spend the next three hours arguing over the
petty cash, critics who will dispute the smallest detail of an interpretation, and who regard reading itself as problematic, if not
impossible, deal confidently in personified abstractions such as
'modernism' and 'postmodernism', apparently secure in the belief that these are precise terms with meaningful referents. In
advanced theoretical discourse, every pivotal term – literature,
language, text, theory, discourse, culture, capitalism, imperialism,
ideology – is reified into a ghostly dance of abstractions. The result, as Roger Poole has shown, is a form of Hegelian grammar,
characterised by

the use of verbs of decision, movement or responsibility which
are illegitimately coupled to grammatical subjects which are
neither animate nor conscious,[44]

and propelled by the 'rhetoric of prosopopoeia':

Prosopopoeia obviously overlaps with other tropes where acts
of feeling, volition and decision are attributed to inanimate objects, but it could just be that the entire critical debate is now
only the invention of virtual objects (or subjects!) due to the

failure to make a necessary logical distinction between entities which *can* think, feel, decide, cancel, proclaim themselves, deny themselves, transform themselves, etc., and those entities which *can not* do so.[45]

By 'the entire critical debate' he means poststructuralist theory, and in particular the work of Paul de Man, who took the procedure to its logical conclusion by attempting to eliminate all *human* subjects from his discourse. But the argument extends well beyond the boundaries of poststructuralism. There may, as Northrop Frye once remarked, be such a thing as being too deficient in the capacity to generalise, but to the extent that agency is attributed to a reified category, trouble invariably follows, as in the case of 'modernism', considered in the following chapter.

1

The Invention of
Modernism

I am now trying an Experiment very frequent among Modern
Authors; which is, to *write upon Nothing.* . . .

Swift, A Tale of a Tub

'We are invited to call it post-modernism . . . but I prefer to
call it *shopping*.'[1]

I

'The fact that defining the modern is a task that now imposes
itself on many distinguished scholars', said Frank Kermode in
1966, 'may be a sign that the modern period is over.'[2] In the course
of his celebrated 'Discrimination of Modernisms', published the
previous year, he turned to the entry for 'modernism' in 'a very
large new *Encyclopaedia of Poetry and Poetics*', only to be told that
it was 'the movement in Hispanic letters which began in the 1880s
in Sp. America, blending Sp., Fr., and other foreign influences'.
'Modernism', in the literary sense, was still covered under 'Modern Poetics'.[3]

In the same essay, he coined a distinction between 'paleo-' and
'neo-' (shortly to become 'post-') modernism, a distinction cited
in turn by Malcolm Bradbury in his extensive entry in *The Fontana
Dictionary of Modern Thought* (1977):

MODERNISM has by now acquired stability as the comprehensive term for an international tendency, arising in the poetry,
fiction, drama, music, painting, architecture and other arts of
the West in the last years of the 19th century and subsequently
affecting the character of most 20th-century art. [4]

The force of that 'by now' is obscured by the accompanying historical sketch. We are accustomed to thinking of 'modernism' as
something that flourished nearly a century ago, but the term itself was not widely employed by literary critics until the 1960s.
The *OED* (1989) offers a more cautious definition:

> The methods, style or attitude of modern artists . . . a style of
> painting in which the artist deliberately breaks away from classi-
> cal and traditional methods of expression; hence, a similar style
> or movement in architecture, literature, music, etc.

The first occurrence of 'modernist', in this sense, is given as 1927,
in relation to painting; 'modernistic' also appears in 1927, in relation to music, followed by 'modernism' in 1929, with reference to
architecture. Though the usage in relation to the visual arts, music,
architecture and design was well-established by the mid-1930s,
and commonplace by the 1950s,[5] 'modernist', in the popular
journalism of those decades, served primarily as a term of derision.
The Times, in 1955, was still framing the word in quotation marks.

However, it is clear that the term was being applied to literature and other arts well before Laura Riding and Robert Graves
published *A Survey of Modernist Poetry* in 1927. Matei Calinescu,
who provides a concise history of the concept of 'modernity' from
the fifth century onwards, thinks it 'safe to assume that in English-
speaking countries the term "modernism" acquired a distinctive
literary significance during the first two decades of our century'.[6]
His earliest citation is 'a short-lived little magazine, calling itself
The Modernist: A Monthly Magazine of Modern Arts and Letters',
published in 1919, but 'more concerned with politics than with
literature or the arts'.[7] We can push this back another four years,
to E. E. Cummings' graduation address at Harvard in June 1915.
'The New Art' is an impassioned, eclectic defence of artistic experiment in literature, painting, sculpture and music:

> The question now arises, how much of all this is really Art?
> The answer is: we do not know. The great men of the future
> will most certainly profit by the experimentation of the present
> period. An insight into the unbroken chain of artistic develop-
> ment during the last half century disproves the theory that
> modernism is without foundation; rather we are concerned with
> a natural unfolding of sound tendencies. That the conclusion

is, in a particular case [Gertrude Stein], absurdity, does not in any way impair the value of the experiment, so long as we are dealing with sincere effort. The New Art, maligned though it may be by fakirs and fanatics, will appeal in its essential spirit to the unprejudiced critic as a courageous and genuine exploration of untrodden ways.[8]

This implies that the word was already in circulation, but one can search long and in vain for 'modernism' in the little magazines prior to 1919; the word does not, so far as I can see, appear even once in *The Egoist*. John Crowe Ransom's 'The Future of Poetry', published in *The Fugitive* in February 1924, begins:

The arts have had to recognise Modernism – how should poetry escape? And yet what is Modernism? It is undefined. Henry James stopped before a certain piece of sculpture to apostrophise 'the beautiful modern spirit'; but he did not attempt a definition where a more incompetent man would surely have done it. . . .
   In poetry the Imagists, in our time and place, made a valiant effort to formulate their program. Their modernist manifestoes were exciting, their practice was crude. . . . They conceived the first duty of the Moderns as being to disembarrass poetry of its terrible incubus of piety. . . .
   But we moderns are impatient and destructive. We forget entirely the enormous technical difficulty of the poetic art, and we examine the meanings of poems with a more and more microscopic analysis . . . and we do not obtain so readily as our fathers the ecstasy which is the total effect of poetry, the sense of miracle before the union of inner meaning and objective form. . . . Modern poets are their own severest critics; their own documents, on second reading, have been known to induce in poets a fatal paralysis of the writing digit. . . . The future of poetry is immense? One is not so sure these days, since it has felt the fatal irritant of Modernism. Too much is demanded by the critic, attempted by the poet . . .[9]

This, according to Calinescu, 'can help us see how modernism was viewed in the early 1920s by an outstanding member of an advanced literary group'.[10] Ransom insists that 'Modernism' can't be reified; Calinescu projects a reified construct, assembled half-a-century later, on to the essay, and assumes that he and Ransom must be talking about the same thing. Riding and Graves, he continues, published their *Survey of Modernist Poetry*

> at a time when the spirit of modernism was asserting itself with full force in English and American literature. Modernism had already produced a highly significant body of works in both poetry and prose. . . . It was, however, too early for a more comprehensive critical synthesis. . . .[11]

Like most historians of 'modernism', Calinescu treats Riding and Graves as pioneers groping their way through the territory he is now mapping. Because the existence of a reified 'modernism' is, to him, self-evident, he regrets that they did not 'try to offer an even remotely systematic definition'. They insist on variety, and use 'modernist' as a portmanteau label for 'advanced contemporary poetry'; he assumes that they have failed to detect unity: 'The fact that the representatives of the "new poetry" are called (and call themselves) modernists is more than just a matter of arbitrary preference.'[12] But, prior to 1927, with the possible exception of Cummings, none of the new poets were calling themselves modernists, in print at any rate; nor did the Graves/Riding usage catch on.

Neither Pound nor Eliot ever described themselves thus. Eliot, by 1916, was familiar with theological debate over 'modernism',[13] but applied the term to literature only once, so far as I know, in 'Contemporary English Prose' (1923) – in a manner wholly at odds with current usage:

> The influence of Walter Pater has continued almost wholly, mingled with the influence of Renan, in a beautifully written but somewhat out-of-date volume of essays by a writer of our own generation, Frederic Manning, entitled *Scenes and Portraits* [1909]. It is an early example of that quality of modernist realistic prose, agitated and dismembered, which culminates and disappears, I believe, in the work of James Joyce.[14]

Literary modernism, according to Eliot, began with Walter Pater and Cardinal Newman, and was demolished by *Ulysses*. Thereafter, he reverted to the theological sense, as in 'Thoughts After Lambeth' (1931):

> You cannot point to one group of 'Modernists': there are Catholics
> who may be called modernist, and Evangelicals who may call
> themselves modernist, as well as a few persons in whom Mod-
> ernism seems to signify merely confused thinking.[15]

'The Humanism of Irving Babbit' (1928) provides an even more
striking instance. Eliot seizes upon Babbit's declaration that 'I
am myself a thoroughgoing individualist, writing for those who
are, like myself, irrevocably committed to the modern experiment.'
'Those of us who lay no claim to being modern', he replies, 'may
be allowed to inquire whither all this modernity and experiment
is going to lead. Is everybody to spend his time experimenting?
And on what, and to what end?'[16] Always alert to nuance, Eliot
is only interested in the theological sense of 'modernity and experiment', and does not allude to any conflicting literary application.

Six years earlier, in a letter to Felix Schelling, Pound had described *The Waste Land* as 'the justification of "the movement", of
our modern experiment since 1900'.[17] 'Modern', unlike 'modernist', was by then well-established in English critical parlance; at
one extreme, the mere phrase 'modern art' had been good for a
populist laugh since the Post-Impressionist exhibition of December 1910, or for that matter the trial of Oscar Wilde; at the other,
'modern' had become the battle-cry of freedom. Padraic Colum,
reviewing the first American edition of Eliot's poems in 1920,
praised him for having 'the modern approach to the soul', and
described the volume as the culmination of a generation of attempts 'to do this kind of thing in English':

> The group in the workshop were aware that he was complet-
> ing a tendency, and for that reason they were speaking of him
> with Browning and Ovid before he had published a book.[18]

The only published comparison with Browning and Ovid was
Pound's, in his review of *Prufrock* for Harriet Monroe's *Poetry*,
which suggests that 'the group in the workshop' was effectively
Pound himself.[19]

But in recent histories of 'modernism', the honorific sense of
'modern' – which by 1913 was commonplace in advanced London literary circles – is almost invariably conflated with 'modernist' – which was rare to vanishing-point before 1927. A reified
'modernism' (the invention of the last twenty-five years), is then

fed back into the period-use of 'modern', of which Pound's 'our modern experiment' is perhaps the most influential instance.[20] The back-projection is now so familiar that the circularity passes unnoticed. 'Modern' and 'modernist' were indeed used interchangeably from the 1920s until well into the 1960s, but 'modernist' was simply shorthand for advanced, experimental, or innovative writing, and most critics agreed that definition was pointless. Janko Lavrin's introduction to his *Aspects of Modernism* (1935), strikes the characteristic note:

> Nothing is more hackneyed and yet more vague than the words 'modern' and 'modernism'. This is why they should be used with caution. In the following essays they stand for the advanced type of consciousness or sensibility, in so far as these are reflected in literature. . . .
>
> [M]odernism comprises trends which seem to have little in common on the surface, although fundamentally they may have a common source. Utter atomisation of the individual, and parallel with this, a passionate though impotent will to achieve at least some balance and harmony in spite of all – such are the two polar trends reflected in European modernism as a whole. And between these two poles one finds a countless variety of writings . . . so great indeed that it excludes beforehand any generalisation.[21]

'Hackneyed' gestures, at least in part, towards the long-running popular debate over 'modern art'. The Very Reverend Dean Inge, in his presidential address to the English Association in 1937, was sure that so far as the visual arts were concerned,

> we all know what 'Modernism' means. It prides itself on a repudiation of all traditions and all developed canons of beauty, and shows an affinity both with the naive artistic attempts of savages, and with the newest proletarianism in Russia. A modernist painter will cover his painting with zig-zags or depict a woman with green hair . . . a modernist architect will put two or three packing-cases together and call it a house or a church. These phenomena are clearly pathological.
> But what is Modernism in literature? This is a much more difficult question to answer.[22]

It was especially difficult for the Dean because, as he cheerfully informed his audience, he had not read any Modernist writing, but he knew that it was 'blasphemy against human nature'.

Neither Louis MacNiece, in *Modern Poetry* (1938), nor George Orwell in 'Inside the Whale' (1940), referred to 'modernism'. Orwell identified a post-war 'movement' which included Joyce, Eliot, Pound, Lawrence, Wyndham Lewis, Aldous Huxley, Lytton Strachey and even Somerset Maugham, but could find no unifying principle other than 'pessimism of outlook': 'the first thing one would notice about the group of writers I have named is that they do not look like a group'.[23] Herbert Grierson and J. C. Smith concluded their *Critical History of English Poetry* (1944) with a disparaging account of 'the modernists': in their version, Hulme was the major theorist; D. H. Lawrence ('in revolt not only against Western civilisation but against reason itself') the most extreme exponent; Hopkins, Owen and Donne were described as major influences, and Edith Sitwell was dubbed 'the pioneer of English modernism', though Eliot 'became lord of the ascendant' with the publication of *The Waste Land*.[24]

Joseph Wood Krutch, writing on '*Modernism*' in *Modern Drama* in 1953, argued that 'the term "modernism" is so vague and general that no two people are likely to use it in the same way, and it ought not to be used at all unless this fact is taken for granted'. This did not deter him from offering his own definition:

> first, the tendency to believe that 'modern' ideas are radically different from any generally entertained before and, second, certain more specific beliefs, doubts, attitudes and judgements which seem to be characteristic of the people who believe themselves to be 'modernists' in the first sense just given.[25]

'Modernism', in his view, was an undesirable tendency, leading to 'intellectual and moral paralysis', though Shaw, as 'a good modernist', escaped censure. Ten years later, William Van O'Connor declared that from 1908 to the Second World War,

> the principles of Modernism dominated letters, in poetry, fiction and in criticism. Eliot, Pound and the Bloomsbury writers were the lawgivers. In poetry the great names, Yeats, Eliot, Stevens and the lesser names, the Sitwells, Marianne Moore and Cummings were recognisably and definably modernists.[26]

But the only common factor he could discern in his list, which included Auden, Dylan Thomas, Joyce, Proust, Faulkner, Ford, Virginia Woolf and Scott Fitzgerald, was that they were all 'innovators'.

So long as we regard such comments as faltering steps toward a later and more sophisticated understanding of 'modernism', they seem to merit only our indulgence. But if we suspend that assumption, what we have (Dean Inge excepted) is several critics of contrasting persuasions and sympathies, grappling with the diversity of innovative writing from the late nineteenth century onwards, searching for a common factor, and acknowledging that while some writers are clearly more 'modern' than others, no unifying principle can be found. So far as I know, the earliest attempt at a systematic definition of 'modernism' in poetry (and one of the few published before the 1960s) is Randall Jarrell's 'The End of the Line' (1942), in which he listed thirteen 'general characteristics of modernist poetry': 'the poetry of Pound, Eliot, Crane, Tate, Stevens, Cummings, MacLeish, et cetera'. His intention, however, was to overturn the assumption 'that almost all modern criticism has emphasised: that modernist poetry is a revolutionary departure from the romantic poetry of the preceding century', and to demonstrate that 'this complex of qualities is essentially romantic, and the poetry that exhibits it is the culminating point of romanticism':

> It is the end of the line. . . . Modernism As We Knew It – the most successful and influential body of poetry of this century – is dead. Compare a 1940 issue of *Poetry* with a 1930 issue. Who could have believed that modernism would collapse so fast? Only someone who realised that modernism is a limit which it is impossible to exceed. . . .

> How could anyone fail to realise that the excesses of modernist poetry are the necessary concomitants of late-capitalist society?[27]

Read in isolation, this seems to imply that 'modernism' was already an established critical reference-point. Yet only two years earlier, Jarrell was using 'modern', framed in quotation marks, to link 'Pound, Eliot, Crane, Tate, Stevens, Cummings, Marianne Moore and so on', before shifting to 'modernist' later in the piece.[28] 'The End of the Line' is a bravura performance, looking back to

Ransom's 'The Future of Poetry' while in some respects foreshad-owing the argument of Kermode's *Romantic Image*, challenging an orthodoxy still in the process of formation. He returned to this theme ten years later in 'The Obscurity of the Poet' (1952), a characteristically embattled defence of difficulty in poetry, in which he assumes that the derisive connotations of 'modernism' will be uppermost in the reader's mind:

> we know that Shakespeare is never *obscure*, as if he were some modernist poet gleefully pasting puzzles together in his garret. . . .

> Modernism was not 'that lion's den from which no tracks re-turn', but only a sort of canvas whale from which Jonah after Jonah, throughout the late '20s and early '30s, made a penitent return, back to metre and rhyme and plain broad Statement; how many young poets today are, if nothing else, plain![29]

Throughout the 1950s, 'modernism' gained little ground among literary critics; Frank Kermode, always an acute observer of criti-cal trends, did not employ the word in *Romantic Image* (1957) except in the earlier, theological sense; like most critics at the time, he was still using 'modern' in the sense now displaced by 'modern-ism'. The same applies to Graham Hough's *Image and Experience: Reflections on a Literary Revolution* (1960), which would now be described as a frontal attack on 'modernism'. 'Modern' remains the preferred term in Harold Rosenberg's *The Tradition of the New* (1959), in which the occasional 'modernism' appears, but with no special emphasis. Even in C. K. Stead's *The New Poetic* (1964), 'modernism' is used infrequently, and within quotation marks. But by the early 1970s, 'modernism' had largely displaced 'mod-ern' in orthodox critical usage.

II

Kermode, in 1965, the year of Eliot's death, was discriminating between 'modernisms' several decades after the 'modernist move-ment in literature' is generally thought to have ended,[30] and at a point when 'modernism' was beginning to replace 'modern' in critical debate. 'Postmodernism', as a literary term, makes its first appearance in the same year. The *OED* gives the first use, in relation to architecture, as 1949; Arnold Toynbee is credited with the first application to history in 1956, but the relevant literary usage begins with Leslie Fiedler's essay, 'The New Mutants' (1965).[31] 'Modernism' and 'postmodernism', in other words, entered general critical parlance almost simultaneously, and have been reified not sequentially, but in parallel.

Whether literary historians fifty years hence will still be using these terms seems doubtful at best: they are unlikely to see themselves as living in the post-beyond-post-modernist era, and the recent proliferation of 'beyonds' suggests that many of the current 'post-' formations are already approaching their use-by date. Leaving 'postmodernism' aside for the moment: if 'modernism' had remained simply a portmanteau label for advanced, innovative, or experimental art, *c.* 1870 and 1930 (or whatever the preferred dates may be), arguments over its continued use could be left for the future to decide. In *The Shock of the New*, for example, Robert Hughes uses the word in the portmanteau sense, meaning no more than 'experimental or innovative art since the late nineteenth century'; his interest is always in what a particular painter or group were doing. But where literature is concerned, its connotations are seldom restricted in this way. Over the last thirty years, the term has been endowed with increasing explanatory and evaluative power. To refer to a writer as a 'modernist' is not simply to identify him or her as an experimental, or innovative, or *avant-garde* author working in the early twentieth century, but to convey a complex value-judgement without recourse to overtly evaluative terminology.

Though no two commentators agree precisely on what 'modernism' means, the competing trends are reasonably clear. The critical literature is now in a very peculiar, not to say schizoid condition. There is, first, a large orthodox industry centred on Pound, Eliot, Joyce and Lewis, in a sense continuous with the mid-century enterprise of 'studies in modern literature', but held together by a reified 'modernism'. By contrast, the elaboration of 'postmodernism' has been dominated by theorists, so much so that 'theory', 'poststructuralism' and 'postmodernism' are sometimes used interchangeably. Some theorists regard 'modernism' as the first step towards the *real* revolution of the sixties and after, when the fog of mystification and logocentricism is finally dispersed by theory. Others – usually Marxist and/or feminist theorists – denounce it as an authoritarian, neo-fascist, male-dominated, totalising, bourgeois ideology.[32] There is little debate between orthodox critics who regard 'modernism' as a good thing, and radical theorists who regard it as a very bad thing, since the arguments have evolved independently, and the two groups seldom communicate. Both, however, assume the existence of a 'modernism' which can be celebrated or damned – and endlessly analysed – according to taste.

At the extreme – as in Marshall Berman's *All That is Solid Melts into Air* (1982) – 'modernism' becomes a key to all mythologies:

> The maelstrom of modern life has been fed from many sources: great discoveries in the physical sciences, changing our images of the universe and our place in it; the industrialisation of production, which transforms scientific knowledge into technology, creates new human environments and destroys old ones, speeds up the whole tempo of life, generates new forms of corporate power and class struggle; immense demographic upheavals. . . . These world-historical processes have nourished an amazing variety of visions and ideas that aim to make men and women the subjects as well as the objects of modernisation, to give them the power to change the world that is changing them, to make their way through the maelstrom and make it their own. Over the past century, these visions and values have come to be loosely grouped together under the name of 'modernism.'[33]

What does one have to do in order *not* be a modernist? 'All forms of modernist art and thought', we learn from a chapter called 'The Modernism of Underdevelopment', 'have a dual character: they are at once expressions of and protests against the process of modernisation.'[34] Berman, swept along on the tidal wave of his enthusiasms, never seems to notice that his central term is so inclusive as to be meaningless. His definitions can scarcely be called definitions, since nothing is excluded.

At first glance, the literary-historical sense is clear and well-established: Pound, Eliot, Joyce and Lewis are the central figures in the 'modernist movement', which flourished during the years 1908–1922. The story has been told and retold many times, from Pound's arrival in London in October 1908 to the publication of *The Waste Land* and *Ulysses* in 1922. 'The forgotten school of 1909'; Hulme and Bergson; Pound and Ford; Pound and Yeats at Stone Cottage; Pound, H. D., Aldington and Imagism; *The Egoist*; *Blast*;

Pound's discovery of Eliot and 'Prufrock'; Pound and Fenollosa; Pound, Lewis, Gaudier-Brzeska and Vorticism: all of these are familiar landmarks in what is now known as the history of modernism.

The problem has less to do with any particular 'modernism' than with the centripetal habits of thought which invariably accompany its use. Most critics, if pressed, will concede that 'modernism' is an academic invention, while maintaining that it contributes to a better understanding of the period to which it has been attached. In practice, however, 'modernism' is frequently personified as an active agent, expressing itself through writers, creating masterpieces, and directing events. 'It is the fault of the dons', said Frank Kermode, reviewing C.K. Stead's *Pound, Yeats, Eliot and the Modernist Movement* (1986)

> that Modernism is both a period and stylistic description. We should have learned long ago of the confusion arising from such practices: Wellek's essay on the baroque is forty years old, and Lovejoy's on the discrimination of Romanticisms (we use the word to mean so many things that it ends by meaning nothing) is over sixty. . . . now 'modernist' is used of the modern works one happens to admire or regard as central or canonical. To be merely a modern author is to have chickened out of Modernism. As for the period, it is thought to have come to an end with *Finnegans Wake* or thereabouts; the admired experimental work that came later, and is judged to be in the same tradition, is called Post-Modernist. Like 'Modernist' it is what is nowadays called a 'valorising' description.[35]

Stead presents Pound and Eliot both as the inventors of a poetic vehicle called 'Modernism', and as having been transported by it: Yeats runs after the carriage, but is left behind; Eliot, despite having composed 'the definitive Modernist poem', disembarks in the late 1920s, leaving Pound alone in the first-class compartment. By the late 1930s, with Eliot 'stalled' and Pound producing 'second-order' cantos, 'one might have been pardoned for thinking that Modernism had run its course'.[36] 'Modernism', nevertheless, is also figured as a tide against which ill-advised poets may choose to swim, and as a vital force transferred during intercourse between poets, so that Yeats's problem, according to Stead, was that he could not 'go all the way with Pound'.[37]

This, however, is merely an overt application of the procedure displayed in hundreds of orthodox studies of 'modernism', in which causal hypotheses and valuations are presented in the guise of studies in sources and influences, textual analysis, history of ideas, and so on. Pound, Eliot and Joyce are central to our understanding of twentieth-century writing because they are modernists; modernism is central because Pound, *et al.* are modernists. This is the dominant mode of commentary. Because 'modernism' has become a valorising term, it can be used to reinforce orthodox valuations of 'modernist' writing without recourse to directly evaluative language. Since it is also used as an explanatory term, it appears to provide an explanation of why Pound, *et al.*, wrote as they did: 'modernism', as it were, was 'in the air' around 1914. Yet in most of these accounts, 'the men of 1914' *were* the 'air' on which 'modernism' is said to have been carried.

To speak of 'Poundian modernism', for example, is to convey a coded signal to initiates, while warning the uninitiated that these are deep waters, not to be crossed without a lifejacket (which the critic is about to offer). Pound, the phrase reiterates, is still at the cutting-edge of poetic practice, both a founder and a full financial member of an exclusive literary club. An ostensibly descriptive category functions as a guarantee of value, underwriting the surrounding exegesis. As the 'modernism' involved tends to be derived from Pound's own writings, one might as well say 'Poundian Poundianism'. Similarly, while Imagism and Vorticism produced (or rather, were invented to promote) some interesting minor works, the significance claimed for them is characteristically underwritten by appeals to the significance of 'modernism' at large. But since, on most accounts, these 'movements' were central to modernism, the claim involves a good deal of circularity.

The distorting effects of this style of argument are especially striking in the opposing cases of Yeats and Lewis. Though Yeats sometimes qualifies as an honorary modernist, he is often excluded from the modernist canon. His early work precedes 'modernism', and his career spans the period which, in the orthodox history of 'modernism', involves a decisive break with the past, centred on the literary revolution led by the 'men of 1914'. He is, from the perspective of the modernism industry, a nineteenth-century poet who lived on into the twentieth without ever quite living *in* it in the approved modernist fashion. A great poet, perhaps, but not in the first division. Such aspersions have impelled some Yeats

enthusiasts who are also believers in 'modernism' to try to rescue Yeats by arguing that he was really a modernist after all.[38]

By contrast, it is taken for granted within the modernism industry that Wyndham Lewis is a major writer, and a more important writer than, say, Kipling. It is hard to imagine a defence of
this position which would not lean heavily on the valorising sense
of 'modernism'. 'His faults were intrinsic with his genius', according to his biographer, Jeffrey Meyers, but the list of 'major
defects' includes: 'his dissipated energy, his lack of form and in-
consistent style, his offensive tone, his negativity' . . . 'repetitive,
undisciplined, digressive and disorganised' . . . 'hasty, careless and
slapdash' . . . 'essential defects of style and structure' . . . 'an elaborate, contorted prose style' . . . 'excessive, extremist and contemptu-
ous' . . . 'long boring patches'.[39] Lewis's genius is evidently a matter
of faith rather than works. On Meyers' evidence, nothing could
persuade more than a handful of Lewis's contemporaries to buy
his books, let alone read them. The publishing figures suggest
that most readers, then and now, would willingly trade the entire Lewis *oeuvre* for *Kim*.

Kipling is routinely condemned for his imperialist sympathies,
and yet everything that can be said against his political stance
can be said, far more damningly, of Lewis. Paranoid megalomania,
fuelled by envy, is the mainspring of Lewis's writing; he was, as
Meyers acknowledges,

> in favour of a powerful authoritarian government in which the
> 'responsible' ruler would permit ordinary people to live the
> comfortable but controlled life of a democracy, but would also
> allow the artists and intellectuals [i.e. Lewis] to have a leading
> role and privileged existence.[40]

The quality of argument mustered in Lewis's defence may be
judged from William Chace's comparison of Lewis and Orwell
on the Spanish Civil War. The comparision, says Chace, 'could
not be more devastating to poor Orwell':

> Where Orwell patiently details the differences between the
> Communists, the Trotsykists, the Anarchists (the F.A.I. and the
> C.N.T.) and P.O.U.M. in Spain, Lewis's strength of mind pre-
> vents him from straining after such gnats. His diagnosis of the
> situation has an elegant simplicity:

> The solution to which we are being driven by our acquiescence
> in present events, is Communism. Consciously or unconsciously
> (it is the latter in Great Britain, where nothing is conscious)
> the puppets who pretend to govern us accept this solution.[41]

By this standard, Senator Joe McCarthy was one of the great
political thinkers of our time. But then, 'Lewis was never as
interested in the determination of the truth as he was in the exercise
of his self-hood'.[42] Frederic Jameson, pursuing 'the affinities between protofascism and Western Modernism', tries to rescue Lewis
by pushing the argument to the opposite extreme: Lewis as Aw-
ful Warning, 'blurt[ing] out in public speech what even in private
was never meant to be more than tacitly understood'.[43] As John
Carey demonstrates with brutal economy, we might as well go
straight to *Mein Kampf*.[44] Within the modernism industry at large,
Lewis's politics are an embarrassment; the incoherence of the
philosophy, and the clumsiness of the novels, is covertly acknowledged; his complete lack of influence is implicitly conceded, yet
he is still presented as a central figure in the modernist canon.[45]

The case of Lewis is only the most striking instance of the way
in which 'modernism' functions as a guarantee of value. With
Pound, the situation is more complex: Pound is invoked to underwrite the importance of modernism, which is reciprocally invoked
to underwrite the importance of Pound, generating a feedback
effect which, when pushed to its extreme by Hugh Kenner and
fellow contributors to *Paideuma*, elevates Pound to the position of
the century's greatest writer. In general, 'modernism' is used by
its promoters to quarantine the approved writers (disputes over
the canon notwithstanding) from strictures applied to their non-
modernist contemporaries. Kipling is disqualified from serious
consideration by association with a repulsive ideology, whereas
adherence to an even more repulsive ideology is, for Pound and
Lewis, a sign of manly independence.

Progress, within the modernism industry, consists of accretion,
complication, and repetition. Argument rages between the exponents
of Pound-centred and Eliot-centred versions; Bergson, we discover
yet again, has been shamefully neglected as an influence; next
year it will be Hulme's turn for another promotion; meanwhile,
Ford's contribution has been undervalued; chunks from all these
investigations are thrown into the pot. Imagism, too, has been
overlooked while we have been worrying about Hulme and Bergson

– but not so disgracefully as Vorticism, which turns out to have been far more central to 'modernism' than anyone had realised, until a new player trumps them both with a Futurist joker. Then there is the Romantic element, the Symbolist element, Kant, Hegel, Schopenhauer and Nietzsche; and meanwhile *everyone* has neglected Wyndham Lewis, without whom, etc.

Such is the reifying power invested in the concept that it tends to dominate even the thinking of those who wish to subvert it. Bonnie Kime Scott in her introduction to *The Gender of Modernism* (1990), starts from the recognition that

> [t]ypically, both the authors of the original manifestos and the literary historians of modernism took as their norm a small set of its male participants, who were quoted, anthologised, taught, and consecrated as geniuses. While the word *modernism* appears in the title of this book, the editors involved in this project have worked restively with it, and introductions to specific authors repeatedly manipulate the term. The 'experimental, audience-challenging and language-focused' writing that used to be regarded as modernism becomes for some of our editors a gendered subcategory. . . .[46]

Despite this collective unease, Scott nevertheless concludes that

> a great deal of energy was subtracted out by gender from modernism. In acknowledging this, and in putting it back, we may be discovering how modernism can continue to 'make it new.'[47]

Her attempt to redefine 'modernism' ends by giving Pound the last word; it would surely have been better to discard the concept altogether.

The unexamined assumption displayed by commentators of all persuasions (theorists and traditionalists alike) is that 'modernism' is larger than the sum of its parts, philosophically elaborate, multifaceted, without precedent, and indispensable to an understanding of the arts in the twentieth century. Sanford B. Schwarz, for example, introduces his *Matrix of Modernism* (1985) with the standard complaint that 'literary historians' have neglected 'the affliations between Modernist poetics and contemporaneous developments in philosophy', thereby justifying the need to take us out for yet another spin with Bergson, Hulme, Nietzsche, Husserl, William James, Remy de Gourmont and company:

> In this book I will propose an alternative to the atomistic approach. Without ignoring specific influences and affinities, I will construct a matrix that brings together a significant number of philosophers and poets, and articulates the relationships among them. This matrix will also provide a new perspective on Modernism itself. It will reveal that the stylistic features of Modernist verse – abrupt juxtaposition, irony, paradox and the like – were not merely accidents of the history of taste; nor were the critical emphases on impersonality, the unified sensibility, and the autonomy of the literary text merely isolated or arbitrary phenomena. Modernist poetics (along with its New Critical offspring) is part of a major intellectual development that produced significant changes in philosophy, the arts, and other fields as well. This study, then, will situate an important literary movement in its intellectual context. . . .[48]

The plight of the scholar trying to find something new to say about 'modernism' from within the established framework is all too apparent. By 1985, the propositions here advanced as novelties had been elaborated by an army of scholars and critics, all concerned to demonstrate that 'Modernism' was part of the 'major intellectual development' he describes. Setting out to 'construct a matrix', Schwarz then personifies this construction as '*the* matrix', an entity capable of providing perspectives, articulating relationships, and revealing connections. This assumes the existence of another, unproblematic entity called 'modernism' which can be 'situated' within the matrix. But since his 'matrix' has long since been incorporated into the edifice of 'modernism', he is in fact pursuing the modernism of Modernism.

Reviewing Dennis Brown's *Intertextual Dynamics within the Literary Group: Joyce, Lewis, Eliot and Pound* (1990) – an attempt 'to reaffirm Lewis's important role within the Modernist venture' – David Trotter observes:

> The idea of Modernism encourages us to think of experiment, not as a constant focus of creativity and self-assertion throughout history, but as the product of a specific (if undefinable) historical crisis.

He notes that to write 'in a Modernist fashion'

> was to write in the conscious or unconscious knowledge that
> things had changed utterly – 1910, or 1914, or whenever. 'If
> the new art is Modernism's dream-child,' Brown writes, 'its birth-
> cry tells of a world where healthy issue has become imposs-
> ible.' Here Modernism is the creator, the work of art a child
> born with the knowledge that things have changed utterly. . . .

Unable to explain literary revolution, Brown portrays it as child-
birth. The metaphor informs us that it would be impossibly
vulgar to enquire about the mechanics of change, the inglori-
ous fumbling compromises of revision and adjustment.

Trotter nevertheless maintains that 'as a label, the concept seems
indispensable'. He wants to see a return to a purely descriptive
usage:

> There is something badly wrong with a concept which elevates
> one writer [Pound] to the status of a tragic hero because he
> worked a successful youth racket, and dismisses another [Vi-
> olet Hunt] because she did not. The solution is to deny the
> concept an explanatory or evaluative function.[49]

This is easier said than done. It is now almost impossible to
use 'modernism' in argument without personifying it as an active agent. Michael Levenson begins his *Genealogy of Modernism*
(1984) with the remark that 'modernism' is a term 'at once vague
and unavoidable', 'a rough way of locating our attention', then
defines his subject as 'the emergence of a literary movement one
of whose own problems was how to name itself', the movement
being 'that associated with Pound, Hulme, Ford, Lewis and Eliot',
and this in turn becomes 'modernism' as the book proceeds.[50] A
few pages later, we learn that

> part of the difficulty with modernism is that it has suppressed
> its origins. As it became an established cultural presence, it re-
> vised its history in line with its present cultural inclinations.[51]

This in fact refers to the way in which *Eliot* shaped his rhetoric as
he became 'an established cultural presence' on the London literary

scene,[52] but once again, 'modernism' acquires a life of its own.

Despite the variety of 'modernisms' proposed, and the continuing disputes over the ranking of the 'men of 1914' and their contemporaries, the overall impression is of hundreds of critics all tramping round the same narrow circle, searching for a unifying principle which does not exist. To change the metaphor, the orthodox edifice of 'literary modernism' resembles an inverted pyramid resting on doctrines largely derived from (or rather attributed to) Pound and Eliot. This produces a feedback effect which has progressively distorted orthodox criticism of Pound and Eliot in several ways. From the late 1920s onwards, the academic promotion of Eliot's poetry was founded on doctrines derived from his polemical essays. Equally, the promotional strategies used by Pound to publicise his 'youth racket' have been elaborated into complex doctrines regarded as central to 'modernism', so that there are now considerable literatures devoted to Imagism and Vorticism, the 'new method of scholarship', the 'ideogramic method', and so on. But as 'modernism' has been elaborated, the work of the early 'modernists' has increasingly been treated as a manifestation of a larger phenomenon, compounding the earlier tendency to present them as philosophers or gurus, and to construe the works of 'the men of 1914' as all having been produced in the same workshop – a notion which Pound, again, had used to promote his own work and that of his protégés.

The structure also includes an ever-increasing mass of material imported from philosophy, historiography, theology, cultural studies, and history of ideas. 'Modernism', ostensibly the subject of these inquiries, is the glue that holds the edifice together, via the assumption that the vast array of works and doctrines are manifestations of a single complex phenomenon. Few scholars would endorse this proposition when put as bluntly, but its effects are everywhere apparent in the characteristic rhythm of argument, where initial caution rapidly gives way to Hegelian assertion in which 'modernism' becomes an active agent, shaping and directing the course of events, 'expressing' itself through artists and philosophers, and so on. Richard J. Quinones, for instance, in *Mapping Literary Modernism* (1985), initially concedes that 'the surprisingly contradictory extent of the testimony points to the multiform range of modernist concern'; within five pages he commits himself to 'the philosophic unity of Modernism' – which then becomes his guiding principle.[53]

All of this activity has less to do with the persuasive powers of Eliot and Pound than with the force of professional imperatives in determining the course of academic debate. Louis Menand has shown, more clearly than ever before, that Eliot did not precipitate a crisis in English letters, but arrived just in time to exploit a situation in which

> it appeared to many of his contemporaries that literary values had somehow lost their authority, that literature had become the victim of its own reputation. To those writers who imagined themselves to be its fomentors, this crisis no doubt seemed in the beginning only the sort of calculated disruption that is likely to attend any major turn of literary generation. . . . But the crisis was not a controlled one. . . .[54]

Jacques Derrida, likewise, arrived in the United States at a time when established *critical* values were losing their authority. By the late 1950s, the immense influence bestowed upon Eliot was a source of growing discontent to a new generation of critics eager to escape from his shadow. The interpretive orthodoxy broadly associated with the New Criticism – and hence with Eliot's essays and, to a considerable extent, the explication of his poetry – was looking increasingly stale; the political upheavals of the mid-1960s added fuel to these discontents. With Eliot's death in January 1965, the sense of a power-vacuum at the centre of American criticism was obviously heightened; the emergence of theory, in its current form, is generally identified with Derrida's appearance at Johns Hopkins in October 1966. The king was dead; long live *l'empereur*.

Derrida would not have been remotely as influential if Eliot had not been canonised by the preceding generation of academic critics. 'Influence' is convenient but deceptive shorthand for a reciprocal process which is primarily directed by the needs of the influenced. For both Eliot and Derrida, success was very much a matter of appearing in the right place at just the right time to exploit an existing crisis. Like Eliot before him, Derrida has become the object of a personality cult; in both cases, this was partly a consequence of the outsider's telling a rising generation what it wanted to hear – and what, in a sense, it already believed. To take up Menand's point that Eliot invented a manner 'perfectly suited to the needs of the modern academic critic', just as a new generation of critics were becoming aware of the need for such a manner: Derrida may be said to have invented a vocabulary and a manner perfectly suited to the needs of a later generation who wanted to sweep away the Eliot-centred orthodoxy, but were not sure how to set about it. The outsider who knows the positions, but is not identified with any of the existing parties, is ideally placed to rally the troops, and thus assume the rank of general almost overnight.

The idea that 'modernism' constituted a radical break with the literary and philosophical past is an important plank in the theoretical platform, because it facilitates the claim that 'postmodernism' involves an even more radical break with the modernist past, putting theorists at two removes from the tradition they claim to have displaced. In *Of Grammatology*, for example, Derrida identifies Pound as one of his precursors:

> This is the meaning of the work of Fenellosa [sic] whose influence upon Ezra Pound and his poetics is well-known; this irreducibly graphic poetics was, with that of Mallarmé, the first break in the entrenched Western tradition. The fascination that the Chinese ideogram exercised upon Pound's writing may thus be given all its historical significance.[55]

The modernists, in this version, become the advance party who soften up the Western tradition, which is then routed by General Derrida and his followers. 'Modernism' must in turn be demoted to make way for theory – hence, in part, radical theorists' hostility to the canonical moderns.

As history, none of this will bear examination. Derrida's assertion that an 'entrenched Western tradition', running from Plato to the late nineteenth century, is first disrupted by Fenollosa, Pound, and Mallarmé, belongs to the history of self-promotion rather than to the history of ideas. Structurally, the claim resembles Eliot's 'dissociation of sensibility', except that instead of a bad break in the seventeenth century, we have an unprecedented disruption in the early twentieth, followed by a Grand Closing Deconstructionist Sale half a century later. The poststructuralist enterprise depends on a reification of the 'Western tradition' – a notion which in its modern critical form is closely identified with 'Tradition and the Individual Talent'. Whether Derrida had heard of Eliot when he wrote *Of Grammatology* is irrelevant: it is not a matter of influence, but of analogous forms of self-promotion. Eliot's comparatively modest strategy was to put three centuries between himself and the last great age of English literature; Derrida's programme requires an undifferentiated logocentric tradition to be superseded by an Age of Deconstruction.

Anyone who claims to have transcended all previous thought needs a reified tradition, suitably caricatured, to serve as a punching-bag. As Frank Kermode observed, in one of the earliest critiques of 'dissociation of sensibility':

> it seems to me much less important that there was not, in the sense in which Mr Eliot's supporters have thought, a particular and far-reaching catastrophe in the seventeenth century, than that there was, in the twentieth, an urgent need to establish the historicity of such a disaster.[56]

By the same token, the assertion that before Derrida, *everyone* was deluded by logocentricism, obviously requires some kind of historical rationale, a tradition in which thinkers such as Nietzsche and Heidegger, struggling to waken from their logocentric slumbers, play John the Baptist to Derrida's Messiah. In the literary version, 'modernism' and 'postmodernism' perform a similar function in preparing the way for theory. But if 'modernism' and 'postmodernism' have no historical substance, the rationale collapses, and we are left with the bald assertion that theorists are the only persons ever to have understood the nature of language correctly.

Theorists, therefore, have a heavy investment in a decisive modernist schism. Though a great deal of critical effort has been expended on distinctions between 'modernist' and 'postmodernist' literature, this is not the central issue. Literary theory, rather than postmodernist literature, is, according to theorists, the true successor to 'modernism'. 'One might conjecture', says Jonathan Culler,

> that the power of innovation and defamiliarization, which previously lay with a literary avant-garde, behind which academic criticism lagged, has now passed to criticism. . . . The quality of the 'modern', the sense of crisis that literature provokes, now inheres in the critical process of exposing the assumptions of prior discourses.[57]

'One might conjecture' is not, I think, meant to qualify the assertion, but only to concede that literature may still have a subordinate role to play in the task of demystification.

This seems to be the standard view among theorists who take their bearings from Derrida (whether or not they identify themselves as deconstructionists), and it has been promoted by way of a sustained attempt to 'free' criticism from its previous subordination to literature, the difference between the two being 'delusive', according to Paul de Man.[58] Whereas the modernist revolution, in the received versions, involves the displacement of one kind of literature by another, the essence of the poststructuralist revolution is said to be the displacement of literature by literary theory. Attempts to defend this territorial claim can have bizarre consequences, as is evident from a recent essay by Christopher Butler:

> the avantgardist attempt to bind an *élite* of critical interpreters to innovatory works of art grows significantly in the Modern period, to the point where the typically Modernist aesthetic, variously understood, is dominant in intellectual circles. Cubist paintings, atonal music, novels and poems like *Ulysses* and *The Trial*, *The Waste Land* and the *Cantos*, are produced for an audience which is capable, not alone of grappling with new ideas, but of decoding the relationships within the work between its stylistic medium and its message. The Modernist epoch thus inaugurates a process of comprehension which, in growing alliance with the Academy, leads inexorably to the theory dominated, abstract and conceptualist art of the postmoderns.[59]

First modernism, then postmodernism and theory: an inevitable progression, according to Butler. In order to justify the claim, he is compelled to invent a spurious genealogical link between contemporary theorists and an unspecified interpretive elite early in the century. But, as his own examples illustrate, there was no 'avantgardist attempt to bind an *élite* of critical interpreters to innovatory works of art', because the avantgardists *were* the *élite*. His emphasis on interpretation is in any case anachronistic. One of the ironies of the history of modern criticism is that while New Critical interpretive theory was founded upon doctrines attributed to Eliot's early essays, the enduring tendency of Eliot's criticism is anti-interpretive. Pound and Eliot were consistently hostile to the notion of the interpreter as mediator; both used their polemical and critical writings as a way of promoting and directing the reception of their work.

Butler's assertion that *Ulysses* and *The Trial*, *The Waste Land* and the *Cantos* were 'produced for an audience which is capable, not alone of grappling with new ideas, but of decoding the relationships within the work between its stylistic medium and its message' is equally misleading, implying as it does that these works were 'produced' with an audience of late-twentieth-century critics in mind. Again, his allegiance to a spurious genealogy propels him to the conclusion that the four works were composed on the same principles, for the same audience. As on numerous occasions, the triumph of theory over observation leads to crudely intentionalist arguments rivalling the worst excesses of old-style exegesis. His argument is underpinned by the standard claim that the modernist experiment is an unprecedented 'Kuhnian revolution' which 'calls into question the viewer's, hearer's or reader's very identity'.[60] Until the late nineteenth century, he implies, all new art was immediately transparent to its audience; but then came the great cultural crisis in which 'even the basic categories of time and space were reinterpreted in a way that affected the very feel and texture of everyday life'.[61] Yet he admits that 'there are many Modernisms . . . and their beginnings and their possible endings are a good subject for endless disputes'. The only way to proceed, he argues, is to start with a list of canonical Modernist works, based on appeal to the 'consensual judgement' of his readers. The concept of modernism, in typically circular fashion, is then fed back into the canon, generating the distortions already outlined.

This is not to imply that Butler's essay is, by the standards of the genre, an inferior piece of work. On the contrary; it compresses the problem into a mere ten pages. The essential confusion is plain: Butler believes in the existence of a complex entity called 'Modernism' which, on his own showing as in numerous others, is the single most important phenomenon in the history of Western literature prior to the advent of theory. Yet when all of its disputed attributes have been canvassed and rejected, the only remaining 'common denominator' of his canonical works is 'experimentalism of technique' – which is where we were in 1927, forty years before the modernism industry began. It is only necessary to return to Malcolm Bradbury's mid-1970s 'definition' to push this to its logical conclusion. An incomplete list of movements sheltering under 'modernism's' capacious umbrella includes: Naturalism, Anti-Positivism, Symbolism, Impressionism, Post-Impressionism, Decadence, Fauvism, Cubism, Futurism, Cubo-Futurism, Constructionism, Imagism, Vorticism, Expressionism, Dada, Surrealism, Atonalism, Vers Libre, Stream of Consciousness, Functionalism, Collage, Non-Objectivism, Orphism, Rayonism, Suprematism, and Zaum.[62]

Even if some of these are rejected as precursive rather than genuinely modernist, it is clear that experimentalism is the only common denominator, and further, that 'experimental' can be defined only negatively: not traditional; not popular; not (in general) conventionally realist, and so on. If 'modernism' is broad enough to embrace the immense variety of works and theories covered by this list, then we are back where we started, with nothing more than a portmanteau label for 'experimental art, *c.* 1870 to 1930'. And since the only things these experiments have in common is difference, from each other as much as from their precursors, the search for some 'essence of experimentalism' is as misguided as that for the 'essence of modernism'. There is no phenomenon, no tendency, no philosophy, and no unity at the heart of it all, but rather a diverse profusion of works, doctrines, groups and slogans which are alike primarily in being *un*like what we vaguely think of as 'traditional' literature – which in this debate means, primarily, nineteenth-century realism, itself an abstraction from a rich variety of literary techniques. Experiment exists only in relation to orthodoxy, which exists only as a background blur; once it becomes foreground, it ceases to be orthodoxy, and resolves into individual works and *oeuvres*: difference, again, becomes prominent.

In order to speak of literary experiment with any precision, we are forced to speak of particular experiments and their contexts. There will be obvious resemblances with neighbouring works, shading into vaguer and vaguer resemblances as the difference increases; as a portmanteau term like 'modernism' is applied to more and more works and doctrines, the content does not increase, but diminishes until it becomes meaningless. To put it another way, Imagism, Vorticism, *vers libre*, Fordian impressionism, Eliotism, Poundianism and Joyceanism do not add up to, or form components of, something called 'modernism' – they do not add up to anything. These 'isms' are themselves abstractions, frequently distorted by attempts to endow them with academic respectability and incorporate them into the larger and seemingly grander structure of 'modernism'.

III

Everything that has been said about the problem of 'modernism' applies, with even greater force, to 'postmodernism'. A term which can be applied indiscriminately to novels, lifestyles, pop stars and shopping malls is a Humpty-Dumpty word: there are as many 'postmodernisms' as there are users. The futile proliferation of 'post-' formations is a striking symptom of the current academic determination to maintain the illusion of control over a vast range of diverse phenomena by coining new definitions which are in fact non-definitions. A short list includes: post-modern, post-structural, post-Marxist, post-industrial, post-cultural, post-Saussurean, post-historical, post-feminist, post-humanist, post-environmental, post-business, post-Fordist, post-bourgeois, and post-colonial – all of which provide the user with the illusion of having made some kind of conceptual advance. The illusory gains are necessarily short-term; we are already moving into the realm of 'post-post-' and 'beyond post-' formations.[63]

As Kermode remarked of 'dissociation of sensibility' in *History and Value* (1988):

> Once a term of this kind takes off there is no knowing where it will go; there are no societies for the preservation of its original sense or even for the prevention of its nonsensical use. That this is as true of megaperiods as it is of minor inventions like 'dissociation of sensibility', a moment's thought about 'Postmodern' and related terms will show. It is as if these terms came into being and then had to be given meanings.[64]

'Postmodernism', however, has been endowed with so many meanings that it has become meaningless: a problem compounded by the fact that whereas 'modernism' has, on the whole, been elaborated by orthodox, if misguided methods, the promotion of 'postmodernism' is largely the work of literary and cultural theorists, so that the definitions proffered by enthusiasts tend to be anti-definitions. 'Postmodernism' is frequently defined as that-which-cannot-be-defined, or that which reveals the futility (and the immorality) of 'totalising' definitions. The range of reference has long since expanded beyond the control of either the promoters or the detractors, so that it now embraces virtually anything which qualifies as rebellious, liberating, and subversive of authority. 'The fact that it doesn't matter to its exponents whether what they say about it is trivial or false', as Kermode remarks, 'is bound to make life difficult for old-fashioned investigators of Postmodernism.'[65]

The advent of 'postmodernism' is characteristically presented by its supporters as a second, decisive break in the historical process, following the failed schismatic rebellion of the early modernists. In the late 1960s, the term was generally applied to artistic experiments of a kind which looked, to the jaundiced eye, very like an inferior re-run of the *avant-garde* experiments of the 1910s and 1920s.[66] Subsequently, the front line of the postmodernist revolution has been occupied by theorists who present their theories as the product of an absolute break with the mystified past, so that Derrida, for example, can imply that we need a new calendar to mark the advent of deconstruction.

It seems clear that the term has outlived whatever usefulness may have been attributed to it. The distinction between 'modernist' and 'postmodernist' literature is often said to turn on a distinction between 'closed' and 'open' form, but critics are unable to agree about what these terms mean, or to define them in any agreed or even intelligible way, or to agree about where 'modernism' leaves off and 'postmodernism' begins, or why. An unindoctrinated reader confronted with *The Waste Land*, *Ulysses*, *Finnegans Wake*, *The Cantos*, *Labyrinths*, *Gravity's Rainbow*, *Self-Portrait in a Convex Mirror* and *Flaubert's Parrot* would find it impossible to separate the 'modernists' from the 'postmodernists' on any basis other than chronology. Late 1960s attempts to define (or gesture towards) the 'essence of postmodernism' tended to converge on silence or incoherence: the blank canvas or page, the concert in which the pianist does not play, or strikes notes at random, the random array of words or letters or blobs of colour – art, as it were, with a minus sign in front of it. Leaving aside the fact that the territory had already been exhaustively – and far more skilfully – explored by Duchamp alone, anti-art is very much a one-off category: one for each genre (or generation). (The second blank canvas, being in a sense a representation of the first, is condemned by its complicity with the ideology of representation, and therefore fails the test.) Even *objets trouvés,* or Campbell's soup-tins, are suspect in so far as there is any evidence of skill or judgement involved in the presentation.

Applied to a sophisticated work like *The Crying of Lot 49* or *The Name of the Rose,* 'postmodernist' is worthless as a descriptive, explanatory, or generic term. Since it is widely used as a synonym for 'self-subversive', once the critic has made the ritual observation that the work is 'self-subversive' (and explained why *A Tale of a Tub, Tristram Shandy* and *Jacques le Fataliste* do not qualify as postmodernist works), it can help the inquiry no further. If the critic is of the deconstructionist persuasion, he or she can use the text as the occasion for another sermon on indeterminacy and demystification, but since, according to deconstruction in its pure form, all literary texts are equally self-subversive, there is again no need for a special category of 'postmodern' works. In reviewing parlance, 'postmodern' is shorthand for a sophisticated, intrusive or disruptive narrative style, but these qualities are frequently discovered in works complicit with the ideologies of lucidity and coherence, such as Russell Hoban's *The Medusa Frequency,* or Amanda Prantera's *The Cabalist.*

Literary critics sometimes write as if 'postmodernism' can be identified with abstract or non-objective painting, in order to argue that some equivalent category must exist in literature – or that the real postmodernist action is always happening somewhere else. Robert Hughes, however, will have no truck with 'postmodernism' in his revised edition of *The Shock of the New* (1991). 'Movements', he observes,

> would be revived with thunderous eclat in the eighties under the sign of post-modernist recycling – neo-Expressionism, *pittura colta,* 'Neo-Geo,' and so forth. But in 1975 all the isms seemed to be wasms and the only people heard talking about 'movements' – wistfully, at that – were dealers. The sixties produced art-world stars with the incontinent frequency of a kid shaking a bag of glitter. The boom market of the eighties would turn this process to parody.[67]

He identifies 'postmodernism', not only with recycling, but with '"Bad Painting" – as the clumsy devices of *lumpen*-post-modernism came to be approvingly known':[68]

Every year in the 1980s, about 35,000 graduate painters, sculptors, potters, and other 'art-related professionals' issued from the art schools of America, each clutching a degree. That meant that every two years the American educational system produced as many aspirant creators as there had been *people* in Florence in the last quarter of the fifteenth century. The result was a Fourierist bad dream. Secure in the belief that no one should be discouraged, the American art-training system had in effect created a proletariat of artists by the end of the seventies, a pool of unemployable talent from which trends could be siphoned (and, if need be, abandoned) more or less at will.[69]

The same applies to 'creative writing' – and to academic criticism. The reification of 'modernism' and 'postmodernism', together with 'the return of Grand Theory' in the humanities and social sciences, seems in part a response to another, less publicised crisis of the 1960s, which, roughly speaking, marks the point where the secondary literatures on canonical modern authors had become so vast that only bibliographers could hope to confront them in their entirety. Not only have the secondary literatures on individual authors become unmanageable; the contemporary canon, so to speak, has been expanding geometrically since the 1960s. Claims that theory, or postmodernism, or any other 'ism', has 'taken over' are therefore misguided; the situation, as Claude Rawson notes, is more like that anticipated by Diderot

> when he foresaw that the number of books in the world would one day become so vast that no one would ever be able to know what was in them, or to know, when embarking on an investigation, whether the answer was or wasn't already available. Modern learning, in most fields, is evidently already in that state. It multiplies itself in such a way that the impossible accumulation of books can only be negotiated with the help of further publications which mediate among them.[70]

It would now be possible to compile an almost day-by-day account of literary life in London, from the time of Pound's arrival in October 1908 to the publication of *The Waste Land*, without going beyond published sources. The appearance of the first volume of Eliot's letters in 1988 filled the last major gap in the published correspondence of the 'men of 1914' prior to 1923;

Humphrey Carpenter's *A Serious Character: The Life of Ezra Pound*, published in the same year, filled an analogous gap in the biographical picture. Anyone who has read Louis Menand's deceptively titled *Discovering Modernism: T. S. Eliot and his Context* (1987), and who still believes that Eliot's early essays present a coherent theory of literature, or that Vorticism is a profound, subtle and conceptually sophisticated doctrine, is unlikely to be persuaded by another book-length demonstration to the contrary. Michael Levenson, in *A Genealogy of Modernism* (1984), had already emphasised the fissiparous nature of 'the movement', though his title and parts of his commentary are, as I have indicated, at odds with his evidence that 'modernism' consisted of many disparate enterprises with no unifying principle. Now that so much of the primary material is readily available, any interested reader can see the force of Pound's exasperated reply to a 'painfully evangelical epistle' from James Vogel in January 1929:

> *If* you are looking for people who agree with you!!!! How many points of agreement do you suppose there were between Joyce, W. Lewis, Eliot and yrs. truly in 1917, or between Gaudier and Lewis in 1913; or between me and Yeats, etc.?
>
> If you agree that there ought to be decent writing, something expressing the man's ideas, not prune juice to suit the pub. taste or *your* taste, you will have got as far as any 'circle' or 'world' ever has.
>
> If another man has ideas of any kind (not borrowed cliches) that irritate you enough to make you think or take out your own ideas and look at 'em, that is all one can expect.[71]

To argue that 'modernism' is a meaningless category is not to deny anything of the range and vitality of literary experiment during the first quarter of the century; only to insist that the changes can't usefully be accommodated within a single conceptual framework – or indeed within anything like the kind of approach employed within the modernism industry. Academic critics, with rare exceptions, tend to reinvent writers in their own image, transforming poets and novelists into *ersatz* philosophers preoccupied with systems, theories, doctrines and methodologies. As the critical population increases, so the doctrines become more complex and multi-layered. When Joyce joked about keeping the professors busy for a hundred years, he could not have imagined how many professors would take up the invitation. Since 'modern-ism' did not exist, it was necessary to invent it – necessary, that is, for theoretical and interpretive critics working within self-im-posed, and very narrow limits. There is a limit to the amount of exegesis that even *Finnegans Wake* can sustain before everyone starts to complain about overcrowding, but once an abstract en-tity like 'modernism' becomes the focus of inquiry, the business of building castles in the air can go on forever.

No revisionist account of 'the movement', however detailed, could *prove* that 'modernism' is not a meaningful category of lit-erary history. But to see the extent of the distortions imposed by the modernism industry, one has only to subtract 'modernism', along with all of the explanatory and evaluative baggage loaded onto it, from the historical picture. 'The movement' can then be seen for what it always was: a string of promotional strategies invented by Pound to boost the reputations of writers he admired, and, by association, his own. Joyce reappears as a solitary worker in his own field, rather than a participant in a larger enterprise; which, again, is not to deny his influence, but to insist that the influence is Joyce's, not 'modernism's'. Lewis dwindles to the status of a cult figure for a small club of male admirers. Pound, Eliot, and Yeats emerge as three very different poets, not as two founding members, and one honorary or rejected member, of the same club.

Yeats, in the 1890s, was much preoccupied with Mallarmé's an-nouncement that 'our whole age is seeking to bring forth a sacred book'.[72] According to many histories of 'modernism', the whole age was seeking to bring forth *Ulysses* and *The Waste Land*. In this evolutionary style of argument, fifteen years' worth of artis-tic experiment culminates in the publication of two great master-pieces in 1922. Most critics, if pressed, will concede that *Ulysses* was composed in relative isolation, and in a spirit of sublime indifference to the London *avant-garde* scene. But *The Waste Land* is central to almost every account of the evolution of 'mod-ernism'; which brings us to the strange and almost accidental history of the century's most influential poem in English.

2

'These fragments you have shelved (shored)': Pound, Eliot and *The Waste Land*

Pound is that curious thing, a person without a trace of originality of any sort. It is impossible even to imagine him being any one in particular of all the people he has translated, interpreted, appreciated.... *By himself* he would seem to have neither any convictions nor eyes in his head.... Yet when he can get into the skin of somebody else... he becomes a lion or a lynx on the spot.

Wyndham Lewis[1]

And it was evident that the writers did not resent the puzzle they thought I had set them – they liked it. Indeed, though they were unconscious of the fact, they invented the puzzle for the pleasure of discovering the solution.

T. S. Eliot[2]

I

The completion of *The Waste Land* in the winter of 1921–22 has long been acknowledged as the crucial moment in the Pound/Eliot relationship. It was Pound, rather than the 'excessively depressed' Eliot, who saw the poem as 'the justification of "the movement", of our modern experiment since 1900'.[3] Until the award of the *Dial* prize, Eliot endorsed Pound's valuation: 'I think it is the best I have ever done, and Pound thinks so too', he wrote to John Quinn on 25 June 1922, but by 15 November he was speaking of it as 'a thing of the past so far as I am concerned'.[4] His notorious disclaimers ('their illusion of being disillusioned'; 'rhythmical grumbling'; 'a personal grouse'; 'bogus scholarship'; 'just as structureless, only a more futile way')[5] are scattered across the following decades, punctuated, from 1933 onwards, by tributes to Pound's editing of the manuscript.

The story of Eliot's effectively disowning his most popular, and by far his most influential poem, is so familiar that its strangeness is worth reflection. He regarded *Four Quartets* as his finest work,[6] but the majority of his readers have not endorsed that judgement. Eliot, as Helen Gardner remarked, 'was willing to talk about [*Four Quartets*] and give direct answers. In speaking of it he never employed the defensive irony that marks so many of his references to *The Waste Land*.'[7] Equally, he had no doubts about the quality of 'Prufrock'; his correspondence during the years 1912–17 returns repeatedly to the fear that he will never be able to equal it.

His preference for the *Quartets* aside, the tenor of his later remarks about *The Waste Land* is to disparage it, and to distance himself both from the poem and from the immense significance attributed to it by its readers. No strategy could have contributed more to the poem's early reputation as an oracular, impersonal, omniscient diagnosis of cultural collapse. Peter Quennell remarked that the Oxford 'intelligentsia' in the mid-1920s

> were as knowledgeable and talkative about the relationship of Mr Ionides [sic] and Phlebas the Phoenician as their Burlington equivalents about the genealogical complications of the Stud Book.[8]

Wallace Fowlie, who first encountered Eliot's work in the early 1930s, maintained that 'it would be impossible to exaggerate Eliot's influence' on his generation:

> Every word he said – and he seemed to speak more and more parsimoniously – had to be construed into a message of profound significance.[9]

Parsimony and profundity were inseparably related. Had Eliot given a string of interviews 'explaining' the poem ('My typist at Lloyd's was always complaining about her carbuncular boyfriend'), much of its mystique would have been dissipated.

The explosive growth of biographical research over the past two decades has had precisely that effect. Peter Ackroyd's work[10] effectively demolished earlier, reductive attempts to explain the life by way of the poem, but the poem can no longer be divorced from the life. Perhaps Eliot's determination to distance himself from *The Waste Land* was, then, simply due to its painful personal associations, to embarrassment at seeing a 'personal grouse' transformed into a document of cosmic significance.[11]

No doubt such feelings played their part. Yet Eliot, it seems, had hoped to produce exactly the kind of work that a generation of readers took it to be. Part of his New Year's resolution for 1920 was to 'write a long poem I have had on my mind for a long time',[12] but, as Conrad Aiken later revealed, he was unable to begin, despite 'every confidence that the material was *there* and waiting'. Homer Lane told Aiken that the only obstacle was Eliot's 'fear of putting anything down that is short of perfection'; Aiken was convinced that this advice, though it infuriated the poet, 'broke the log-jam'.[13]

The source of the inhibition may have been rather more specific. Throughout 1919 and 1920, he was reading instalments of *Ulysses* and admiring it 'immensely'.[14] In an interview with Anthony Cronin in the 1950s, Eliot said that the instalments made him feel that

> [w]hat he was tentatively attempting to do, with the usual false starts and despairs, had already been done, done superbly and it seemed to him finally, in prose which without being poetic in the older sense, had the intensity and texture of poetry.[15]

'Ulysses, Order, and Myth', however, suggests quite the opposite; his account of the 'mythical method' seems to put *The Waste Land* on the same footing as *Ulysses*. The proposition that Eliot had succeeded in 'giving a shape and significance to the immense panorama of futility and anarchy which is contemporary history'[16] dominated exegesis of the poem for the next forty years. He had, from the point of view of his readers, succeeded in effecting a complete separation between the man who suffered at Clarence Gate Gardens and the poet who received the *Dial* prize. He had, for all public purposes, rivalled *Ulysses*, and thereby achieved what he had despaired of doing. Pound's knowledge of the manuscript had in no way qualified his sense of Eliot's achievement. Why, then, disown it?

Any approach to this question must focus on Pound's role in the composition of the poem. Ronald Bush, for example, considers that 'Pound altered it relatively little'.[17] Yet he has already conceded that Eliot 'imposed' the 'mythic organisation' on the poem 'in the last stages of composition'.[18] That 'organisation' is, on his own account, central to the impact of *The Waste Land* – and it was 'imposed' not by Eliot, but by Pound. The priority of the published version makes it hard to shake off the illusion that the poem was already 'there' in the manuscript. Reading the manuscript, we cannot avoid privileging *The Waste Land*, seeing the rejected lines and passages as flaws and excrescences. We cannot now avoid seeing what Pound saw, and sharing his assumption that the 'real' poem must have been equally apparent to Eliot, that it was the poem Eliot had meant to write but had not quite arrived at. The circularity of the argument is obvious; such is the force of consensus that circularity looks more like inevitability.

Pound's perception of it as Eliot's masterpiece has further obscured the point: 'I am wracked by the seven jealousies.'[19] This was not, however, self-sacrifice or excessive modesty. The assurance with which he transformed the manuscript testifies to his clarity of purpose; he must, given the tenor of his comments, have assumed that Eliot, too, could 'see' the final version in the 'sprawling, chaotic' manuscript.[20] Pound's belief that he was performing a 'caesarian Operation', rather than radical reconstructive surgery, is one of the most powerful factors in sustaining the belief that Eliot 'intended' to arrive at the printed text.[21] Another is, of course, the fact that the poem was published under Eliot's name, and had already generated a vast critical literature, much of it concerned with the minutiae of Eliot's intentions, by the time the manuscript reappeared. Twenty years later, little has changed in this regard. The critical consensus is still, overwhelmingly, that Pound realised *Eliot's* conception of the poem.

From Eliot's point of view, his situation when he requested Pound's assistance must have looked something like this: for nearly a decade he had been unable to improve on the achievement of the 'Prufrock' period. Though he could write to his mother, in March 1919, that '[t]here is a small and select public which regards me as the best living critic, as well as the best living poet, in England',[22] his reputation rested squarely on the poems of 1909–12. Pound had given him a good deal of assistance with the drafts of his poems from at least 1917 onwards: 'Whispers of Immortality' is virtually a joint production.[23] In his last week in Lausanne, 'Prufrock' was still the best poem he had written; he did not know where his 'long poem' was heading, or whether it would work.

On 19 December 1921, Eliot told Sydney Waterlow, in a letter from Lausanne, that he was 'trying to finish a poem – about 800 or 1000 lines. *Je ne sais pas si ça tient*'.[24] Five weeks later,[25] after Pound had been through it, the poem had been reduced to around 500 lines. 'Trying to finish' are not, one feels, the words of a man who is about to discard half his manuscript. Pound generously refers to 'your instinct' in commending the improvement, but it is apparent that even after the first critique, Eliot could not distinguish between the best and the worst passages. He retained the lifeless 'Exequy' and the repulsive 'Dirge', and had to be persuaded to leave them out. In 1928 he remarked that Pound had induced him 'to destroy what I thought an excellent set of couplets' (the 'Lady Fresca' passage) on the ground that Pope had done it better.[26] He gave up the shipwreck in the original Part IV only reluctantly, and then asked Pound whether he should jettison Phlebas the Phoenician as well – as if he could see nothing, in terms of quality, to choose between the two. To say that he had lost control of his material would be misleading, since there is no evidence that it was ever under his control.

Pound, editing the 'sprawling, chaotic' manuscript on Fordian principles ('never comment: state') changed it not merely in quality but in kind. The manuscript version is dominated by an all too 'personal' author, an interested party much concerned to judge his 'characters' in terms which are frequently 'doubtful', or 'over the mark' in ways that subvert the authority they seek ('make up yr. mind'). This applies not only to the crass intrusions ('London, the swarming life you kill and breed . . .') but to the 'Nighttown' opening, the Lady Fresca passage, the shipwreck passage and the appended fragments. While traces of this 'personality' remain in the final version (most obviously in 'The Fire Sermon') they are (or were) effectively displaced by allusive strategies which are swamped by the 'personal' voice in the manuscript.

Though a few enthusiasts have tried to rescue something from the detritus of 'He Do the Police in Different Voices', it is generally conceded that the rejected passages are very bad indeed. The hallmarks of bad Eliot are fairly consistent: overinsistence, at times bordering on hysteria; prurience; portentousness; a shrill condemnation of the loathed Other (characteristically female, Jewish, or both). All are prominently displayed in the manuscript; as in the misogynist portrait of 'Fresca' (Ottoline Morrell?):[27]

(The same eternal and consuming itch
Can make a martyr, or plain simple bitch);
Or prudent sly domestic puss-puss cat,
Or autumn's favourite in a furnished flat,
Or strolling slattern in a tawdry gown,
A doorstep dunged by every dog in town,

and the 'doubtful' gloating over Bleistein's corpse:

Full fathom five your Bleistein lies
Under the flatfish and the squids.
Graves' Disease in a dead jew's eyes!

Anti-Semitism and envy of Joyce here form an unholy alliance as Bleistein/Bloom becomes the drowned corpse in Dublin Bay.[28] The juxtaposition of good and bad Eliot throughout suggests that the line between the two is much narrower than it seems, and that the oracular gravity of his best work was always something of a tightrope act.

Just as the belief that Eliot must have known what he was doing derives from the priority of the published text, so *The Waste Land*'s reputation rested, in part, on an illusion: the 'presence' of an omniscient, oracular author, 'like the God of creation ... invisible, refined out of existence, indifferent', and closely identified with the forensic authority of the early essays. That illusion is shattered in the manuscript, and threatened in 'The Fire Sermon', principally in the encounter between typist and clerk, which survived for many years under the umbrella of Tiresias, but became exhibit A in the case against the poem as it developed in the 1960s and early 1970s.[29] This passage is also the one most heavily reworked by Pound, who seems to have been on the verge of rejecting it altogether ('not interesting enough as verse to warrant so much of it') before setting out to salvage what he could.

The manuscript suggests that Eliot, in so far as he had any notion of where he was going, was attempting to compete with Joyce by composing in as many different styles as he could muster, but without any clear sense of his subject, or of his limitations. Among the worst passages are those which allude directly to *Ulysses*: Fresca's morning defecation; the drowning of Bleistein/Bloom; and the opening attempt at 'Nighttown':

And old Tom took us behind, brought out a bottle of fizz,
With old Jane, Tom's wife; and we got Joe to sing
'I'm proud of all the Irish blood that's in me,
'There's not a man can say a word agin me'.

Pound then transformed the manuscript on principles whose application Eliot was unable, in any practical sense, to follow. By
focusing on quality, rather than quantity of voices, Pound rescued
the poem from certain failure in the contest. In the process, he
also arrived at the five-part structure,[30] resonant with echoes of
Shakespearean tragedy, the 'omniscient' opening and closing lines,
and perhaps even the title.[31] The much-praised dramatic quality
is a matter of poise and control, rather than range (the Cockney
voices in the second half of 'A Game Of Chess' became the other
most vulnerable target when the reaction of the 1960s set in).

Granted that Eliot had been 'excessively depressed' after his
return to London,[32] all of this suggests an extraordinary lack of
judgement – verging on tone-deafness – on the part of a man
whose ambition was to rival Joyce's mastery of style. Lyndall
Gordon attributes his confusion, his 'submissiveness to Pound's
idea of the poem', to the frustration of 'Eliot's impulse to exhibit
the whole truth – the strength as well as the sickness of a suffering soul':

> When Eliot left Lausanne, he was master of his autobiography,
> but from the time Pound revised the manuscript in Paris there
> was a recrudescence of Eliot's depression.[33]

Much of this is implausible: his depression seems an obvious consequence of his return to the miseries of his London life, and
Gordon's reading of the manuscript reflects her own determination to discover the later Eliot in the earlier. But she is right, in a
way, to describe the published *Waste Land* as 'Pound's idea of
the poem'. Eliot's 'submissiveness' – which seems more like surrender – suggests that he had little idea of what he was aiming
for ('*Je ne sais pas si ça tient*'). *The Waste Land* emerged from an
uncanny convergence of the two poets' strengths and weaknesses.
Pound could not have produced the raw material; Eliot could
not tell the difference between good and bad passages, nor, evidently, could he separate the impersonal voice from the 'merely
personal' one. Edmund Wilson, writing in 1971, thought that Pound

had 'produced from Eliot's rough version a more or less Poundian work more successful than anything on a similar scale he had been able to do himself'.[34]

Eliot's subsequent ambivalence towards the poem, therefore, surely had much to do with the question of ownership. Throughout the negotiations for the poem's publication, he was occupied with practical (and financial) details. In September 1922 he wrote to Quinn, who had negotiated the award of the *Dial* prize:

> My only regret (which may seem in the circumstances either ungracious or hypocritical) is that this award should have been given to me before it has been given to Pound. I feel that he deserves the recognition much more than I do, certainly 'for his services to Letters',[35] and I feel that I ought to have been made to wait until after he had received this public testimony. . . . I think that this manuscript is worth preserving in its present form solely for the reason that it is the only evidence of the difference which his criticism has made to this poem. . . .[36]

Despite this ambiguous acknowledgement of his debt to Pound, Eliot was clearly very nervous about any public indication of its scope. Having decided not to use Pound's 'Sage Homme' as a preface, he had instead dedicated the poem to '*il miglior fabbro*', a phrase which the public naturally construed as a gracious bow from one master (or 'literary bolshevik')[37] to another, rather than a covert acknowledgement of services rendered. The dedication, furthermore, did not appear in either the first English or the first American printing of the poem; it was added, along with the notes, to the Boni & Liveright edition of 15 December 1922. A few months later, Pound's allusion to *The Waste Land* in the opening line of what became Canto VIII ('These fragments you have shelved (shored)') provoked a reaction from the editor of *The Criterion* which was, in the circumstances, fraught with irony:

> I object strongly on tactical grounds to yr. 1st line. People are inclined to think that we write our verses in collaboration as it is, or else that you write mine & I write yours. With your permission we will begin with line 2.[38]

'These fragments you have shelved'; indeed.[39] Yet, writing to Aldington a few months earlier, he had described *The Waste Land* as 'a thing of the past so far as I am concerned'.

Eliot's published comments about *The Waste Land* prior to the publication of *Collected Poems 1909–1935* are cryptic, equivocal and evasive. In 'The Function of Criticism' (1923) Eliot was much concerned to present himself as the masterly technician, tireless in his pursuit of perfection:

> Probably, indeed, the larger part of the labour of an author in composing his work is critical labour; the labour of sifting, combining, constructing, expunging, correcting, testing: this frightful toil is as much critical as creative;[40]

remarks which his readers could hardly have failed to apply to the composition of *The Waste Land*. Readers of 'Thoughts After Lambeth' (1931), after digesting the lofty rebuke: 'I may have expressed for them their illusion of being disillusioned, but that did not form part of my intention', would have construed the mysterious 'intention' as something too subtle and profound for the likes of I. A. Richards (or themselves) to comprehend.[41]

The scope of his debt seems to have been first publicly acknowledged in 1933, in a tribute to Pound's *Cantos*,[42] and more fully in 1938, when he declared that the dedication to Pound was meant to 'honour the technical mastery and critical ability manifest in his own work, which had also done so much to turn *The Waste Land* from a jumble of good and bad passages into a poem'.[43] (No one, in the absence of the manuscript, could have known that the 'excellent set of couplets' mentioned in Eliot's preface to Pound's *Selected Poems* (1928) had any relation to *The Waste Land*.) Such an admission in 1922 would have severely damaged, if not destroyed, the poem's mystique, whereas by 1938 Eliot's reputation was secure beyond doubt. Significantly, the declaration was prompted by an attack on Pound by G. W. Stonier, which suggests that Eliot still felt the need to redress a past injustice.

His debt to Pound was again acknowledged in a 1946 tribute, published as part of the campaign to save Pound from himself (and the electric chair).[44] But the equivocation continued. In the *Paris Review* interview in 1959, he described Pound as 'a marvellous critic because he didn't try to turn you into an imitation of himself. He tried to see what you were trying to do.'[45] His comment that 'I wasn't even bothering whether I understood what I was saying' in *The Waste Land*[46] suggests that he might have added,

'even if you had no idea of it yourself'. A little later he responded
to the question: 'Did the excisions change the intellectual structure of the poem?' with 'No, I think it was just as structureless,
only in a more futile way in the longer version.'[47] The interviewer
then questioned him directly about his intention, received a completely evasive answer, and changed the subject.

Eliot's published comments on the poem, then, suggest that he
did not share his readers' valuation of it, was embarrassed by it,
and wished that it had not become a *cause célèbre*. There are at
least three possible explanations. First, as I have suggested, he
may have felt that despite Pound's transformation it was too
personal, too self-revelatory.[48] But if so, why quarrel publicly with
interpretations which in effect protected his privacy – and in the
process contradict his own repeated assertion that the reader is
the final arbiter of meaning?

Second, Eliot's change of manner shortly after the publication
of *The Waste Land* was, as Louis Menand says,

> so dramatic – it almost seems possible to date it within a month
> or two – that some commentators have suggested that only a
> single, decisive personal crisis can explain it.[49]

While not dismissing that possibility, he argues that Eliot became,
in effect, the victim of his own success. After *The Waste Land*, 'the
received conception of literary values was no longer an anonymous cultural given, but . . . to a considerable extent identifiably
his own'. He could no longer operate as the outsider, subjecting
those values to 'the critical force of a relentless irony'; once he
began to assume 'definite positions' (as in 'The Function of Criticism', published in October 1923, in which the later manner is
already ascendant), much of that force was dissipated:

> It is somehow fitting that of the many attitudes that Eliot the
> cultural critic found in need of correction, a few could be traced
> to the work of his younger self – a writer for whom the notion
> of prescriptive cultural criticism would have seemed only another
> opportunity for irony.[50]

But if he disowned *The Waste Land* because it belonged to a phase
which he wished to put behind him, why did he exempt the earlier poems from this dismissal?

There is, finally, the matter of ownership and control. This is the only factor which applies specifically and solely to *The Waste Land*, and here there are several strong possibilities: guilt and anxiety at having profited so much from Pound's labours without full and prompt public acknowledgement; chagrin at not having 'modernised himself *on his own*',[51] in Pound's phrase; resentment of the debt itself; unease about the constant requests for insight into the work. Given his propensity to inflate small irritations into nightmarish anxieties, these possibilities cannot be discounted.

Having signed the poem, he was, in any case, saddled with it, and was therefore obliged to endure a chorus of complaints, throughout the years separating *For Lancelot Andrewes* from *Collected Poems 1909–1935*, from admirers who wanted more waste land and less royalism, classicism and Anglo-Catholicism. Philip Blair Rice's lament, uttered in 1932, is characteristic:

> He occupies the position of a *directeur du conscience* – at least in matters of taste – for a number of people, and they may be pardoned for feeling a little wistful if he, to use his own words, goes on 'playing possum'. Should he continue in this slumbrous pastime, it will be necessary to conclude that he is capable of leading out of the waste land only those who already agree with him and not those who come to him for light.[52]

As the monographs began to appear, *The Waste Land* became the hub around which his *oeuvre* was made to revolve. Ironically, it compelled respect for the religious poems from critics who clearly found them neither enjoyable nor comprehensible. *The Times Literary Supplement*'s notice of *Ash-Wednesday* echoes the valedictory tone of the reviews at large:

> The pale flowers that spring from this soil of dejection will remain as 'evidence of character' for a period which looked so earnestly to Mr. Eliot for poetic wisdom.[53]

All of this, occurring in what were, even by Eliot's standards, exceptionally miserable years, cannot have been easy to swallow. His gnomic attempts to distance himself from the poem's mystique were counter-productive. The closest he came to any public acknowledgement of his curious plight is in the closing chapters of *The Use of Poetry and the Use of Criticism*, where, after another attempt to shake off I. A. Richards' veneration of *The Waste Land*, he proceeds to an oblique acknowledgement of his loss of inspiration, launches into an extended retraction of what he has just said, and proceeds, via a glancing blow at 'the exaggerated repute of *Kubla Khan*' to leave us with a bow to 'the sad ghost of Coleridge' – who has been rattling his chains ever since his appearance in the fourth chapter.[54] Though Eliot's recent separation from Vivien obviously contributes to the gesture, it also evokes 'Wordsworth' in Rapallo, the man responsible for the 'exaggerated repute' of *The Waste Land*, not only 'droning on' about Social Credit, but pressing reams of cantos, pamphlets, tracts and letters upon his 'ruined' publisher. In 1934, Pound attacked *The Use of Poetry* in the *New English Weekly*, to which Eliot then wrote in support of Pound's judgement, comparing the book unfavourably with *After Strange Gods*.[55] Compounding these ironies, one reviewer declared that *The Use of Poetry* 'is prodigiously seductive ... but half its seduction comes from the fact of its author being also the author of *The Waste Land*'.[56]

The completion of *Four Quartets* meant that Eliot had at last, in his own eyes and those of his more respectful critics, surpassed *The Waste Land*, and thereafter he was able to take a more relaxed view of it. 'The intolerable wrestle with words and meanings' was, in any case, over. Even if he had openly admitted that *The Waste Land* was not, in a very real sense, his poem, no one would have believed him. No one, after all, had taken any notice of his previous disclaimers. It would have been put down to another characteristic excess of modesty. As the *Observer* remarked on the award of the OM: '[t]hat Eliot is the most famous living poet perhaps only he himself would be found to doubt'.[57]

II

Pound wanted no credit for his contribution to *The Waste Land*: '[m]y squibs are now a bloody impertinence'.[58] His delight in being present at the birth of 'the longest poem in the English langwidge' is obvious: '[i]t is after a all a grrrreat litttttterary period'.[59] It was the culmination of eight years of unstinting effort on Eliot's behalf. But the moment of 'the movement's' triumph was also the moment at which Pound finally lost control of it.

Humphrey Carpenter has admirably documented the decline

of Pound's influence in London, the darkening of his attitudes, the gradual dispersion of his energies which began as early as 1916, and was largely complete by 1919. Eliot wrote to Quinn in January 1920: 'I know that Pound's lack of tact has done him great harm. But I am worried as to what is to become of him.'[60] And in May 1921: 'I have had no news of Pound, beyond two postcards with no address, since he left this country. He appears to be avoiding communication with England, and to consider the country hopeless.'[61] Yet unfinished business remained. When Pound left England in January 1921, there was no single poem to which he could point as 'the justification of "the movement", of our modern experiment since 1900'. '1900' gestures in Yeats's direction, but 'the movement' (like the pronoun) surely centres on Pound's London career as (in Ford's equivocal phrase) 'the greatest discoverer of literary talent the world has ever seen',[62] from 'the forgotten school of 1909' to the 'two authors' who decided in 1917 that 'general floppiness had gone too far and that some countercurrent must be set going'.[63]

The dynamics of Pound's London career as the P. T. Barnum of 'the movement' have yet to be fully explored. He was, according to Eliot, 'so passionately concerned about the works of art which he expected his protégés to produce that he sometimes tended to regard them almost impersonally, as art or literature machines to be carefully tended and oiled, for the sake of their potential output'.[64] This seems to me to capture something of the paradox: Pound's generosity, his subordination of his personal interests to his work for 'the movement' is indisputable, and yet his campaign was, equally, propelled by his identification of himself with 'the movement'. Thus, when Amy Lowell succeeded in capturing 'Imagism', Pound immediately disowned it. At around the same time, he was engaged in a dispute with F. S. Flint over the ownership of 'the forgotten school of 1909'.[65] No one, perhaps, could have engaged in such a protracted and intense campaign without some degree of identification. But in Pound's case the issue was complicated by the symbiosis between his own poetic ambitions, and his aspirations for 'the movement' at large.

Pound, in 1912, recalled his initial ambition: 'I knew at fifteen pretty much what I wanted to do. I resolved that at thirty I would know more about poetry than any man living.'[66] The contrast with Yeats at sixteen is striking: 'my peculearitys ... will never be done justice to ... until they have become classics and are set for examinations'.[67] Yeats intended to write 'classics'; Pound sought an unrivalled knowledge *of* them. As Carpenter notes, 'there is no clear evidence of [Pound's] having composed much serious poetry until he was eighteen, and when he did start, he wrote chiefly about the idea of being a poet'.[68]

'The idea of being a poet' was, perhaps, as close as Pound ever got to a central subject. His supporters have always faced at least two essential difficulties in their attempts to present him as 'the greatest poet of the twentieth century' (as he is routinely described in the pages of *Paideuma*): the recurring perception that his work is dependent on its sources, or models, in a way that the work of a major poet is not, and the absence of any thematic coherence, or development (unless one regards his surrender to belief in a global Zionist conspiracy as a development). Pound's stylistic improvement after Ford's celebrated reaction to *Canzoni* in 1911 is obvious, at least from the perspective of *Cathay*. But to speak of the 'development' of his style is again misleading; what happens is more like fragmentation, leading both to the emergence of a range of disparate voices, some archaic, some prosaic, some 'modern', and to the dissolution of style into 'Ezz-eze'. As George P. Elliott put it, 'the more poets he is like, the less one is sure who Pound is'.[69]

The issues of style, subject, and 'translation' are inseparably related. Whereas Eliot devoted himself, in 1909–12, to swallowing Laforgue, Pound was consumed by his models:

> Thus am I Dante for a space and am
> One Francois Villon, ballad-lord and thief
> Or am such holy ones I may not write,
> Lest blasphemy be writ against my name;
> This for an instant and the flame is gone.[70]

His involvement with his sources takes many different forms: free translation, imitation, *hommage*, ventriloquism, pastiche, mimicry, parody, and plagiarism. In the broadest sense of 'translation', Pound remains a translator by default. The absence of any core of subject-matter which is identifiably his, the lack of thematic continuity or development, ensured that his sources would always tend to dominate him, rather than the reverse. In Bloomian terms, he is a prime example of the weak poet, the son overwhelmed by the father(s).[71] The fatal attempt at epic in the *Cantos* may be seen as a self-destructive rebellion (ironically encapsulated in his father's name) against his poetic destiny. Much energy has been expended on the identity of the lady in 'Portrait d'une Femme', and yet the poem is also a self-portrait:[72]

> No! There is nothing! In the whole and all,
> Nothing that's quite your own.
>   Yet this is you.[73]

The issue of 'translation' has been clouded, first by his supporters, who have strenuously resisted the charge (as they see it), and secondly by the striking and sometimes bizarre stylistic effects that characterise Poundian reworking. The promotion of Pound the poet, in its confusion of ambition with achievement, has also directed attention away from the links between Pound the verse 'translator', and Pound the editor, promoter and entrepreneur of 'the movement'. In both capacities, he conducts a series of rescue operations on remote, forgotten, or neglected works and forms, striving to secure public attention for his protégés in Provence or China, Oxford or Trieste. The message, as he admits himself, is always the same: 'Joyce is a writer, GODDAMN your eyes, Joyce is a writer, I tell you Joyce, etc. etc.' or

> Say that I believe in Lewis, spit out the later Rodin,
> Say that Epstein can carve in stone,
> That Brzeska can use the chisel,
> Or Wadsworth paint:
>   Then they will have my guts. . . .[74]

The accompanying doctrines, which have been subjected to such exhaustive analysis, are equally polemical, opportunistic, part of the business of capturing the audience's attention.

Carpenter remarks that though Pound 'had an acute ear for weak lines in other people's work, it is striking that he did not apply it to much of his own' – a paradox he attributes to Pound's 'impatience . . . to set other poet's houses in order'.[75] It surely has more to do with Pound's uncertainty about his own poetic identity, which in turn bears on Eliot's remark that Pound 'didn't try to turn you into an imitation of himself. He tried to see what you were trying to do.'[76] There was, in a sense, no 'self' to imitate. His tendency to be absorbed by his models in his own verse was precisely what made him a good editor of his contemporaries' work.

Pound's London career clearly centred on his ambition to 'know more about poetry than any man living' by the time he was thirty – and to be recognised in that capacity. It must have seemed to him, as he turned thirty in 1915, that he had come close to achieving it. He was, at least in *avant-garde* circles, a household name. He had won Yeats's approval; and in his own view had 'modernised' the master. He had got 'our little gang' of Imagists into print, along with Joyce and Eliot, and had published *Cathay*, his finest volume, to considerable acclaim. He had begun his 'endless poem'. Yet by December 1918 he was remarking bitterly to Joyce that he was 'perhaps better at digging up the corpses of let us say Li Po, or more lately Sextus Propertius, than in preserving this bitched mess of modernity'.[77]

Many explanations have been advanced for the rapid decline of his influence on the London scene after 1915. He was later inclined to blame an establishment conspiracy against himself as leader of 'the movement'.[78] The increasing violence of his assaults on the 'dungminded dungbearded, penny a line, please the mediocre-at-all-cost doctrine', obviously did not help:

> HERE is the taste of my BOOT,
>   CARESS it, lick off the BLACKING.[79]

Nor did the exclusion of many of 'our little gang' from his list of 'serious' artists after Amy Lowell's hijacking of Imagism.[80] But, as Michael Levenson observes, the very success of the 'new poetry' ensured that no individual would be able to control it:

> A year . . . after the publication of *Some Imagist Poets*, Imagism became vastly fashionable in the United States, and Lowell was confronted with the circumstance that had tormented Pound, the loss of literary identity in the wash of imitators.[81]

By 1917, Pound's 'gang', so far as poetry was concerned, had been reduced to two members: himself and Eliot. But while Pound was excoriating the opposition, Eliot was cultivating them, lunching with J. C. Squire, frequenting Bloomsbury and Garsington, working his way steadily towards writing for *The Times Literary Supplement*: 'the highest honour possible in the critical world of literature'.[82] Pound certainly encouraged Eliot in this pursuit; as he remarked to Mencken in March 1918, regarding *Ezra Pound: His Metric and Poetry*:

> Eliot wrote it, but it would be extremely unwise for him, at this stage of his career, with the hope of sometime getting paid by the elder reviews, and published by the godly, and in general of not utterly bitching his chances in various quarters, for him to have signed it.[83]

Pound's fall is almost inversely related to Eliot's rise to the ranks of 'the godly'. Even as late as 1925, he seems to have construed Eliot's ascent in terms of infiltration:

> I pointed out to him in the beginning there was no use of two of us butting a stone wall; that he wd. never be as hefty a battering ram as I was, nor as explosive as Lewis, and that he'd better try a more oceanic and fluid method of sapping the foundations.[84]

Breaking and entering provides another well-known metaphor (later deployed by Eliot in *The Use of Poetry*): 'You let *me* throw the bricks through the front window. You go in at the back door and take out the swag.'[85] Eliot, however, seemed more intent on taking over the premises. Pound complained that *The Criterion*, even in 1923, had to be 'so heavily camouflaged as Westminster Abbey, that the living visitor is not very visible'.[86] As Levenson comments, 'What Pound took as camouflage was not camouflage at all; it was Eliot himself.'[87] He argues that Pound was the chief 'agent of provocation' in the cause of 'modernism' from 1908 to 1922, whereafter Eliot took over as the agent of consolidation – but 'modernism', as usual, serves only to confuse the issue.[88]

Louis Menand has crystallised the unease which pervades many discussions over the last two decades: the increasing recognition that the 'programme' so confidently discerned by mid-century critics in Eliot's early essays is self-subversive, contradictory in ways that have remained just beyond the threshhold of articulation. Menand demonstrates that those essays are

> a kind of skeptic's guide to the literary values of early modernism – which is to say in many cases to the literary values, in boiled-down or attenuated forms, of the nineteenth century.[89]

A central rhetorical tactic is the use of 'the power of the received idea' against itself, in ways that allow readers to project their own programmes into the void thus created:

> It is part of the peculiar design of Eliot's early criticism that the received language of aesthetic theory is used to make arguments whose theoretical content is practically zero – as much as to say, I offer these explanations for my aesthetic preferences, but I am not (though others may be) ready to claim anything of greater significance for them.[90]

Because Eliot and Pound, in their early essays, were often attacking the same targets ('the annual scourge of the Georgian anthology'),[91] the natural assumption is they were also arguing *for* the same things (hence the common later belief that Eliot domesticated Pound's 'insights' for academic consumption).[92] But Eliot never supported 'the movement'; Pound, Joyce and Lewis were, rather, exempted from his attacks on it. 'Isolated Superiority' (as his 1928 essay on the award of the *Dial* prize to Pound was entitled), is the characteristic note.

The subtext of Menand's demonstration is inescapable: the one consistent goal of Eliot's early essays is the single-handed 'conquest of literary London':

> The task of the usurping practitioner is to make his discourse seem not a new, but in fact the traditional discourse, and to make the language of the amateur he is supplanting appear to be an aberration. . . . In the case of Eliot's criticism, the mode to be exposed as specious was the mode identified with the Georgian anthologies; the mode to be revealed as traditional was, of course, his own.[93]

Eliot employed the same strategy against 'the movement' itself in 'Reflections on *Vers Libre*' (1917), exposing the revolution as specious whilst implicitly declaring that he *was* the revolution.

Though the tension between Eliot's personal ambition and his loyalty and gratitude to Pound never really surfaced, London by 1919 would hardly have been big enough for the two of them had it not been for Pound's self-subversion – which was, in turn, an inevitable consequence of his identification with 'the movement'. The accelerating dissipation of Pound's literary energies and ambitions from 1919 to 1922 seems closely linked to the loss of his entrepreneurial authority, to his sacking by one journal after another. His increasing bitterness, and his growing susceptibility to conspiracy theories about his expulsion from the realms of 'the godly', surely reflect his inability to recognise the extent to which 'the movement' had become a projection of his need to dominate it. The contrast between the increasing violence of his attempts to maintain that control (or the illusion of it) and the essential passivity of his early poetic stance is so extreme as to suggest a form of self-division, some principle of opposites at work in the resolutely extroverted Pound.

What follows is complicated by the ideological dispute which still rages around the *Cantos*. Warwick Gould has recently examined the course, and the eventual collapse, of Pound's own attempts to defend the work.[94] Outside of the 'Pound cult', as Robert Casillo calls it,[95] critical defence of the poem since the 1960s amounts to a series of strategic retreats, culminating in Jerome McGann's attempt to shift the responsibility, not only for Pound's anti-Semitism, but for the incoherence of the work at large, on to the reader.[96] While Pound was still alive, it was always possible for his supporters to claim that he might yet produce some miraculous ending which would unify the *Cantos* – though no other work of that length has ever depended on its closing passages to rescue it from disaster. As Donald Davie put it, reviewing *Section: Rock-Drill* in 1957:

> In short, the gamble continues. The method is being pressed to its logical conclusion. Either this is the waste of a prodigious talent, or else it is the poetry of the future.[97]

Much of the confusion springs from the promotion of the *Cantos* as an *avant-garde* work – 'modernism' being, once again, the glue that holds the image together. Hugh Kenner's principal tactic has always been to identify objections to the work with hostility to innovation itself: those who would deny Pound the title of greatest poet of the century must be closet supporters of Arthur Waugh and Shane Leslie (the man who dubbed *Ulysses* 'an Odyssey of the sewer'). Even Pound's severest critics have generally accepted the premise, thereby undermining their own case. What we see in the *Cantos* is surely not the birth of a new form but the disintegration of an old one – a nineteenth-century epic in a state of terminal collapse. As Carol T. Christ observes, the 'motivating epistemology' of the *Cantos*,

> that seeing the object as it really is, without the interfering or falsifying ego, reveals a structure implicit in the order of things – develops directly from Victorian poetics. And like the Victorians, Pound relies upon a didactic commentary at many points in the poem in order to make it all cohere, as if the welter of particulars he has juxtaposed generated some compensatory need for overdetermination.[98]

But he could not make it cohere. Straining for significance, Pound characteristically lapses into archaic diction ('Pull down thy vanity'); for all his insistence that he was 'making it new', he remained a nineteenth-century poet obsessed with the *idea* of being modern, who became, in the later cantos, a ghastly parody of a Victorian sage.

Even as the *Cantos* receded into the past, it was still possible to hope that the scholars would rescue the work. 'Pound's readers are still waiting for a description of the poem's major form', said Ronald Bush in 1976.[99] Three years later, Leon Surette began his study with the observation that, after the publication of the last fragments, 'students of the *Cantos* should have stopped seeking a ghostly poem somehow concealed in a text that grew ever longer but never clearer':

> It should have been recognised that the scholarly challenge presented by the poem did not lie in the search for some key which would render the cryptic, opaque and heterogeneous text at once lucid and coherent, but rather in discovering why the poem is so intractable, why Pound could not make it fit his account of what he wished it to be.[100]

No serious critic now believes in the existence of a 'key'. It seems hopeless to claim, as some enthusiasts still do, that the figure in the carpet will emerge when a variorum edition is completed – or when the last scrap of paper in the mountainous archive has been subjected to microscopic scrutiny.

Within the 'Pound cult', the problem has been defined out of existence by the critical equivalent of moving the goalposts; Hugh Kenner, for example, once claimed that Pound's 'principal achievement' was to 'dispense with' subject, plot, and 'line of philosophic development'.[101] Along with this we have the various forms of special pleading derived from Pound himself, centred on the 'ideogramic method', the 'new method in scholarship' and the 'luminous detail'.[102] Here the strategy is to claim that these 'techniques' work in opposition to, or on a higher plane than, normal logical or narrative structures, whereas the chaos of the *Cantos* is a compelling demonstration of the fact that they only work in conjunction with more mundane forms of organisation and understanding. As Carpenter observes:

> The Ideogramic Method would perhaps have been highly productive . . . if, having 'heaped together' his facts, he had then troubled to find 'organisations' to fit and explain them. Unfortunately, he generally stopped at the first stage, judging that the facts themselves, without any kind of organisation or interpretation being imposed on them, were self-evident of some larger truth. . . .[103]

Similarly, until the publication of Robert Casillo's *The Genealogy of Demons* in 1988, it was (just) possible for critics bent on rescuing the *Cantos* to hold to the line that though the poet might have been fascist and anti-Semitic, the poem was not. This defence has always depended on the double standard built into the argument that poems exist above and beyond real-world-politics. If – as Pound's admirers invariably argue – the *Cantos* embody wisdom, historical insight, and other positive qualities, then by the same token they can also embody pro-Fascist, anti-Semitic attitudes. Despite its flaws,[104] Casillo's demonstration that

> [f]ar from being extraneous to Pound's texts, anti-Semitism is a characteristic manifestation of Pound's thought and language, a virtually inescapable response to the most pressing intellectual and poetic difficulties[105]

has pushed back the line of defence to McGann's cry of '*hypocrite lecteur!*' – a retreat anticipated by Martin Kayman in 1986.[106] While efforts to salvage something from the wreck of the *Cantos* will doubtless continue, the trend is clear.

Casillo's study of the 'transformation of Pound's enemies and obstacles into the single form of the demonic Jew' links the virulence of Pound's anti-Semitism to a fear of 'infection' from his own unconscious, figured as feminine, passive, chaotic and threatening: 'Pound most frequently associates the Jews above all others not only with the fluidity of the body's inner life but with the diseases that afflict it.'[107] This paranoid complex of associations is also manifest in Eliot's early writings;[108] close variants are apparent in the writings of Lewis and T. E. Hulme. The links between their stress on 'masculine' qualities in art ('classicism'; 'hard, clear outlines') and their corresponding fear of feminine qualities (characteristically defined by Pound as 'slop'), and of women as anything other than passive receptors for the 'thrust' of male genius, have been largely ignored by the (male) historians of 'modernism', who until recently have been content to take the sexual boasts of Pound and Lewis, in particular, as information rather than symptom. One consequence has been that the political philosophies of Pound and Eliot have been subject to much fruitless scrutiny, propelled by the mistaken belief that this will somehow explain why 'modernism' and right-wing, authoritarian, anti-democratic attitudes are so closely entangled. It does not occur to such investigators that the mutual alliance between Pound, Eliot and Lewis may have been initiated and sustained by temperamental, more than intellectual, affinities.

Pound, as the extreme case, is the most illuminating. His bizarre sexual theories of the early 1920s, in which women are mere passive receptors, and the (male) brain becomes 'a great clot of genital fluid',[109] are part of a larger, systematic, malignant pattern of self-delusion. The speed with which Pound embraced global paranoia accelerated more or less in proportion to the decline of his literary influence from around 1916 onwards; Major Douglas was, effectively, an accident waiting to happen, since Pound immediately construed Social Credit as a conspiracy theory. In 1922, this expanding complex of obsessions intersected with the *Cantos*. From that point on, the die was cast. 'There is no other verse available, and will be none', he told James Watson in October 1927, when declining to accept the *Dial* prize 'except on Cantos or on my verse as whole'.[110] Carpenter argues, persuasively, that Pound's interview with Mussolini in January 1933 was the terminal point in his surrender to obsession. But the editing of *The Waste Land* marks an earlier stage in the process.

III

When Pound set about transforming Eliot's manuscript in the winter of 1921, his literary energies had dissipated into dubious ventures like the Villon opera, amateur attempts at music and sculpture, and the elaboration of his deranged theory of sexuality. A year earlier, he had published something very like an elegy for an earlier self who had hoped, by *'l'an trentuniesme/ [d]e son eage'*, 'to know more about poetry than any man living'. Despite his equivocal assertion that 'of course I'm no more Mauberley than Eliot is Prufrock',[111] the autobiographical element is, as Carpenter observes, unmistakable. 'Mauberley' laments not only Pound's 'final/ [e]xclusion from the world of letters', but also the 'death' of the prewar Pound; 'Envoi' looks back to *A Lume Spento*, dedicated to 'such as love this same beauty somewhat after mine own fashion'. 'Mauberley' is, as he acknowledged, 'distinctly a farewell to London'.[112]

Given the increasing eccentricity of Pound's day-to-day activities in Paris throughout 1921, the balance and sanity evident in his approach to Eliot's manuscript is remarkable; nowhere more so than in his rejection of the anti-Semitic 'Dirge'. Like 'Hugh Selwyn Mauberley', the editing of *The Waste Land* evokes an earlier Pound, and stands both as coda to, and the culmination of, his London career. In presenting Eliot with 'the poem of a generation', Pound unexpectedly achieved his goal as the entrepreneur of 'the movement', producing its 'justification' while at the same time handing over the last of his authority. Eliot the essayist had already displaced Pound; he now possessed the poem around which his essays would shortly be arranged by its admirers.

Pound's ambivalence about collaborating with Eliot on *The Criterion* surely reflects the difficulty of coping with the reversal; after eight years of unstinting support from Pound, Eliot had succeeded in gaining control of his own review, an ambition that had always eluded his sponsor. (Pound's revival of the impractical 'Bel Esprit' scheme in 1922, though generous in spirit, may also be seen as a last-ditch effort to maintain his role as Eliot's 'minder'.) The publication of *Ulysses* within days of *The Waste Land*'s completion must have increased the sense of finality. Having done little or no work on the *Cantos* for over two years, Pound started again in February 1922, almost immediately after completing work on *The Waste Land*. The connection with his sudden determination to 'bust all records' in his 'endless poem' is impossible to ignore. When he began work in 1915, it was merely one of a sheaf of projects, a relatively harmless diversion from his labours on be- half of 'the movement' and the writing of other verse. By 1920, work had come to a halt. It seems clear that the completion of *The Waste Land* triggered a fundamental change in his attitude to the *Cantos*; that they became, in or soon after February 1922, his personal bid to achieve poetic immortality by rivalling Dante and Homer (along with Eliot and Joyce). As Carpenter points out, the purpose of his revision of the first sixteen cantos in 1923

> was not to clarify, rather the reverse – to remove what Ezra now evidently regarded as the damaging admission, made by the narrator of 'Three Cantos', that the 'endless poem' was simply a 'rag-bag' in which he could 'stuff' all his ideas.[113]

The 'ideas', however, were already swallowing up the poet. The Hell Cantos, composed in mid-1922, present a coprophilous parody of *The Waste Land*'s despair: Pound later claimed that the subject was 'specifically LONDON, the state of the English mind in 1919 and 1920',[114] which suggests some confusion between the two works.

After all Pound had done for him, Eliot could hardly condemn the *Cantos*. Ironically, he was more or less compelled to support Pound in a venture about which he clearly had serious doubts. (It might be said that he also had to refrain from criticising Pound's malignant political fantasies, but Eliot seems to have been more amused than alarmed by Pound's politics in the 1920s and 1930s, though he was sceptical about the economics.) As Pound's London publisher, his support was crucial. Something of the strain, from Eliot's perspective, is already evident in a letter to Quinn in October 1923:

> It is harder to help Pound than anyone else. Apart from the fact that he is very sensitive and proud and that I have to keep an attitude of discipleship to him (as indeed I ought) every time I print anything of his it nearly sinks the paper. And he offers more than I want, thinking he is helping. I am willing to sink the ship for things like the cantos, which are great stuff whether anyone likes them or not, but it goes against the grain to do it for his articles.[115]

'I have to keep an attitude of discipleship to him (as indeed I ought)' admits several interpretations: recognition of the size of his debt; the awareness that Pound's pride will otherwise be wounded; and fear that he may turn against Eliot if crossed. But the 'attitude' is already a matter of past indebtedness ('as indeed I ought') rather than present conviction. The fear that the *Cantos* will 'sink the ship' is plainly at odds with the description of them as 'great stuff'. His comments to Pound on individual cantos became increasingly negative as the work rolled on into the 1930s. Though he always publicly defended the *Cantos* at large, his praise remained curiously vague: 'I am certain that in [Pound's] later work is to be found the grand stuff', he told Donald Hall in 1959[116] – which could be taken to mean that he himself was still searching for it. At about the same time, he admitted to F. R. Leavis that he found the bulk of the *Cantos* 'arid and depressing'.[117] But then, his view of *The Waste Land* was scarcely more enthusiastic.

Though Eliot accepted the fame it brought him, he was evidently unhappy with the terms. Had they published *The Waste Land* under both names, its authority (and Eliot's) would have been much diminished, but Eliot could have lived more happily with the poem, and Pound, his 'services to letters' justly acknowledged, might have been diverted from his attempt to 'bust all records', and hence from the fatal convergence of the *Cantos* and the paranoid fantasies that destroyed him.

Pound persuaded Eliot to drop the original epigraph from *Heart of Darkness*, but it was, after all, 'weighty enough to stand the citation'. Its proleptic application to Pound is grimly appropriate; he did indeed 'live his life again' in the 1960s, when he came to realise what he had done with the last four decades of it, and that all that survived of the *Cantos* was a few late 'fragments shored against ruin'.[118] Not the least of the ironies surrounding *The Waste Land*'s composition is that Pound's finest and most influential feat of editing should have had such destructive consequences for the editor.

3

Death by Exegesis

I was rather pleased one year in China when I had a course on modern poetry, *The Waste Land* and all that, and at the end a student wrote in the most friendly way to explain why he wasn't taking the exam. It wasn't that he couldn't understand *The Waste Land*, he said, in fact after my lectures the poem was perfectly clear: but it had turned out to be disgusting nonsense, and he had decided to join the engineering department. Now there a teacher is bound to feel solid satisfaction; he is getting definite results.

William Empson[1]

I

'No contemporary poem', declared G. S. Fraser in 1953 'has been subjected to more detailed analysis than *The Waste Land*, yet no critic has either confidently assigned it to one of the traditional kinds of poetry or, if he considers it as the invention of a quite new kind of poem, has invented a new name for that kind.'[2] Reviewing the situation in 1962, Fraser observed that the critical discussion was 'still very largely inconclusive'; there was still no agreement about the genre, mode of coherence, or influence of the poem.[3] A decade later, the question of genre had apparently been resolved. *The Waste Land* was now, by general consent, a 'modernist' poem; the task, therefore, was to locate it within the larger structure of 'modernism'.

But the elaboration of 'modernism' depends, as we have seen, on the presumption of coherence: precisely the assumption that dominated academic interpretation of *The Waste Land* from the outset. Like most of the premises on which mainstream Eliot criticism was founded, this one derives, in a curiously ironic way, from a hint provided by Eliot himself: that *Ulysses* and *The Waste Land* are as macrocosm and microcosm. By 1926, I. A. Richards had reduced it to two sentences which more or less encapsulate the ensuing history of orthodox explication:

> Allusion in Mr Eliot's hands is a technical device for compression. *The Waste Land* is the equivalent in content to an epic.[4]

Like 'modernism', the poem has been put together in so many ways that there are, on one level, as many interpretations as there are interpreters. But of all the critics who have attempted a 'full treatment' – and they must now be numbered in thousands – no one, to my knowledge, has resolutely rejected the assumption that the fragments can and should be assembled into an integrated whole which is, in some sense, objectively 'there' in the poem. On many such accounts, Eliot fails to complete the pattern discerned by the interpreter, but the presumptive unity of the poem remains effectively intact. Which is hardly surprising, for a close analysis dedicated to proving the incoherence of *The Waste Land* would be almost a contradiction in terms: not an analysis, but an inventory of fragments.

It would also be a pointless exercise. Whenever a reader discovers the unity of *The Waste Land*, the unity is there – for that reader. But to the extent that such readings are objectified, and presented as 'research findings' rather than personal responses, trouble invariably follows. Richard Poirier's diagnosis in 'The Literature of Waste' (1967) has lost none of its force:

> Eliot and Joyce have been made assertive where they are vague, orderly where they have chosen to remain fragmentary, solemn where they are comic, philosophically structured where they are demonstrating their disillusionment with philosophical as much as with literary structures. The literary organisations they adumbrate only to mimic, the schematisations they propose only to show the irrelevance of them to actualities of experience – these have been extracted by commentators from the contexts that erode them and have been imposed back on the material in the form of designs or meanings.[5]

The history of Eliot criticism – or rather explication – in the academy is largely one of misreading by systematisation. By this I don't mean to imply the existence of some ideal reading; on the contrary, the conviction that there must *be* an ideal reading is responsible for much of the trouble. The problem is not that, with a handful of exceptions, commentators have simply misunderstood the nature of the work. As I hope to show in this and the following chapter, it is much more the consequence of a spectacular mismatch between the poetry and the demands of orthodox academic explication, regardless of the explicator's theoretical orientation.

Eliot criticism began, seemingly unpropitiously, in October 1916, with a tirade directed by Arthur Waugh (the novelist's father) against Pound's *Catholic Anthology* in general, and 'The Love Song of J. Alfred Prufrock' in particular:

> If the fruits of emancipation are to be recognised in the un-metrical, incoherent banalities of these literary 'Cubists' the state of Poetry is indeed threatened with anarchy.... From such a catastrophe the humour, common-sense and artistic judgement of the best of the new 'Georgians' will assuredly save this generation; nevertheless, a hint of warning may not be out of place. It was a classic custom in the family hall, when the feast was at its height, to display a drunken slave among the sons of the household, to the end that they, being ashamed at the ignominious folly of his gesticulations, might determine never to be tempted into such a pitiable condition themselves.[6]

This might have been just another forgotten salvo in the poetry wars of 1914–18 if Pound, seizing the moment, had not immortalised 'the silly old Waugh' as the man who had called Eliot a 'drunken helot'.[7] The phrase was Pound's, and its promotional value cannot be overestimated. Waugh, with Pound's assistance, had solved the problem that confronts any young writer – how to stand out from the crowd – by branding him the most dangerous and revolutionary of the new poets.

Almost everyone who reviewed *Prufrock and Other Observations* arrived at the same conclusion: here was something so remarkable, or outrageous, or offensive, as to defy categorisation. *The Times Literary Supplement* came closest to lofty dismissal:

> The fact that these things occurred to the mind of Mr. Eliot is surely of the very smallest importance to anyone – even to himself. They certainly have no relation to 'poetry,' and we only give an example because some of the pieces, he states, have appeared in a periodical which claims that word as its title.[8]

But the *New Statesman* (in which Eliot had just published his 'Reflections on *Vers Libre*') turned the same point into a backhanded compliment:

> Mr. Eliot may possibly give us the quintessence of twenty-first century poetry. Certainly much of what he writes is unrecognisable as poetry at present, but it is all decidedly amusing; and it is only fair to say that he does not call these pieces poems. He calls them 'observations,' and the description seems exact; for he has a keen eye as well as sharp pen, and draws wittily whatever his capricious glance descends on.[9]

The *Southport Guardian* was much taken with J. Alfred Prufrock,

> the expectant, undecided youth who enters, an eternal question to life and experience, self-conscious of his clothes and appearance, his emotions strangely stirred yet not definitely expressed, save as they are memories of the erotic imagination. . . .[10]

Robert Lynd, in *the Daily News*, found the volume 'witty and dissatisfying', but many of the images 'quite startling in their originality':

> Mr Eliot is still playing with his talent, and though the book is original and amusing, one feels that this is only the first heels-in-the-air prancing of a young and clever writer.[11]

The *Athenaeum* retired behind the epithet, 'Beardsleyesque'.[12] The *Literary World (and Reader)* suspected a hoax: 'Mr. Eliot is one of those clever young men who find it amusing to pull the leg of a sober reviewer.'[13]

Whatever Mr Eliot was writing might not be poetry, but it was certainly distinctive, as Babette Deutsch emphasised in the *New Republic*:

> the language has the extraordinary quality of common words uncommonly used. Less formal than prose, more nervous than metrical verse, the rhythms are strung along a tenous thread of sense.[14]

May Sinclair – no doubt encouraged by Pound – detected a 'journal-istic conspiracy' against Eliot, manifest in Arthur Waugh's perora-tion and the *New Statesman* review: 'Mr Eliot is dangerous.'[15] Eliot's detractors might, with justice, have returned the compliment. Early in 1918, Harriet Monroe invited the English novelist Edgar Jepson to write an article celebrating her *Poetry* prize-winners, princi-pally Vachel Lindsay and Edgar Lee Masters. Jepson's essay heaped praise upon Pound and Eliot at the expense of the 'Mid-Western School', presenting Eliot, rather than Lindsay and Masters, as the true voice of American feeling. Monroe refused to print it; Jepson placed it with Austin Harrison's *English Review* instead.[16] Pound then shortened the essay and persuaded Margaret Anderson to reprint it in the September *Little Review*, along with a 'supporting note by E. P.'.[17] His already strained relationship with Harriet Monroe was virtually severed in consequence, but Eliot did well out of the ensuing controversy, which lasted for over a year.

William Carlos Williams complained, in May 1919, that 'there is always some everlasting Polonius of Kensington to rate highly his eternal Eliot',[18] but by then Eliot no longer needed Pound's support. 'Is This Poetry?', the *Athenaeum*'s notice of his second volume, contrasts strikingly with the two sentences it had de-voted to *Prufrock* in 1917. The answer this time was a resounding reproof to the 'jeering laugh which is the easy reaction to any-thing new and strange':

> Mr. Eliot is always quite consciously 'trying for' something, and something which has grown out of and developed beyond all the poems of all the dead poets.... The poetry of the dead is in his bones and at the tips of his fingers: he has the rare gift of being able to weave, delicately and delightfully, an echo or even a line of the past into the pattern of his own poem. And at the same time he is always trying for something new, some-thing which has evolved – one drops instinctively into the scien-tific terminology – out of the echo or the line, out of the last poem of the last dead poet....[19]

The authors of the anonymous review were Leonard and Virginia Woolf, the volume's publishers. This passage precisely anticipates – and may, as Louis Menand suggests, have helped Eliot formu-late – his 'notion of the irruption of the truly original from the mass of tradition', first articulated in the fourth of his 'Reflections on Contemporary Poetry' (July 1919) and developed two months later in the first part of 'Tradition and the Individual Talent'.[20] But it is just as likely that Eliot had been working out his argument in conversation with the Woolfs.

The success of *The Sacred Wood* reinforced his critical authority.[21] It also provided, in a conveniently accessible form, what appeared to be an explanation of the principles upon which his poetry was founded. An essay published in January 1921 by Desmond MacCarthy, whom Eliot had known for some years, illustrates the rapidity with which the essays were adopted as a guide to the poems. 'Whenever two people are discussing modern poetry together the name of T. S. Eliot is sure to crop up.' Young readers had already been won over by 'the exciting concision of his phrasing', but their elders were still unconvinced. MacCarthy, *The Sacred Wood* at his elbow, set out to reassure them. Eliot, he explained, 'does not steal phrases; he borrows their aroma':

> He is like a dumb man... taking up one object after another and showing it to us, not intending that we should infer that the object is the subject of his thoughts, but that we should feel the emotion appropriate to it. . . .

> He belongs to that class of poets whose interest is in making a work of art, not in expressing themselves.

Besides, he was only 'doing the same thing as Browning for a more queasy, uneasy, diffident, complex generation'.[22]

Richard Aldington's 'The Poetry of T. S. Eliot', published simultaneously in London and New York in January 1922 (and written more or less at Eliot's direction) pushed the argument a stage further. The association of Eliot with Laforgue was, he declared, verging on cliché; an 'affinity of mind' had been misconstrued as imitation. Eliot had as much in common with Rimbaud and Corbière; he was a direct descendant, not an imitator, of the younger Symbolists. As for his 'so-called obscurity':

> The comparisons instituted show that Mr. Eliot's poetry is traditional, linking up on the one hand with the ironic French poets and, on the other, with the stately, subtle-minded Englishmen of the Renaissance.

Aldington's (which is to say, Eliot's) declared objective was 'merely to surprise the reader into admitting how "traditional" this "revolutionary" poet is'.[23] The programme that would dominate Eliot criticism in the academy from the late 1920s through to the 1960s was now effectively in place.

Yet, outside the circle of Eliot's influence, a perception shared by conservative and *avant-garde* reviewers alike was that the poems were not so much redefining as mocking the established conventions of seriousness in poetry. 'There can be no doubt of his talents', said Arthur Clutton-Brock, reviewing *Poems* (1919) for *The Times Literary Supplement*:

> They are evident in 'The Hippopotamus' and even in 'Sweeney Among the Nightingales', where he carries the game of perversity as far as anyone has ever carried it. But poetry is a serious art, too serious for this game.[24]

The reception of his first American collection, published by Alfred Knopf in February 1920, covered the full spectrum of opinion on this issue. 'Even here,' Eliot wrote to his brother as he waited for the notices, 'I am considered by the ordinary Newspaper critic as a Wit or satirist, and in America I suppose I shall be thought merely disgusting.'[25] *The Boston Evening Transcript* took its revenge:

> Reading these poems (?) is like being in a closed room full of foul air; not a room in an empty house that is sanctified with mould and dust, but a room in which the stale perfume of exotics is poisoned with the memory of lusts.[26]

R. M. Weaver, in the *Bookman*, though just as hostile, wondered if the book was a send-up:

> The 'Poems' – ironically so-called – of T. S. Eliot, if not heavy and pedantic parodies of the 'new poetry,' are documents that would find sympathetic readers in the waiting-room of a private sanatorium.[27]

Louis Untermeyer, who counted himself among the 'new poets', thought Eliot's work 'related to poetry only at rare intervals'; it was, rather, 'a species of mordant light verse'[28] – precisely the quality most admired by the *Nation*'s reviewer:

He is the most proficient satirist now writing in verse, the uncanniest clown, the devoutest monkey, the most picturesque ironist; and aesthetically considered, he is one of the profoundest symbolists.[29]

Mr Eliot did not seem to belong to any of the current factions; he was variously identified as parodist, satirist, ironist, plagiarist and fraud; one of the main points at issue was whether this sort of thing – whatever it might be – could legitimately count as poetry, but the reviewers were more or less agreed on one thing: he could not be taken straight. By 1919, Eliot was well aware that in order to extend his reputation as 'the best living poet' in England beyond a 'small and select public', he would have to shed his revolutionary image. The orthodox defence advanced, at his instigation, by the Woolfs, MacCarthy and Aldington, and later adopted in the academy, conceded from the outset that great poetry had to be serious. Arthur Waugh and Co. had provoked an equal and opposite reaction: they would be answered, again and again, by a legion of scholars and critics bent upon proving just how traditional – and serious – Mr Eliot really was.

In 1923, however, Eliot the parodist and fraud was still very much alive. Within months of *The Waste Land*'s publication, the rumour was circulating, on both sides of the Atlantic, that the poem was a hoax.[30] Some admiring reviewers conceded the possibility, but declared that it would make no difference even if true. 'If this is a trick,' said the poet Elinor Wylie,

> it is an inspired one. I do not believe that it is a trick; I think that Mr Eliot conceived *The Waste Land* out of an extremity of tragic emotion.[31]

Burton Rascoe went further. 'He may, and I think he does, even play practical jokes on his readers, but that is in character with the curious, variable mood of this fine poem . . . perhaps the finest poem of this generation':

> [It] contains enough sheer verbal loveliness, enough ecstasy, enough psychological verisimilitude, and enough even of a readily-understandable etching of modern life, to justify Mr. Eliot in his idiosyncrasies.[32]

Though the story of *The Waste Land*'s composition remained a closely-guarded secret, the rumour had, with a certain ironic justice, coalesced around the question of authorship. Eliot admitted, decades later, that he had added the notes 'with a view to spiking the guns of critics of my earlier poems who had accused me of plagiarism'.[33] But the notes merely reinforced the impression, shared by several reviewers, that the whole thing was a collage of quotations, a parody of scholarship dressed up as a poem. 'The main function of the notes', said F. L. Lucas,

> is, indeed, to give the references to the innumerable authors whose lines the poet embodies, like a mediaeval writer making a life of Christ out of lines of Virgil. But the borrowed jewels he has set in its head do not make Mr Eliot's toad the more prepossessing.[34]

This highlights the paradox at the heart of the poem's reputation. Eliot's thefts and borrowings have been indefatigably pursued, in the guise of allusions, by two generations of scholars. The greater the range of allusion uncovered, the more meaning he is generally credited with having loaded into *The Waste Land*. Yet if Lucas could have been confronted with their findings, he would have dismissed *The Waste Land* as all jewel and no toad; an anthology, not a poem. His conception of originality, so effectively countered in 'Tradition and the Individual Talent', was untenably naive. But so is the opposite view, in which allusion always works to Eliot's (or 'modernism's') advantage.

The *Dial*'s editors seem to have assumed, correctly as it turned out, that they could take an *avant-garde* success for granted. In December 1922, Gilbert Seldes, the editor primarily responsible for the award of the $2000 prize to Eliot, published a review in *The Nation* which was clearly aimed at securing the middle ground, anticipating objections which had yet to be fully articulated. The promotion of *The Waste Land* as a modern epic in miniature begins with this essay. 'In turning to Mr Eliot as a poet,' he began, 'I do not leave the critic behind since it is from his critical utterances that we derive the clue to his poetry.' One had only to consult 'Tradition and the Individual Talent' to see that *The Waste Land* was a serious, traditional poem, and though it seemed 'at first sight remarkably disconnected', a closer view would reveal 'the hidden form of the work'. As with the Woolfs' review of

Poems in 1919, Seldes drew out the implication of an essay that Eliot had not yet published:

> It will be interesting for those who have knowledge of another great work of our time, Mr Joyce's *Ulysses*, to think of the two together. That *The Waste Land* is, in a sense, the inversion and the complement of *Ulysses* is at least tenable.[35]

'*Ulysses*, Order and Myth' appeared in the *Dial* eleven months later. Whether Seldes was actually writing under direction from Eliot scarcely matters; he might as well have been. His review, together with Edmund Wilson's 'The Poetry of Drouth', did for *The Waste Land* what Richard Aldington's 'The Work of T. S. Eliot' had done for the earlier poems, mapping the boundaries within which mainstream interpretation would operate for the next half-century.[36] Though Leavis presented *New Bearings in English Poetry* (1932) as a pioneering work, the conceptual substance of his chapter on Eliot is contained in these three essays.

Yet Wilson and Seldes were, at the time, in the minority. Critical opinion was, again, polarised, ranging from 'World's Greatest Poem' (John Drury), to 'a masterpiece of decadent art' (Harriet Monroe), to 'so much waste paper' (Charles Powell), but there was near-unanimous agreement on one point: *The Waste Land* broke all the rules.[37] John Crowe Ransom lamented its violation of traditional unities, 'good for some purposes, but not for art'. Eliot's difficulty was, he thought, typically American – a concern with formal novelty at any price – but the poem had consequently won 'a spectacular triumph over a certain public'.[38] Among the converted, Louis Untermeyer struck the characteristic note:

> As an echo of contemporary despair, as a picture of dissolution, of the breaking down of the very structures on which life has modelled itself, 'The Waste Land' has a definite authenticity.

His reservations were similar to Ransom's: 'Even the process of disintegration must be held within a pattern'.[39] But the surviving testimony suggests that for many early readers, dissolution of form was the signature of the poem's authenticity.

Conrad Aiken's 'An Anatomy of Melancholy', published in February 1923, must have been something of a setback to the *Dial*'s promotional campaign; though he did not name Seldes, Aiken demolished his case point by point, focusing on the 'illusion . . . that *The Waste Land* is, precisely, a kind of epic in a walnut shell; elaborate, ordered, unfolded with a logic at every joint discernible':[40]

> [T]he poem must be taken – most invitingly offers itself – as a brilliant and kaleidoscopic confusion; as a series of sharp, discrete, slightly related perceptions and feelings, dramatically and lyrically presented, and violently juxtaposed (for effect of dissonance), so as to give us an impression of an intensely modern, intensely literary consciousness which perceives itself to be not a unit but a chance correlation or conglomerate of mutually discolorative fragments.[41]

The parallel with *Ulysses* presumed full authorial control, every allusion woven into a grand design apparently sketched in the notes. Aiken had the advantage of inside information (though I doubt that he knew the full extent of Eliot's debt to Pound):

> *The Waste Land* is a series of separate poems or passages, not perhaps all written at one time or with one aim, to which a spurious but happy sequence has been given. This spurious sequence has a value – it creates the necessary superficial formal unity; but it need not be stressed, as the Notes stress it. Could one not wholly rely for one's unity – as Mr Eliot has largely relied – simply on the dim unity of 'personality' which would underlie the retailed contents of a single consciousness?. . . We reach thus the conclusion that the poem succeeds – as it brilliantly does – by virtue of its incoherence, not of its plan, by virtue of its ambiguities, not of its explanations.

He need only have gone a step further to dispel the last illusion. The idea that the poem was held together by a unifying consciousness became, with Richards and Leavis, a device not merely for saving, but for reversing the appearances. Though *The Waste Land* might look like a heap of broken images, it was really a perfect whole in which Mr Eliot, like the God of creation, was everywhere present and nowhere visible. Aiken came within striking distance of the opposite conclusion, that the unifying consciousness is not Eliot's, but the reader's. *The Waste Land* succeeded by virtue of its incoherence because any reader could assemble fragments borrowed from dozens of familiar or half-remembered works to his or her own satisfaction. Readers on the lookout for an inclusive expression of cultural and spiritual dislocation were bound to be captivated by what was, in effect, an identikit portrait in which they discovered, as in a glass darkly, the features of their own preoccupations.

E. M. Forster remarked in 1929 that for young readers, Eliot was 'the most important author of their day . . . they are inside his idiom as the young of 1900 were inside George Meredith's.' Yet, though they were 'far better qualified than their elders' to expound the poetry, they seemed 'averse to answering leading questions: "What is *The Waste Land* about?" provokes no enthusiastic reply'.[42] Whereas established reviewers and first-generation academic critics in the 1920s dwelt largely upon bleakness, disillusion and despair, another group of readers, many of them undergraduates, responded with such exuberance that they seemed to be reading a different Eliot.[43]

The first group were reading him straight, taking the irony as a device for controlling or heightening the vision of desolation; the challenge, as they saw it was to decode the irony, construe the allusions, and fill in the gaps in the 'narrative', in order to get the message right. Hence the burden of complaint over Eliot's obscurity: we know he's saying something important, but why won't he tell us what it is? (Forster thought that Eliot had 'seen something terrible', and 'declined to say so plainly'). But the difficulties attributed to obscurity often sound more like difficulties with irony, manifest in the recurrent unease over the status of whatever was being said. Edwin Muir, for example, disturbed by the expression of an 'anguished vision of the world' in 'light verse', was driven to conclude that *The Waste Land* failed the test of seriousness, and therefore could not qualify as great poetry.[44]

Yet, according to the other group, Eliot was neither difficult nor obscure. 'The language', Hugh Sykes-Davies recalled in his obituary essay, 'struck me with that tang which, in the last analysis, can perhaps only be tasted fully from writing which is deeply and even violently contemporary':

[T]he effect of Eliot's poetry on me was in some ways oddly like what I had been assured I should get from *Dracula* and had failed to find in it. The main structure of its comment on the age, the suggestive drift of its remedies, were almost wholly lost on me, but from the imagery of deserts and waste places I got the kind of direct thrill which had failed to emerge from werewolves, ruined abbeys, and the rituals of necrophily. . . . The words were common, everyday, but what of that? They had behind them, to my mind, the terrific suggestiveness of words heard in dreams, of phrases spoken in nightmares. And my delight in this poetry was enhanced when my Englishmaster picked up the book from my desk one day, glanced at it for a few minutes, and then handed it back with the advice that I should not waste my time on such 'Bolshevik' stuff. My own unspeakable and unreadable verses were, of course, full of desert scenery, red rocks, and rats' feet slithering over broken glass. Eliot's images for the barren waste of English culture lent themselves very readily to an indulgence in the facile melancholies of adolescence which was, in those days, a very long-drawn-out affair. . . . I came up to Cambridge with a fair stock of verses in this manner, and here, of course, I met many other young men with similar portfolios.[45]

Davies' ironic contrast between the 'direct thrill' of those first encounters and what was, in 1965, pretty much the standard academic reading ('comment on the age'; 'barren waste of English culture') is part of the subtext of his obituary. 'Mistah Kurtz: He Dead' is both a warm tribute to Eliot's personal kindness, and an implicit lament for a lost leader – a man who, having 'spoken to the condition of a small minority . . . with enormous force', had ceased to explore the frontiers of consciousness, and chosen instead to become a celebrity. Davies saw the first performance of *The Rock* in 1934 as the turning-point:

Scattered thinly through the auditorium were a few of those to whom Eliot was already as eminent as he could be; surrounding us, quite swamping us, were those with whom it clearly lay in his power to be eminent in a slightly different fashion. He can hardly have been unconscious of the possible change, the possible choice – I never remembered him missing much subtler points than that.[46]

The 'enormous force' of the poetry was enhanced, for Eliot's early readers, by a sophisticated balancing-act in which Eliot managed to infiltrate the literary establishment while maintaining – or appearing to maintain – a subversive relation to it. The sense of betrayal aroused by his notorious declaration of faith in *For Lancelot Andrewes* was an inevitable consequence of this strategy. In *becoming* the establishment, Eliot was bound to betray the readers who, as Davies saw it, ought to have mattered most to him. Hence the allusions to *Heart of Darkness* in Davies' tribute, the implication that despite the kindness, and the eminence, the later Eliot was hollow at the core.

The Waste Land, as I remarked in the previous chapter, set the standard by which the religious poems were judged by reviewers from the late 1920s through to the mid-1930s. Mr Eliot, in the view of the majority, had sold out, and yet the sheer volume of protest testified to the strength of the investment in him. 'All we have before us', said Richard Church, reviewing *Ash-Wednesday*, 'is something that confuses our minds and works up our nerves into a frenzy. We are a generation waiting for news; and here comes one broken figure staggering across the empty desert'.[47] His output was fiercely debated, volume by volume; *After Strange Gods* temporarily alienated even his most committed admirers.

But even as one sector of his audience was still coming to terms with the apostasy of Mr Eliot the jazz-age prophet, F. R. Leavis was rewriting history, offering himself as the sole champion of an Eliot hitherto misrepresented and despised. *New Bearings in English Poetry*, he would complain for the next thirty years, had been savagely condemned, spitefully ignored, and basely pillaged by critics who had even had the gall to accuse him of exaggerating the opposition to Eliot. *New Bearings* in fact received a favourable notice in the *Cambridge Review*; Geoffrey Grigson called it 'the best book of criticism . . . since the lifetime of Coleridge'; it was praised in the *TLS*, and by Richard Church in the *Spectator*.[48] This did nothing to inhibit Leavis, whose success in distorting the history of Eliot's reception was truly remarkable.

On the other side of the Atlantic, Hugh Kenner has spent the last forty years doing for Pound what Leavis had done for Eliot. It is still received wisdom among Pound enthusiasts that Pound found London a cultural desert, 'modernised' Yeats single-handed, created the modernist movement in the teeth of entrenched opposition, was universally reviled by the British, and driven into exile for his pains. Some cultural misprision is involved; to be satirised in *Punch*, as Pound was in 1909 and again in 1911, is a mark of success, not failure,[49] and, as Barbara Everett observes, Kenner 'takes over the Leavises' territory and tries to see the culture as a whole, British Rail and all',[50] so that even the notorious BR cuisine becomes a symptom of British hostility to 'modernism'.

It is only in the last decade or so that literary historians and biographers have reversed the emphasis, focusing on the rapidity of Eliot's ascent, and the success of Pound's entrepreneurial ventures in the years 1909–17. Even in 1972, Donald Davie was able to claim without apparent irony that the young Kenner, in writing *The Poetry of Ezra Pound* (1951),

> took appalling risks. He was chancing his arm, and his professional future, time and again. And he was in any case making enemies. For by assuming that a tradition of criticism existed, assuming the existence of a consensus of information and opinion, Kenner was goading, almost taunting the rest of us into finding out whether such a consensus was possible.[51]

Given the furore over the award of the Bollingen Prize to the *Pisan Cantos* in 1949, the aborted treason trial, and Pound's confinement in St Elizabeths, 'appalling risks' may sound plausible. But the controversy had mobilised numerous influential supporters, including Eliot, Auden, Robert Lowell and Allen Tate, in Pound's defence. His postwar reputation in the academy was partly a consequence of that notoriety; some of the most influential of the critics who established the Pound industry took their instruction at the master's 'Ezuversity' in St Elizabeths. And, with McCarthyite paranoia rampant, it was a good deal safer to praise a poet who had lapsed into fascism than one who had leaned the other way. Pound was, at least, sound on Communism.

Davie's remark that *The Poetry of Ezra Pound* was written 'as though out of access to a critical tradition that in fact had never existed', also obscures the extent to which that 'tradition' derived from Pound's own attempts to justify the *Cantos*. Kenner, assessing the *Cantos* on Poundian principles in 1951, not surprisingly reached the conclusion that Pound was the presiding genius of the century, as Pound himself had been saying for the past forty years.[52] As Davie inadvertently acknowledged, Kenner also established, for academic purposes, the Pound-inspired categories of special pleading (such as the 'ideogramic method', the 'new method of scholarship' and the 'luminous detail') on which the defence of the *Cantos* has since depended. Though the circularity of the arguments advanced by Poundians is no doubt obvious to most outsiders, Eliot's case is far more complex, since his critical authority extended far beyond the boundaries of his poetry. For many academic critics, from the 1930s through to at least the mid-1960s, the poetic canon was largely determined by Eliot's valuations, as reified in Leavis's *New Bearings* and his *Revaluation* (1936), and Cleanth Brooks' *Modern Poetry and the Tradition* (1939).

Eliot's immense influence in the academy has usually been ascribed to the power and cogency of his judgements, buttressed by his reputation as one of the century's greatest poets. How one man could have retained so many eminent advocates, and held his position for so long, was always something of a puzzle to reflective observers. But as Louis Menand has recently emphasised, Eliot's authority was not so much imposed upon the academy as co-opted by it. 'To answer the charge that literary criticism belongs to the history of taste rather than the history of ideas ... it was necessary that critics be considered not as practitioners or propagandists, but as theorists':

> [A]n interpretation or evaluation of a work of literature that is based on a theory of literature (or of interpretation) can claim standing as a contribution to knowledge in a way that a more personal or methodologically ad hoc judgement cannot. It is essential to the institutional status of the academic literary critic that criticism be regarded as a discipline which produces results that can be evaluated 'objectively' – or else how can literary critics be professionally certified and rewarded within the university system?.... Eliot's criticism recognised literature as an object of study on its own terms; it was anti-impressionistic and scientific-sounding; it had the look of being theoretical and rigorous rather than journalistic or belletristic.... and was thus an ideal model for an academic literary criticism....[53]

Eliot, therefore, had to be located within a reconstituted history of criticism 'intended to reveal the twentieth-century academic critic to be the latest edition in a line of critics that reaches back (usually) to Aristotle':

> There is a sense in which the establishment of literature as a field was not a precondition for the establishment of literary criticism as a discriminable field of endeavour, but the other way round.... What the academic historian most needs to

establish ... is that the history of criticism is a series of writings that not only hangs together, but leads directly to the work of his or her own colleagues.... The figure who, in most of these histories, stands historically between the sequence of critics writing before the emergence of the research university – Pater, Arnold, Hazlitt and so forth – and the first generation of academic critics – Richards, Empson, Leavis, the New Critics – is, conventionally, T. S. Eliot. In the academic critics' effort to construct a genealogy for their work that extends back prior to the formation of the modern university, Eliot is, in effect, the link.[54]

He was, in other words, elevated to the position of dominant theorist by first-generation academic critics precisely because he was not an academic. He had to be endowed with a coherent theory of literature because the founding fathers could not afford to be seen (even by themselves) as cutting their coat to suit the institutional cloth. It is ironically appropriate that a man who made his reputation partly by inventing his own tradition should have been enlisted, despite his continued objections, as principal backer and guarantor for a critical enterprise which had never existed in the form necessarily adopted to secure its place in the academy.

II

During the 1920s and 1930s, academic critics were still reading literary journalists, but as the volume of academic writing on Eliot increased, this sort of interchange diminished, and by the late 1940s had more or less ceased. Leavis's determination to be seen as the first in the field no doubt reinforced the separation, also encouraged by the institutional demand for original work, a requirement more easily accommodated on the assumption that only professional criticism counts. F. O. Matthiessen's *The Achievement of T. S. Eliot* (1935) is generally regarded in the academy as a pioneering book, but the *TLS* rightly declared that Matthiessen 'had nothing very original to say on this well-worn theme'.[55]

By the mid-1950s, critics were complaining vociferously about overcrowding and sterility, as the paraphrases became longer than the texts and the putative 'sources' and 'influences' proliferated without end. Interpreters laid bets as to whether Eliot had intended a particular allusion; a few emerged triumphant, brandishing a letter from the oracle.[56] Reading a 1958 note on 'Eliot's Incorrect Note on "C.i.f. London"',[57] one can hardly avoid the reflection that the critics were scraping the barrel. In 1955, discussing 'the craze for writing books and articles about T. S. Eliot', Malcolm Cowley observed:

> So much has been written about his poems that apparently there is nothing left to say except a few of the simplest things. So much has been written that the poet's rather slender production . . . seems to be buried deep under an accumulated mass of commentaries, glosses, exegeses, and explications. More interesting than any new essay that followed the established lines would be a psychological and sociological study of Eliot's critics; at some universities they include almost every member of the English department who hasn't written or planned a book on Herman Melville.[58]

Allen Tate made the same point a year later:

> Within five years of the appearance of *Four Quartets*, we knew more about the poem than Mr. Eliot knew – and quite predictably, for if a poet knew all *that*, he wouldn't have had to write the poem and mankind would not need poetry.[59]

Yet the other most striking feature of orthodox academic exegesis was its narrowness. No one paused to comment on the exclusion of history in every form other than the literary (which then amounted largely to the reiteration of Mr Eliot's views on the subject). Biographical approaches were then considered reductive, and besides, as John Peter and F. W. Bateson discovered, Mr Eliot would sue if you engaged in rash speculation. The nineteenth century was still largely a depressed area so far as Eliot criticism was concerned. Popular culture (apart from approved references to music-halls) was out; the quest for the One True Meaning, the Holy Grail of exegetical criticism, was only for the pure in heart, those who had renounced the world for literature, philosophy and comparative religion.

It seemed, too, that the poetry had lost a good deal of its flavour since Hugh Sykes-Davies bought his copy of *The Waste Land*. Herbert Gorman, reviewing the poem in 1923, had said:

'The Waste Land' . . . arouses a troubled, twisted ecstasy in the reader, a regret that is like a sob in the throat beneath its glittering surface of ironic nuances. . . . For my own part, 'The Waste Land' is an unusual poem, for it shook me violently.[60]

But in the 1950s, *The Waste Land* seemed to be arousing not so much ecstasy as anxiety about where the next allusion was coming from. As the book-length exegeses of *Four Quartets* began to appear, each writer would begin with the obligatory Critical Health Warning: the following commentary is not, of course, to be confused with 'the real meaning', nevertheless it is humbly offered as a 'way in' to the poem, etc. 'Way out', or 'No Entry', would have been more appropriate. Why anyone would want to read a work as pedestrian and sententious as the exegetes made it sound was a question none of the hapless authors wanted to answer.

Their rivals, however, were only too willing to ask it. Opposition to source-oriented exegesis crystallised around Grover C. Smith Jr's *T. S. Eliot: A Study in Sources and Meanings* (1956). 'No reader', complained G. S. Fraser in the *TLS*,

> and almost certainly not Mr Eliot either when he was writing the poem [*The Waste Land*] or when he is re-reading it now could hold in his head at once such an extraordinary jumble of influences, some no doubt in some degree relevant, but some flatly contradictory of each other.[61]

Ironically, Smith had merely taken the methods employed by hundreds of his fellow exegetes to their logical conclusion. None of his academic reviewers, however scathing, realised that they were confronting a *reductio ad absurdum* of their own procedures. Staffan Bergsten, having denounced the book in 1959 for unprincipled source-hunting, and as an example of 'the dangers of academic criticism',[62] went on to perpetrate one of the worst examples of the genre in *Time and Eternity: A Study in the Structure and Symbolism of Eliot's Four Quartets* (1960), which was in turn savaged by Helen Gardner, who had also savaged Smith, but who herself had succumbed to the temptations of exegetical paraphrase in *The Art of T. S. Eliot* (1949) after forswearing such methods in a highminded introduction. The dullness and futility of the exegeses was matched only by the fury with which the combatants assailed one another, as if the fate of civilisation hung on the exact meaning of 'the bath symbol' in 'Mr Eliot's Sunday Morning Service'.

One of the implicit grievances about Grover Smith's book was that he had included what then appeared to be every conceivable (and inconceivable) 'source', thereby threatening to put rival exegetes out of business.

The New Criticism figures largely in the demonology of current literary theory, as a controlling ideology behind Anglo-American 'formalism'. So far as mid-century Eliot criticism was concerned, New Critical principles were honoured mainly in the breach. Cleanth Brooks's essay, 'The Waste Land: Critique of the Myth' in *Modern Poetry and the Tradition* (1939) was, ironically, the *fons et origo* of postwar Eliot exegesis.[63] His 'critique' of *The Waste Land* is an extended, adulatory paraphrase which flatly contradicts his theoretical injunctions to avoid paraphrase and respect complexity and ambiguity. Having attacked other critics for imposing logical structures on 'metaphysical' poems, he proceeded to impose one on *The Waste Land*, treating it, in what was to become the standard postwar fashion, as a crossword puzzle to be completed by the critic according to clues thoughtfully provided in the notes. Madame Sosostris, it seems, is unable to see the Hanged Man because he is hooded; we know he is hooded because Eliot says so in a note. The Dog in 'O keep the Dog far hence' is 'Humanitarianism'; the 'fishmen' in 'The Fire Sermon' have a more meaningful life than the upper classes because they happen to be drinking next to a church. His unconvincing assertion that all this must not be 'substituted for the poem itself' was reiterated by a generation of exegetes.

It may seem that I am flogging some very old carcases. But the point has less to do with the shortcomings of Brooks's analysis than with the unexamined assumption that 'the full treatment' is better than the partial treatment – which in turn is better than no treatment at all. Whereas an outsider like Henry Reed, writing in 1953, could condemn 'laborious, detailed analysis' at large, arguing that it was a hindrance, rather than a help, to *all* readers,[64] the insider's complaint was always that rival analyses were wrong, or incomplete – thus establishing the need for more of the same.

There was, further, the pervasive assumption of Absolute Greatness. The Eliot industry was underwritten, not merely by the insistence that these were canonical, indeed sacred texts, but by the Holy Writ of his essays, systematised into dogma. Orthodox exegesis until the early 1960s was founded on the premise that Mr Eliot never nodded, never blotted a line. Explication, as Gerald Graff observes, had become a 'protection racket'. He argues that when it comes to modern literature, this protective way of dealing with literature was initially necessitated by a cultural climate in which that literature was ignored, despised, and persecuted. The ease, however, with which modern literature has become assimilated into the curriculum suggests that changes in the culture may have lessened the need for protection.[65]

So far as Eliot was concerned, the need for protection had more or less vanished with the award of the *Dial* prize and the founding of *The Criterion* in 1922. By the late 1930s he had been dubbed 'the undisputed literary dictator of London'. Harold Bloom describes the atmosphere at Yale in the late 1950s as

An Anglo-Catholic nightmare. Everyone was on their knees to Mr T. S. Eliot, and, no matter what you read or how you taught it or how you wrote, you were also supposed to gravely incline the head and genuflect to the spirit of Mr Thomas Stearns Eliot, God's vicar upon earth, the true custodian of Western tradition.[66]

J. Hillis Miller reinforces the point:

The real precursor for Bloom is T. S. Eliot: anybody can see that. It's not Frye at all. . . . The real person he was obsessed with at the beginning, and continues to be obsessed with, is the man he calls 'the abominable Eliot'. . . . For all of us, when we were going to graduate school, the really looming figure was T. S. Eliot. If you wanted to make your way, you had to do something different from Eliot.[67]

Graff sees the conflict between scholarship and criticism as a central part of his story. For the mid-century Eliot industry, the distinction hardly existed. The scholars, like their critical counterparts, were in the business of extended paraphrase; the only difference was that the scholarly paraphrases were interspersed with laborious accounts of the philosophical, theological and literary 'sources' they had uncovered. The effect, on both sides, was to present the poetry as *ersatz* philosophy – or religion. 'Intentional fallacies' were cheerfully perpetrated by all parties; the real consequence of that injunction was that few critics bothered to do much biographical or historical research. Intentions were instead attributed to an omniscient 'Eliot' evoked by the interpreters to underwrite their paraphrases.

This being (who also appeared in what passed for biography during his lifetime, presented in successive *festschriften* and numerous opening chapters) knew and had read everything, and therefore could always be said to have 'intended' the 'meaning' displayed in any given analysis. The range of 'sources' and 'influences' was sufficiently large to permit infinite variations on the standard pattern (in the sense that the number of intervals between zero and one is infinite). Further insurance could be sought by consulting the oracle, who might tell you that yes, he had read *Crime and Punishment* before writing 'Prufrock', but in a French, not an English translation, thus upsetting your attempt to date its composition in 1914, when Constance Garnett's translation first appeared, and destroying the 'intended' parallels with the Garnett translation.[68] Given the assumption of Mr Eliot's omniscience, the procedure (with or without a letter from the oracle) was both self-validating and circular. This was not, of course, how the players described the game. The text was the official arbiter of 'meaning', a commodity with strong religious affiliations. Harold Bloom's 'Anglo-Catholic nightmare' is no exaggeration: Eliot-worship in the 1950s was virtually an academic religion, and much of the reaction since his death amounts to blaming him for not living up to the standards of divinity required by his congregation.

The role of literature as a substitute religion in the mid-century, with criticism as its theology, has received more condemnation than attention in recent years. Radical theorists tend to present the old criticism as the tool of a repressive establishment, and to dismiss the religious (or religiose) element as mystification for reactionary political purposes, as part of a broader argument that (Western) religious or metaphysical discourse can and should be reinterpreted as political manipulation of one kind or another. Yet some of the hostility to religion evident in the writings of theorists derives, perhaps, from the extent to which literature served as a displaced religion for their teachers in the preceding generation.[69]

The Eliotic cathedral, for example, suited those of a depressed, aesthetic or catholic temperament, whereas the worshippers of D. H. Lawrence were all for 'life' as promised by the high priest Dr Leavis; the Yeats cult provided a haven for those attracted to 'the perennial philosophy'; Pound enthusiasts could imbibe a heady mixture of extreme right-wing politics, Confucianism, and the promise that he would 'write paradise'. While many of the faithful were also declared Christians, agnostics were, for obvious reasons, the most fervent, as in R. P. Blackmur's response (in 1956) to the passage beginning 'a woman drew her long black hair out tight' in 'What the Thunder Said':

> The exegetes tell us, and it is true, that we are in the Chapel Perilous and the Perilous Cemetery is no doubt near at hand.... But for myself, I muse and merge and ache and find myself greeting with the very senses of my thought greetings and cries from all the senses that there are.[70]

According to Blackmur, the 'enabling act of criticism' is that of total submission to the work, the literary equivalent of the mystic's surrender to God. 'Serious writing', of criticism as of poetry,

> is done under the full tolerable weight of mind and sensibility. Imagination is in that sense absolute.[71]

'Imagination' was to mid-century criticism what the Holy Ghost is to devout Christians, just as Eliot and Lawrence were to their devout mid-century readers what Shelley and Byron had been to their nineteenth-century counterparts. Lionel Johnson, searching for a portrait of Shelley in 1884, wrote to a friend:

> I have hunted all London, and can't light upon what I want. It is for a cousin who almost literally prays to Shelley, having lost all her other gods.[72]

Much of Eliot's animus toward Shelley was, I think, provoked by this kind of veneration. The obvious irony of his assault on poetry-as-substitute-religion is that he became the object of a cult as fervent as the Shelley-worship he had so successfully displaced. But whereas literary religion in the late nineteenth century was relatively straightforward, the academic version in the 1950s was inextricably entangled with a pseudo-science of textual analysis.

Though the explicators continued to add new layers to the pyramid (and are still doing so today), it was clear not only to observers but to some insiders that the edifice was inherently unstable. The publication of the unfortunate Grover Smith's book in 1956 was, as indicated, the occasion for some misdirected soul-searching. As the reaction against Eliot gathered momentum in the late 1960s, Smith's work was frequently identified as the nadir of exegesis.[73] 1956 was also the year in which Eliot lectured on 'The Frontiers of Criticism' to an audience of 14 000 at the University of Minnesota's baseball stadium, 'the largest assembly ever gathered to attend a literary lecture'.[74] This was clearly an ideal opportunity for him to throw a very large spanner into the exegetical works, an opportunity the Eliot of 1920 would have seized with both hands. But despite his evident distaste for 'the lemon-squeezer school of criticism', he was careful not to leave his audience with the impression that he wished 'to condemn the criticism of our time'.[75] He had become the captive of his reputation.

Frank Kermode's *Romantic Image*, with its revisionist critique of 'dissociation of sensibility', and its willingness to consider Eliot and the 1890s side by side, may be said to have inaugurated the long process of dismantling the edifice of dogma assembled around Eliot's *oeuvre*. Though the attack on 'dissociation of sensibility' and the related devaluation of the nineteenth century had begun some years earlier,[76] it was Kermode who first pulled the threads of the argument together. The notion of a seventeenth-century crisis was always a distraction, a way of validating the decisive schism supposedly heralded (or caused) by the literary revolution of 1914, but in 1957 it was necessary to attack the seventeenth-century version first. If one had to write the history of Eliot criticism – as opposed to explication – on a postcard, one might say that the first generation of critics applied themselves, at Eliot's instigation, to disconnecting him from his nineteenth-century English precursors, and that the second generation set about restoring the connections, so that with Louis Menand's *Discovering Modernism*, Eliot criticism arrives at more or less the point from which it started, but in a way that turns its subject inside-out.

From the perspective of the 1990s, it is easy to look down on the narrowness, the naïveté, the tunnel-vision of the *ancien régime*. The reader who is convinced that we have got beyond all that is invited to substitute 'theory' for 'exegesis', and 'Derrida' for 'Eliot' (along with a string of parallel quotations), in the above account, and to reflect on whether a log of claims against current practice, lodged in twenty years' time, is likely to look much different.

4

The Case of the Missing Subject

'I thought about what progress I'd made on the Larisch case ...'
                                        Martin Rowson, *The Waste Land*

It is necessary to understand
That a poet may not exist ...

                                        Ern Malley, 'Sybilline'

I

Eliot's poems, as Hugh Kenner remarked in 1959, 'differ from reader to reader to an unusual degree, posed between meaning nothing and meaning everything, associating themselves with what the reader thinks of, and inclined to wonder whether Eliot was thinking of'.[1] Unusual, that is, in terms of the kind of reading they invite; compared to John Ashbery, Eliot seems, at first sight, a model of discursive clarity. Each component is so precisely turned as to suggest, to the reader who takes up the challenge, that there can be only one right way of fitting them together. The trouble, as witness the collective record of interpretation, is that they combine all too readily into whatever pattern the interpreter is bent on discovering.

Christopher Ricks provides a nice illustration in showing how critics, confronted with

In the room the women come and go
Talking of Michelangelo,

read their own prejudices into the lines, converting 'an impalpable smell' into 'a palpable dossier':

Robbed of their prey, or rather, robbed of the assurance
that certain of the people put before them may unmisgivingly
be considered prey, the critics write the recriminatory
novel which Eliot succeeded in not providing.[2]

Louis Menand, in a recent essay, counters this by arguing that

if historical scholarship has any use at all in interpretation, it surely
gives us grounds for supposing that Eliot intended the lines to invoke an image of cultural debility, and precisely for the reason that
they refer to women and not to men.[3]

A strong point, but, metre aside, substituting 'men', or 'guests', for
'women' would not banish the hint of cultural debility; as Ricks goes
on to demonstrate, if what is wanted is a couplet describing women
moving about a room, talking of Michelangelo, it would be hard to
compose anything *less* prejudicial.[4]

The lines are elusive for another reason. If, on opening Hugh
Kenner's *The Invisible Poet*, one's eye were to fall upon the following couplet:

Dans la pièce les femmes vont et viennent
En parlant des maîtres de Sienne,[5]

the reaction might well be, 'so even *that* was stolen', rather than
instant identification of Eliot's couplet in translation. The extent,
and the foregrounding, of thefts and borrowings is such as to
render every phrase suspect; the early poems achieve their peculiar effects by way of repeated hints that not only the feeling, but
the provenance of the phrases selected to convey its inadequacy,
is suspect. But the tactic cuts both ways: in declaring his poem
suspect, the poet casts suspicion upon the ideal of authenticity,
exploiting precisely the habit of reading he seems to scorn.

For some readers, elusiveness is the defining characteristic; yet
the temptation to interpret it as covertly expressive remains compelling. Eliot, says Richard Poirier, 'can never take anything in
his stride; he moves, falteringly, towards the formation of images
and concepts that dissolve as soon as he has reached them'; an
observation preceded by an explanation, that this is 'a poet who,
for reasons that have nothing necessarily to do with the twentieth
century, could not commit himself to narrative destinations of a

kind imagined if not experienced daily in a life more determinedly sexual than his was'.[6] The poems rush, as it were, to assist him: the repeated progression from street to door to stair to the (non)encounter with a woman or women in an upstairs room and back on to the street is a textbook Freudian dream-sequence, soliciting the view that sexual and emotional inhibition is Eliot's central subject. But one could hardly describe the poems, from this vantage-point, as faltering: 'transparent' would be more appropriate. It is a key which, with very little effort, will unlock every door in the house. The trouble, again, is that we are offered not one key, but a whole bunch of them, with assorted religious, philosophical, and cultural labels, and they all function as master-keys.

Interpreters bent on extracting thematic coherence from the early poems are doomed to succeed, because the qualities generally identified as Eliotic – fragmentation, isolation, affectlessness, bleakness, meaninglessness – can scarcely be described without reference to their opposites. Louis Menand calls the 'Preludes' an *In Memoriam* without a Hallam: 'the ghost fails to appear because the machine has broken down'.[7] But the device is double-edged; every reader is invited to discover his or her own ghosts in Eliot's half-deserted streets. Whatever fancies *I* am moved by will curl around these images, and cling. The poems read like filleted casehistories: every sign presents as a symptom, and each interpreter divines a different malady. Eliot's remarks, in *The Use of Poetry*, about 'the difficulty caused by the author's having left out something which the reader is used to finding', seem directly applicable:

> the reader, bewildered, gropes about for what is absent, and puzzles his head for a kind of 'meaning' which is not there, and is not meant to be there.[8]

In his case, however, the difficulty is quite the opposite. Faced with a poet who seems to have nothing to declare but his symptoms, the interpreter is more or less compelled to offer a diagnosis, whereupon the symptoms obligingly cluster around it. Interpretation becomes a quest for the missing subject; the poems map the geography of absence with such apparent precision that they seem to invoke the absence *of* something in particular: faith, hope, charity, sexual fulfilment, love, God, the organic community, an integrated personality, or what you will. And so the systematising critic naturally seizes upon the 'notion of some infinitely gentle, infinitely suffering thing' in the fourth 'Prelude' and converts 'these images' into tokens of an absent deity who nevertheless, like Berkeley's God, keeps an eye on the sequence in order to hold it together. The poet can then be endowed with a fully-fledged crisis of belief, and shelved alongside Kierkegaard, Nietzsche, Heidegger, and other philosophers of cultural or epistemological crisis. Yet when one returns to Eliot's shuttered rooms and vacant lots in search of the organising principle thus created, it is nowhere to be seen; the poem resembles a ring described by Peter Beagle, 'a simple pattern of turquoises set into what at first seems to be some polished black stone and is actually only carved emptiness'.[9]

The difficulty with such readings is not that they are demonstrably wrong, but that there is no way of choosing between them. Systematic explication necessarily proceeds by appeal to 'what is absent', for how else can absence be interpreted? Menand, who has written better than anyone else about the problem, argues that if the 'Preludes', and their unpublished drafts and companion-pieces, have a drama,

> it is the drama of much modernist writing, performed with unrelenting irony by Joyce and wearisome bravado by Hemingway – the drama of a style in search of a subject.[10]

'Modernist', in Menand's usage, gestures towards a minimalist aesthetic quite unlike the grand reifications discussed above: it is what, if anything, remains after the literariness has been subtracted from literature. Abstractly speaking, it is an impossible ideal, 'for a thing that is suspect for looking like itself is an onion that can be peeled indefinitely'.[11] But 'like many problems of identity . . . it is no less consequential for being metaphysically indeterminable'. Eliot – alone among his contemporaries in 'the movement' –

> grasped the particular fatality of modernism's predicament with (to borrow one of his own praise words) a clairvoyance that is even now a little disquieting.[12]

Even in this stripped-down version, 'modernism' remains a distraction. Menand's argument gains force and precision if we refine it down a stage further. Eliot, by the time he set to work on 'He Do the Police in Different Voices', had grasped the fatality of his *own* predicament, which can best be framed as a question: what kind of a poem remains after everything that, in nineteenth-century terms, makes poetry 'poetic' has been discarded? It was not, as Pound, Ford and Aldington thought, simply a question of modernising poetic diction. Throw out every archaism, 'every book word', every superfluous word, and you arrive, not at the unmediated Image, cashable in full against a real-world object, but back at the terminus of Paterian aestheticism:

> In its enthusiasm for ridding itself of the literary, Imagism ended by getting rid of everything *but* the literary; it moved the quality of literariness to the centre of the poem, and then began to trim away what was left around the edges.[13]

Eliot, in his early poems and essays, sought to push the question to its limit by discrediting, as far as possible, every quality that, in nineteenth-century terms, makes poetry 'poetic'. In so far as style functioned as a guarantee of literary value – and in the aesthetics of Pater and Wilde, his immediate point of departure, style was already the *only* remaining guarantee of value – it had to go, not only in the Paterian sense, but in any form capable of assimilation under the heading of self-expression. To put the question another way: what is original about a poem from which everything that, according to Pater and Wilde, makes poetry original, has been eliminated?

This was not a coherent, theoretically-grounded project, systematically developed, not only because Eliot didn't in fact pursue it in that way, but because he couldn't have; it can be defined only negatively, as an anti-theory, an anti-aesthetic. His programme was to expose the futility of all programmes, including those he apparently espoused. In a compelling reversal of the style of interpretation which gives the Bradley dissertation 'a prescriptive character . . . it seems determined not to possess', Menand argues that the author of *Knowledge and Experience in the Philosophy of F. H. Bradley* devoted himself to constructing the philosophical equivalent of a wrecking ball, 'a weapon, not a tool', guaranteed to demolish any theoretical structure in its path:

> we might feel equally justified in attributing to the Eliot of the dissertation not the despair of someone facing an unwished for crisis of belief, but the exhilaration of a young man who, bent

on the cultivation of an unassailable ironism, suddenly finds in his hands an instrument whose touch turns every post-Cartesian philosophical brick into straw. . . .[14]

Exactly the same can be said of the young poet discovering, by way of an almost symbiotic identification with Laforgue, that he is writing poems which are, so to speak, fireproof, disarming by incorporation every device which might be turned against them. In one common variant, endlessly and tediously reiterated in 'experimental' writing throughout this century, this ambition issues in a refusal of meaning, by way of extreme disruptions of sense and syntax, whereas Eliot achieved it in what appeared to be a poetry of plain, unvarnished statement.

Whereas Tennyson was infuriated by John Churton Collins's massive inventory of his 'obligations to his predecessors', Eliot, as Menand puts it, insists on his 'failure (there is a struggle, to be sure, but it seems to be conducted with only half a heart) to keep his feelings from becoming literary cliches' – to the point where it becomes a literary technique:

> a poem that professes to find in the received forms of literary language only the means for the production of secondhand sentiments will rely on its objects becoming real to its readers by the mechanism that makes a person seem most real to us when we are searching for the words to describe him.[15]

Which is to say that the peculiar effect of these poems does not depend on the reader's recognising that the opening lines of Laforgue's 'Crepuscule' provide a scenic and structural blueprint for the 'Preludes'; this is a poetry which repeatedly insists on its inadequacy to the task apparently assigned to it:

> insofar as readers of Eliot's early poetry . . . feel that this is the way the city really is for a particular consciousness at a certain pitch of *aboulie*, it is perhaps the consequence not of the creation of a new form but of the shattering of an old one, and if so, it is important to the effect that the damaged vessel not be mistaken for a new and more adequate container. . . .[16]

Familiar though the urban lyric was by the time he began to publish, a poet was expected to make something of his cityscape; what was new in Eliot was the declaration that he could make nothing of it. He sought, as it were, to disable every mechanism which, in nineteenth-century terms, underwrote the sincerity of a poem by appeal to the experience of the poet, and thereby to suggest that *his* sincerity consisted in renouncing any claim to it. In refusing to tune himself up to the required pitch – required, that is, by the reader's sense of what a poem is: for what is all this intensely-observed urban detail doing here, if not to convey some equivalent intensity of feeling on the part of the poet? – Eliot enlists the reader in a struggle to which he declares himself unequal. And so the refusal becomes heroic; personality returns by the back door, and the poet's declared inadequacy of response becomes the signature of a feeling too intense to be captured in words. Yet if he is ever called to account for any presumed *excess* of feeling, he need only sketch one of his weary gestures of dismissal: he keeps his countenance, he remains self-possessed; if there is any overflow of powerful feeling, it has nothing to do with him.

At its best, the conjuring-trick is worked with an aplomb and an elegance unsurpassed in twentieth-century poetry. But in spurning the quest for sincerity, Eliot was implicitly condemning the established devices for attaining it – devices which, to the advanced reader in 1910, had already begun to sound mechanical and tired, like the street-piano in 'Portrait of a Lady'. The early poems work by discrediting the conventions on which they depend for their effects. On most accounts, Eliot is in the established business of exploiting the work of his predecessors in order to develop a new kind of poetry, which in turn will become part of the tradition. On this argument, he is dismantling the work of his predecessors and selling off the pieces, shattering old forms rather than creating new ones; not, as conservative critics like Arthur Waugh assumed, as an act of cultural vandalism, but because he saw – or at least wrote as if he believed – that the machinery of 'the poetic' had broken down so irreparably that there was nothing left to do but exploit the conditions of its collapse.

II

Many readers have felt that Eliot, in 'Tradition and the Individual Talent', is writing from his own experience of composition, most vividly described only a few months earlier in the last of his 'Reflections on Contemporary Poetry', in which he described poetic maturity as the product of

> a feeling of profound kinship, or rather of a peculiar intimacy, with another, probably a dead author. It may overcome us suddenly, on first or after a long acquaintance; it is certainly a crisis; and when a young writer is seized with his first passion of this sort he may be changed, metamorphosed almost, within a few weeks even, from a bundle of second-hand sentiments into a person. The imperative intimacy arouses for the first time a real, an unshakeable confidence. That you possess this secret knowledge, this intimacy, with the dead man, that after a few or many years or centuries you should have appeared, with this indubitable claim to distinction; who can penetrate at once the thick and dusty circumlocutions about his reputation, can call yourself alone his friend: it is something more than *encouragement* to you. It is a cause of development, like personal relations in life.[17]

By this, Menand argues, Eliot 'means something he can describe only on the analogy of personal experience': that the writer's 'private affair has plugged him, whether he consents or not, into a public thing' – namely 'tradition' – so that this passage 'leaves us on the doorstep of "Tradition and the Individual Talent"'.[18] But to speak of an *analogy* with personal experience seems odd; this is Eliot's account of the experience of finding a voice through the agency of Symons and Laforgue in 1909.[19] The power of the essay depends, in part, on its compressed, urgent appeal to an experience authoritatively presented as paradigmatic rather than merely personal. The concentration, and the air of scientific precision combine to suggest that something new and unprecedented is being said, whereas the argument, as Menand shows, is underpinned by the critical tradition it appears to supplant:

> if we open up 'Tradition and the Individual Talent' and replace 'tradition' with 'experience,' the sequence of texts with the stream of sensations, we will find ourselves with something very like Pater's essay on 'Style'; and we will discover at the centre of both arguments a similar model of the mind, one that seems both reductive, because such passivity is ascribed to it, and extravagant, because it is required to generate such an exalted

kind of truth. The mental eyeball Pater borrowed from the empiricists to explain how the input of random sense data is corrected against the fixed structure of the 'inner vision' reappears in 'Tradition and the Individual Talent' as the famous 'shred of platinum'. . . .[20]

With Zen-like aplomb, Eliot attacks the idea of art as the expression of personality by using 'the intensity of the artistic process' to underwrite the impersonality of the product. The intensity is located in 'the mind which creates', but when we look around for 'the mind of the poet', all we are offered is a 'medium', inscrutably compared to a shred of platinum, quite distinct from the 'personality' which supplies 'the passions which are its material'. The shred of platinum, however, appears to be a chip off a larger block called 'the mind of Europe', into which the impersonal poet disappears by 'surrendering himself wholly to the work to be done'. He is, in other words, visible only when invisible.

In most of the received versions, Eliot is presumed to be saying that poets learn by rewriting their predecessors (as in Harold Bloom's theory of influence); everything has already been done, but the strong poet will always see the need for – and will wrest from his or her precursors – a new way of doing it, appropriate to the historical moment. Once again – though the point is seldom emphasised, or even recognised – we are back with Pater on style, and with style as the expression of personality, which is precisely the argument that Eliot seems most concerned to demolish by reduction. 'Tradition and the Individual Talent' does not, of course, read like an essay on style; the vocabulary of the second and third sections is resolutely experiential, and the argument is conducted by way of fine distinctions which are as impressive as they are inscrutable. What is the difference between an impression and an experience, or a feeling and an emotion? What counts as a new emotion, as opposed to an ordinary one? How can a poet work with 'emotions which he has never experienced'? How can there be 'feelings which are not actual emotions at all'? We will evidently have to work hard to keep up with Eliot, for whom these distinctions are apparently so obvious as to require no explanation. The rhetorical tactic is analogous to that deployed in the poems: a heap of precisely-carved, bafflingly-shaped pieces is tossed to the reader, along with the hint that they are parts of a whole which, if it can only be got together, will form a clear picture. The effectiveness of the device can be measured by the sheer amount of critical effort invested in attempts to unscramble Eliot's terminology.

So long as we accept the gambit, and continue to wrestle with impressions and experiences, feelings and emotions, personalities and mediums, the effort to make sense of it all is fruitless; on this level, the argument is counterfeit, the essay a cunningly-contrived, parodic facsimile of what it purports to be. Understandably, some readers have dismissed it as an exercise in dissimulation on the part of a didactic or confessional poet seeking to cover his tracks; a response that Eliot, in framing the argument in experiential terms, and especially in his cryptic remarks about the necessity of suffering, may be said to have courted.[21] But, from a writer's point of view, impressions and emotions are usable only when put into words, and if we transpose the experiential vocabulary into linguistic terms, the essay makes a great deal more sense – though of a rather different kind. The link to Pater and Wilde is immediately uncovered; it becomes, after all, an essay on style, on writing as rewriting. Eliot half-concedes as much in describing the poet's mind as 'a receptacle for seizing and storing up numberless feelings, phrases, images'. But the argument for impersonality – which depends upon Eliot's conjuring with minds, personalities and catalysts – dissolves in consequence. My poem can perfectly well be a tissue of other poets' phrases *and* a direct expression of my personal feelings and opinions. Which is very much the position that orthodox Eliot criticism has consistently occupied, taking 'impersonality' as more or less synonymous with 'sublimity' or 'greatness'. 'You see', says Eliot, 'how completely any semi-ethical criterion of "sublimity" misses the mark', but we seem, for the most part, to have seen nothing of the kind.

Once the substitution is effected, the essay, construed as an argument about poetic process, apparently boils down to a few paragraphs-worth of commonplaces. It is, from this perspective, a striking illustration of Menand's point that the theoretical content of the early essays is 'practically zero'. Yet few readers would happily dismiss the entire performance as fraudulent or merely self-aggrandising. Nor, I think, did Eliot deliberately set out to deceive his audience; the device of pushing a familiar argument to its extreme and presenting the result as the only reasonable position to hold was second nature to him; it is the principal strategy of the Bradley dissertation. I suggest that the experiential component of the essay is confused for the simpler reason that Eliot did not fully understand it himself, even though, as usual, he was able to derive a rhetorical advantage from his uncertainty. 'The point of view which I am struggling to attack is perhaps related to the metaphysical theory of the substantial unity of the soul' is not, I think, a strategic refusal to declare a fully-worked-out position, but a genuine admission of uncertainty. Equally, it appeals to the reader's vanity: this is all very difficult, he seems to say, and must be got right; together, perhaps, we can work it out.

'Tradition and the Individual Talent' makes much better sense when read as a personal report – and a progress report – on the experience of composition, elaborately disguised as a prescription. This, again, is not a new idea, but the general tendency has been to stress – as the essay invites us to stress – how much Eliot has in common with other poets by, for example, invoking Keats's celebrated letter to Woodhouse: 'A Poet is the most unpoetical of any thing in existence, because he has no Identity – he is continually infor[ming] and filling some other Body',[22] or the passage cited in *The Use of Poetry*:

> Men of Genius are great as certain ethereal chemicals operating on the Mass of neutral intellect – but they have not any individuality, any determined character – I would call the top and head of those who have a proper self Men of Power.[23]

The effect of such associations is to restore the prescriptive character of the essay, whereas its most striking feature is the extremity of the position taken. Eliot's 'impersonality', as Menand demonstrates, is 'the nineteenth century doctrine of sincerity at its most extreme stage of attenuation: being has become a physiological condition, and its sentiment a symptom':[24]

> In giving the self so little to express, in making the literary work the symptom of conditions, inner and outer, for which the writer's pen serves only as a kind of unconscious conduit, Eliot gave his criticism a powerful vocabulary for revisionism, since what the writer *intended* to say could now be safely ignored in favour of what he could not *help* saying. . . .

> It is one of the ironies of literary history that some twenty-five years after Nordau used this analysis of the artistic process as

the basis for an attack on the forerunners of modernism, 'Tradition and the Individual Talent' made the same notion of creativity part of an argument that seemed to many readers a defence of art's autonomy and value.[25]

In seeking to destroy the notion of poetry as inspired self-expression, Eliot had arrived at its exact opposite, which, as often in such cases, looks remarkably like the thing rejected. For what is inspiration, as conventionally defined, if not a condition in which 'the writer's pen serves only as a kind of unconscious conduit'? What is to stop the writer's personality from seizing the pen and transferring its 'conditions' nakedly to the page? Only, it would seem, the shred of platinum, 'the catalyst that adjusts the experience of the contemporary world to the "ideal order" of tradition and guarantees that the result will be "impersonal"'.[26] Eliot's appeal to tradition simply blocks any approach to the question, for 'tradition' means anything we want it to mean, and nothing in particular. Construed as practical advice it is, like most of Eliot's prescriptions, entirely useless. Having bought a device guaranteed to render our work impersonal, we discover, when it fails to operate, that the manufacturer has neglected to supply an address.

On most views of inspiration, necessity and intention merge into identity: what the writer could not help saying turns out to be what the writer most wanted to say, as Kafka discovered on the night of 22 September 1912:

> This story, 'The Judgement', I wrote at one sitting. . . . The fearful strain and joy, how the story developed before me, as if I were advancing over water. . . . How everything can be said, how for everything, for the strangest fancies, there waits a great fire in which they perish and rise up again. . . . The conviction verified that with my novel-writing I am in the shameful lowlands of writing. Only *in this way* can writing be done, only with such coherence, with such a complete opening out of the body and the soul.[27]

The same exultant note can be heard in Eliot's account, written almost ten years after the event, of his encounter with Laforgue: 'The imperative intimacy arouses for the first time a real, an unshakeable confidence.' But the contrast is equally striking: Kafka discovers his voice in his story; Eliot finds a voice in Laforgue.

All writing may be rewriting, but not equally so, and in this regard, Kafka and Eliot are at opposite ends of the spectrum. The
mature Kafka can certainly be equipped with precursors, but only
in the most paradoxical fashion. Borges goes to the heart of the
matter in two pages:

> At first I had considered him to be as singular as the phoenix
> of rhetorical praise; after frequenting his pages a bit, I came to
> think I could recognise his voice, or his practices, in texts from
> diverse literatures and periods.

The half-dozen instances offered are as eclectic as can be imagined.
'If I am not mistaken,' he concludes:

> the heterogeneous pieces I have enumerated resemble Kafka; if
> I am not mistaken, not all of them resemble each other. . . . In
> each of these texts we find Kafka's idiosyncrasy to a greater or
> lesser degree, but if Kafka had never written a line, we would
> not perceive this quality; in other words, it would not exist. . . .
> The fact is that every writer *creates* his own precursors. His
> work modifies our conception of the past, as it will modify the
> future.[28]

The last sentence is accompanied by a footnote referring us to
'Tradition and the Individual Talent'.

The fact is that very few writers create their precursors in this
sense; Kafka (like Borges) remains as singular as the phoenix,
whereas in the best of Eliot we have a poet in whom we can
hear, from one angle, nothing *but* the voices of his precursors.
This is not intended as a value-judgement, but as a distinction in
kind. Eliot did not create Laforgue; Laforgue created Eliot. Again
with no pejorative intent, we might reverse Eliot's terms and say
that, as a poet, he was metamorphosed from a person into a bun-
dle of second-hand sentiments – and that this, though in a costly
and ultimately self-defeating way, was the making of him.

Perverse though this may sound, it relates to a perception which,
in a less categorical form, recurs constantly in Eliot criticism: that
wherever the moralist gets the better of the ironist, as in *The Rock*,
or the plays, or the discursive passages of *Four Quartets* – or the
rejected portions of 'He Do the Police in Different Voices' – the
quality of the writing is markedly inferior. When this perception

collides with the belief that Eliot is always and everywhere a great poet, the result can be very strange, as in Donald Davie's notorious attempt to prove that *The Dry Salvages* is a deliberately bad poem.[29] Numerous rescue attempts on the *Quartets* have been run along similar, though less dramatic lines, striving to show that what looks didactic is actually ironic, but they sound, to me, like special pleading. By this I don't mean to identify the moralist with the 'real' Eliot, but to say that the ironist can't be pinned down in this way, which is not in the nature of Eliot, but in the nature of irony.

His problem, on this view, was to find a way of not being himself. Laforgue provided the solution; Eliot became, in a handful of poems, the finest French poet in the English language. 'The Love Song of J. Alfred Prufrock' is, by any standard, an extraordinary achievement for a 23-year-old writer; just as extraordinary, in its way, is the sheer dreadfulness of 'The Love Song of St. Sebastian', evidently part of an attempt to escape the Laforguian manner, completed some three years later. What is remarkable is not that he should have written it, but that he should have shown it to anyone, let alone Conrad Aiken, who was just about to publish his first volume. Of the accompanying pieces, 'Oh little voices', and the first section of 'Appearances', are equally, though less melodramatically, bad; it is as if the poems of 1909–12 had never been written – or had been written by someone else. The concluding 15 lines of 'Appearances' are salvageable (several fragments appeared, eventually, in *The Waste Land*), and recognisable; but they are also a lame redaction of the third 'Prelude'.[30]

'I am disappointed in them', he told Aiken, wondering whether he should 'knock it off for a while', but nevertheless asked *whether* 'St. Sebastian' was 'morbid, or forced', and if it all seemed 'very laboured and conscious'. By the time the hoped-for reassurance arrived, he was unable to accept it:

> The devil of it is that I have done nothing good since J. A[lfred] P[rufrock] and writhe in impotence. The stuff I sent you is not good, is very forced in execution, though the idea was right, I think. Sometimes I think – if only I could get back to Paris. But I know I never will, for long. I must learn to talk English.[31]

Getting back to Paris is not a matter of changing his address (though that might have helped), but of recovering the symbiosis with

Laforgue. Talking English means, I think, seeking a voice of his own, a natural but self-defeating response to his plight. Desperation is, and remains, the keynote until April 1917, when he gave up and returned to Paris by composing in French, using Corbière as a model, though without achieving the 'saturation' which, as he put it in his 1919 account of the Laforgue period, 'sometimes combusts spontaneously into originality'.[32] Those poems look more like imitations, partly because he did not have the same degree of inwardness with Corbière, and partly because they *are* in French; the effect of the earlier work depends, to a considerable extent, on his playing one language off against the other.

In a letter to Robert Nichols in August 1917, he declared that 'the best promise of continuing' was to forget what he had already written,

> to be able to detach it completely from one's present self and begin quite afresh, with only the technical experience preserved. This struggle to preserve the advantages of practice and at the same time to defecate the emotions one has expressed already is one of the hardest I know. . . .[33]

It is hard to see, either on this account or in the poems of 1917–19, any sense in which the technical experience *was* preserved; the quatrain poems are not an advance on the earlier work, but a new beginning. In the Laforgue period, he had not come into possession of a style, but been possessed by one, and when the symbiosis failed, he was left with nothing to go on with. It was not, he later insisted, 'a deliberate choice of a poet to mimic, but writing under a kind of daemonic possession by one poet'.[34] His accounts of poetic process are frequently conducted by appeal to idiom of the uncanny (haunting, visitation, possession, clairvoyance), 'Tradition and the Individual Talent' being no exception. For if we reject the chemical analogy, his assertion that 'the poet has, not a "personality" to express, but a particular medium' acquires a new precision, less to do with science than with seances.

The common view of Eliot the poet as, above all, a great stylist seems to me true, but only in a paradoxical sense. For all his stress on the virtues of technique and professionalism, Eliot at his best is always the amateur, in the strict sense of the word, never knowing where his next poem is coming from, compelled to wait upon inspiration, painfully aware that he can do little or nothing on his own initiative. He is, in this regard, the antithesis of Yeats, a professional poet if ever there was one, constantly and purposefully rewriting his earlier work as the *Collected Poems* expanded. One cannot imagine Eliot crying, '[m]onths of rewriting. What happiness!'[35] Once the impulse was exhausted, or the poem published, that was the end of the poem.

Unlike Yeats, he can never be said to have commanded a style (apart from the loose, inferior verse of the late poems and plays); style – or rather a procession of styles – commanded him. Yeats's career invites developmental treatment; Eliot's will scarcely accommodate it. Even to speak of a career is misleading: from 1909 until the mid-1930s, it amounts to a series of new starts – the Laforgue period; the poems in French; the quatrain poems; 'Gerontion'; *The Waste Land*; 'The Hollow Men'; *Sweeney Agonistes*; the Ariel poems; *Ash-Wednesday*; 'Difficulties of a Statesman'; 'Burnt Norton' – followed by a steep decline *caused* by planning (whether his own or someone else's), in *The Rock*, the five full-length verse plays, and the later *Quartets*, where much of the trouble stems from his subsequent adoption of the formal scheme of 'Burnt Norton.' This is not a view that appeals to the reverent, but it has always been, and remains, the standard complaint of those who take their bearings from the Eliot of 1909–22.

The view that, with whatever false steps and local failures, there is a coherent progression from *Prufrock and Other Observations* to 'Little Gidding' is no more than a projection of the great-poet stereotype. This might be called the authorised version, and its most influential exponent is, of course, Eliot himself. He is, in this guise, always the professional, the expert practitioner at war with British amateurism and slackness: 'Surely professionalism in art is hard work on style with singleness of purpose.'[36] In the first part of 'Tradition and the Individual Talent', a thinly-disguised rendition of his own career is offered as a paradigm of artistic development. No poet, he tells us, can continue beyond his twenty-fifth year without acquiring 'the historical sense'; Eliot's twenty-fifth year was 1912–13, the year in which the Laforguian symbiosis collapsed.[37] The ideal artist 'cannot form himself wholly on one or two private admirations' (Laforgue and Corbière), 'nor can he form himself wholly upon one preferred period' (the Jacobean idiom of the quatrain poems and 'Gerontion'), though this is 'a pleasant and highly desirable supplement'; he must tune himself to 'the mind of Europe' – and go on, as the authorised version would have it, to write *The Waste Land*.

This suggests yet another reading in which natural selection, rather than chemistry, powers the scientific terminology of the essay. Once again, Eliot managed to impart some extra spin to an authoritative idea whose implications were, at first sight, inimical to his purpose. The poet, once connected to the 'main current' of tradition, cannot help but evolve; equally, he is not merely the beneficiary, but the agent of natural selection, advancing 'the mind of Europe' with each new synthesis. Necessity and intention fuse: scientific determinism becomes, not the negation, but the ultimate source of (im)personal power and authority. Eliot, though apparently scrupulous in denying any implication that the work of the past is rendered obsolete or inferior, does not close the door entirely: 'this development, refinement perhaps, complication certainly, is not, from the point of view of the artist, any improvement'. But an assiduous reader of *The Egoist*, familiar with Eliot's polemic against the nineteenth century and 'the annual scourge of the Georgian anthology', could scarcely have missed the point: 'If our predecessors cannot teach us to write better than themselves, they will surely teach us to write worse.'[38]

'Tradition and the Individual Talent', like the early poems, remains an elusive performance, accommodating numerous incompatible readings and privileging none. It is simultaneously an essay on the psychology of inspiration, an attack on Romantic poetics, a recipe for creative plagiarism, an excursion in literary Darwinism, a shameless exercise in self-promotion, and more; everything by turns and nothing long. The systematising critic will always find what he or she seeks; like Bradley's philosophy (in Eliot's version) it gives you everything you want and renders it not worth the having. Eliot liked to say that the poet's business was not to think, but to deliver the emotional equivalent of thought; 'Tradition and the Individual Talent' delivers not precision, but the illusion of precision: the ironist's equivalent of theory.

III

Most interpreters construe *The Waste Land* on the analogy of a powerful magnet drawing fragments captured from half-a-dozen traditions into an intricate pattern: a portrait of the artist, or the essence of modernism; a vision of cultural or spiritual desolation (or enlightenment). This style of interpretation requires a unifying principle, a problem generally solved in two moves. The pattern discovered turns out to *be* the principle of organisation, which is then attributed to Eliot. But *The Waste Land* – as witness the collective record of interpretation – will happily accommodate any number of unifying principles, from the decline of the West to relativity theory to mystery religions to the state of the Eliots' marriage. Every interpreter is convinced that his or her reading is there in the poem, waiting to be discovered. As in a way it is, but only in the sense that a reflection is always waiting to be discovered in a mirror.

This aspect of *The Waste Land* was for a long time obscured by academic reverence for the poem as a cultural monument, a new link in the chain of tradition rather than a scrapyard auction of the pieces. From a strict conventionalist point of view, a poem is whatever the prevailing consensus takes it be, but for all the reverence, the frenzy of unconvincing explication is a measure of collective unease about its standing, and there have been too many dissenting voices along the way. And if it were an orthodox monument, it would by now have been surpassed by a new synthesis, whereas it remains (with one strange exception, as we shall see) a poem without descendants – necessarily, in my view, for the logical extension of *The Waste Land*'s technique would be a poem entirely and manifestly composed of borrowed fragments. It would be, in its most extreme form, the verbal equivalent of a Duchamp readymade; not scrambled words, but stolen words:

No Spitting.
No Hawking.
Gentlemen lift the lid.
                    T. Eliot

The trick is really only worth doing once: a gallery displaying nothing but Duchamp urinals is not an art gallery, but a plumbing store. Yet *The Waste Land*, for all its apparent sophistication, is also a trick that can never be repeated (or at least hasn't been repeated) to the same effect.[39] Like the best of the earlier Eliot, it is perfectly poised between scrapheap and synthesis; its power depends on its symbiotic closeness to what it exploits and in a sense parodies, the poem of grand cultural synthesis, of epic perception. 'These fragments I have shored' – the pattern remains a jumble, every fragment visible for what it is, but it still looks like a pattern, shored up by the habit of reading it both invites and mocks. The effect is not simply doubled-edged, but Janus-faced; like the broken spring in the factory-yard in 'Rhapsody on a Windy Night', it exists on the verge of disintegration. The substance is corroded, but the form remains; hard and curled and ready to snap, it has not snapped yet. Not to see the rust is to miss one-half of the effect, to see only the rust is to miss the other half. Push the technique any further towards fragmentation, and the pieces will fall apart (as in the *Cantos*); push it the other way, and the crazed surface will blur into seamlessness.

Frank Kermode once called *The Waste Land* a poem of 'decreation' – 'the deliberate repudiation (not simply the destruction) of the naturally human and so naturally false "set" of the world' – but in regarding it as a work of existential diagnosis he was still, in my view, endowing the poem with a coherence it does not possess:

> one can think of [*The Waste Land*] as a mere arbitrary sequence upon which we have been persuaded to impose an order. But the true order is, I think, there to be found, unique, unrepeated, resistant to synthesis.[40]

It is, rather, the illusion of true order, like the illusion of true perspective in an Escher drawing, not resistant to synthesis but endlessly accommodating of it. Fifty years after Conrad Aiken, A. Walton Litz declared the Grail plot 'spurious', but it is no more, and no less spurious than any of the innumerable plots attributed to the poem.[41] Straight readings dissolve into self-parody because *The Waste Land* is not, in the sense that detailed explication always makes it out to be, a serious work. The more the interpreter babbles of corn-gods and Jessie Weston and the decline of the West, the more the parodic spirit of the poem (and the notes) seems to rise up in mockery. Martin Rowson's graphic version strikes me as by far the most illuminating commentary ever produced: darkly, parodically menacing, teeming with 'significant' detail lifted from disparate contexts, it defies categorisation in precisely the way the poem does.[42]

Menand suggests that if *The Waste Land*

> was indeed intended as a kind of deliberate dead end, an explosion of the nineteenth-century metaphysics of style leaving nothing in its place, this ambition was perhaps one of the things Eliot learned from Joyce. *Ulysses*, Eliot told Virginia Woolf in a

famous conversation, 'destroyed the whole of the nineteenth century. It left Joyce with nothing to write another book on. It showed up the futility of all the English styles. . . . [T]here was no "great conception": that was not Joyce's intention. . . . Joyce did completely what he meant to do.'[43]

Eliot, surely, *projected* this ambition on to Joyce, who after all did have a 'great conception' in Bloomsday, and went happily on to *Finnegans Wake*. That conversation took place on 23 September 1922, two days after Eliot had written to John Quinn to thank him for finalising the American publication of *The Waste Land* and the award of the *Dial* prize. Whereas the application to *Ulysses* is at best oblique, the application to *The Waste Land* is immediate and striking. With the extended and rancorous negotiations over prize and publication finally resolved, he was beginning to realise that the poem would be a very hard act to follow.

Two conflicting impulses are apparent in Eliot's comments on *Ulysses* in 1922–23. On the one hand, he seems to be using the novel as a vehicle for promoting the poem, notably in his account of 'the mythical method' (an altogether appropriate irony) in '*Ulysses*, Order and Myth'. Once dutifully applied to *The Waste Land*, that passage has come to be seen as evasive, designed, in Richard Poirier's view, to 'dissuade readers from discovering, with I. A. Richards, that his poem was as much about sexual sterility as about immense panoramas',[44] or from recognising, with A. Walton Litz, that the Grail plot is spurious. But Eliot, in 1923, could not have foreseen that this particular passage would become so influential. His conflation of *Ulysses* with *The Waste Land* was surely a subliminal recognition of the predicament in which Pound, for the most admirable reasons, had landed him.

In declaring, repeatedly, that he could not have produced *The Waste Land* on his own, Eliot was effectively acknowledging that it was not the poem he set out to write. He could not see *The Waste Land* in the manuscript; he could not follow the logic of Pound's editing. 'He Do the Police' is not an inferior version of *The Waste Land*, but a different kind of poem. One could hardly speak of a chorus of voices in 'He Do the Police', because it has no central theme, or rather, its theme is diversity. Eliot's method of composition, as I have suggested, seems to have been to add more and more styles and voices, in the hope of arriving at a verse equivalent of what he took to be Joyce's achievement in

Ulysses. He had, evidently, little interest in Joyce's material (he first read *Ulysses* in instalments, partly out of sequence, and had not seen the whole work when 'He Do the Police' was submitted to Pound). *Ulysses*, for him, was not so much a novel as a dramatic poem, an encyclopaedic display of stylistic virtuosity in which the writer had managed the ultimate disappearing-trick, rendering himself everywhere present and nowhere visible.

If Eliot's ambition in 'He Do the Police in Different Voices' had been to show up 'the futility of all the English styles', it would have fallen so far short of the mark as to leave the ambition unrecognisable. In the latter stages of its composition, Eliot had effectively abandoned the ironic-exploitative mode of the earlier poems, as is apparent in the shipwreck passage in the original 'Death By Water', and above all in the first forty or so lines of 'What the Thunder Said'. Few commentators seem to have noticed that those lines (described by Eliot as the best in the poem)[45] are stylistically out of key with the rest of *The Waste Land*. Unpunctuated, cadenced rather than metrical, and heavily end-stopped, they anticipate the chant-like rhythms of *Ash-Wednesday*. In *The Waste Land*, the ironic force of the whole contains the departure; in 'He Do the Police' the passage simply foreshadows Eliot's later manner.

'He Do the Police in Different Voices' is, like *The Waste Land*, a collation of fragments written (or stolen) over a ten-year period; unlike *The Waste Land*, it reads like a transitional work. 'Gerontion' (completed in July 1919) is already moving away from the ironic-subversive mode of 1909–12, and the satiric-subversive mode of the quatrain poems; it does not exploit the conventions of seriousness in either the style of 'Prufrock' or that of 'A Cooking Egg'. In July 1919, he told Mary Hutchinson that 'Burbank with a Baedeker', like 'Sweeney among the Nightingales', was 'meant to be *very serious*!' whereas 'The Hippopotamus' and 'Whispers of Immortality' were not. Though the distinction is by no means convincing, he repeated it to his brother on 15 February 1920 (in the letter lamenting his being 'considered by the ordinary Newspaper critic as a Wit or Satirist').[46]

Eliot, as we have seen, knew that he had achieved something remarkable in the poems of 1909–12, without ever being sure of what he had done, or how he had done it. It could hardly have been otherwise; exploiting, as opposed to parodying the conventions of seriousness in poetry is a delicate business, a matter of being only just off-key – which goes far to explain why the distinction between good and bad Eliot is so unstable. His intuitive response to Laforgue was perfectly pitched, but never, so far as I know, explicitly formulated. If he had been consciously committed to a poetry of exploitation, he would presumably have worked it up into a technique (as Laforgue, in a way, had done) applicable to any subject. Rich pickings were certainly to be had in the field of nature poetry, but once established as a method, it would have been subject to the law of diminishing returns. In the letters of 1914–17, he seems equally troubled by the loss of the Laforguian impulse, and the fear that even if he were able to recapture it, he would only be repeating himself. Without a commitment to seriousness *and* an accompanying sense that the established means of generating it had ceased to function effectively – if only for him – the result would have been much closer to explicit parody, rather than the knife-edge poise of 'Prufrock' or the 'Preludes'.

The quatrain poems, furthermore, are in no sense a development from the *Prufrock* volume. Satire and melodrama are uneasily and often violently yoked together, rather than fused; without the strict form, the elements would fly apart (as they do in 'Ode', which appeared only in *Ara Vos Prec*). *Prufrock and Other Observations* on one side, and *The Waste Land* on the other, exert a sort of gravitational pull, hauling them back toward the exploitative mode, but the strain is apparent. 'Burbank' could hardly be defended as unassailably ironic; even Christopher Ricks declines the brief,[47] citing a revealing passage from Eliot's review of Murry's *Cinnamon and Angelica* (1920):

Why these grocery names? It is a movement of protection against the cultivated audience. Whoever is acutely sensitive of the pressure of this intruder will have his own grimace of buffoonery, to avoid sentiment or to decorate sentiment, so that it will no longer appear personal, but at most – safely fashionable. The concealment is a 'give-away'; but we cannot safely say that Mr Murry has given himself away either, for his 'close-knit intertexture' is a maze of such subtilised and elusive feelings as will hardly be threaded by any but those whom he would be willing to admit.[48]

Many readers have felt that Eliot, in the poems of 1917–19, gives himself away in precisely this fashion. A defining characteristic of the exploitative mode is that it disarms the question of intention by throwing it back at the reader, and though the case stands up for 'The Hippopotamus', 'A Cooking Egg', 'Mr Eliot's Sunday Morning Service' and 'Sweeney Among the Nightingales', it sounds far less convincing when applied to 'Lune de Miel' or 'Whispers of Immortality', and breaks down entirely with 'Burbank' and 'Ode'. 'Grimace of buffoonery' encapsulates the problem: no weary gesture of dismissal, but a defensive mannerism.

Dissatisfied with the character of 'Wit or satirist', he seems equally bent on maintaining it as a hedge against intruders, an uneasy truce which could not endure for long. 'Gerontion' can certainly be read as ironic from start to finish, but only against the grain. Christopher Ricks is willing to go to court this time:

> the consciousness in 'Gerontion' after all is not offered as healthy, sane and wise; who would wish to be he, and what endorsement then is being asked for the thoughts of his dry brain in its dry season?[49]

Almost convincing, but where is the frame of reference? The immediate context does not help; little in the consciousness of *Ara Vos Prec* could be described as healthy, sane or wise. Gerontion, at best, sounds uncomfortably like his creator, whereas Prufrock's title sets him free; the poem trades on its resemblance to a love song, not on Prufrock's resemblance to T. S. Eliot. 'Dramatic monologue', appeals to Browning notwithstanding, lacks the required precision. Nor does 'Gerontion' exploit its quasi-Jacobean idiom as the *Preludes* exploit the poetry of urban squalor. Eliot uses the authority of his borrowings to heighten Gerontion's: 'I that was near to your heart', for example, is straight rewriting, not subversion of Middleton. Gerontion speaks in the voice of the moralist, with nothing to gainsay him; if the reader is expected to supply all of the health, sanity and wisdom here, why not in 'Burbank'?

To enter one *caveat* on Ricks's behalf: with *The Waste Land* in near-final shape, Eliot thought of 'printing Gerontion as prelude in book or pamphlet form'.[50] Pound dissuaded him, but it would have been an interesting, if damaging contest between moralist and ironist. Read through the lens of *The Waste Land*, 'Gerontion' looks vaguely suspect, whereas in the context of *Ara Vos Prec* it assumes an oracular gravity. But if Eliot had published 'He Do the Police' more or less as it stood, or broken it up into separate poems, *Prufrock and Other Observations* would seem the exception, followed by a prolonged, fitful struggle in which the moralist gradually displaces the ironist. That struggle is enacted in the 'sprawling, chaotic manuscript' of 'He Do the Police in Different Voices'. In what Eliot intended – in so far as it makes sense to speak of his intention – as a decisive break with his earlier manner, Pound discovered the culmination of it, and presented him with the poem against which his later work would be judged, and found wanting, by many of his most committed readers.

Eliot, once *The Waste Land* had assumed its final form, always insisted on its absolute superiority over 'He Do the Police'; he was equally consistent in declaring it, for his own purposes, a dead end. On 12 November 1922 he wrote to Gilbert Seldes: 'Nov. no. [of the *Dial*] just received. Poem admirably printed. But I find this poem as far behind me as Prufrock now: my present ideas are very different.'[51] Three days later, he wrote to Richard Aldington: '*The Waste Land* ... is a thing of the past so far as I am concerned.'[52] His 'present ideas', in fact, had been very different since the middle of 1919; he had been 'feeling toward a new form and style' even before work on 'He Do the Police' had seriously begun.

The Waste Land would have been a hard act to follow even for a poet who had done completely what he meant to do. For Eliot, it was an impossible act to follow, and he had every reason to distance himself as thoroughly as possible from 'his' achievement. Embarrassment over the debt to Pound is a sufficient explanation, but not, I think, the only explanation. Eliot saw in *Ulysses*, as in a glass darkly, something he could not afford to acknowledge even to himself. As he said to Virginia Woolf (with a few substitutions):

> Eliot is a purely literary writer. ... *The Waste Land* destroyed the whole of the nineteenth century. It left Eliot with nothing to write another poem on. It showed up the futility of all the English styles. ... But there was no 'great conception': that was not Eliot's intention. ... Pound did completely what Eliot [the ironist] meant to do.

Unless you believe that *Ulysses* and *The Waste Land* are as macrocosm and microcosm, this must surely be taken as unwitting self-revelation. Any thoroughgoing ironist – such as the early Eliot – is 'a purely literary writer', because unconstrained irony feeds off what it destroys; it lives by undermining 'great conceptions', not by advancing them. The early poems work by exploiting worn-out nineteenth-century poetic conventions of sincerity and moral earnestness; *The Waste Land* treats the entire poetic tradition ('all the English styles') in similar fashion. Its sheer stylistic, allusive, and thematic inclusiveness left him with nowhere to go; he could pursue the exploitative mode no further, and without Pound's intervention he would never have got so far. He had claimed it as his major work, but it was also a no-thoroughfare sign in the way of the poetry of high moral seriousness to which (with what-ever ironic defences) he was now committed:

> For at my back from time to time I hear
> The sound of horns and motors, which shall bring
> Sweeney to Mrs. Porter in the spring.

Destroying the reputation of the nineteenth century had been a high priority in the polemical essays of 1917–21; with a handful of exceptions, he had been just as dismissive of his *avant-garde* contemporaries. As covert self-promotion, it had been an extra-ordinary success. So long as he remained the outsider, the ironist whose only position was to expose the futility of all positions, he had nothing to lose. But in seeking to secure the position of 'the best living critic, as well as the best living poet, in England',[53] he was also converting his strongest assets into liabilities – a pro-cess encapsulated in the dismal history of *The Criterion*. From mid-1921 onwards, he squandered his energies on the project, always on the defensive, agonising over the smallest detail. A dedicated ironist might have adopted that title, but Eliot was – in every sense – deadly serious.[54] Having made his reputation by tearing up the agenda, he was now determined to set it, no matter what the cost in health, strength and sanity.

In the space of five years, Eliot moved from uncompromising attack to entrenched defence. His change of manner immediately after *The Waste Land*, dramatic though it seems, was the final step in a change of stance which began no later than 1919. Menand, for all the precision of his analysis, finds Eliot's 'conquest of lit-erary London. . . . still, as a social fact, a little hard to account for',[55] but the one thing underplayed in his account is the sheer

force of Eliot's ambition. The letters tell the story: as Eliot's reputation grew, so did his preoccupation with it; by 1919 it had become an obsession which grew, over the next four years, to
monstrous proportions. Marital unhappiness, and his consequent
determination to prove to his family that he had not made a mess
of his life, obviously contributed. But, illness aside, the marriage
did not deteriorate markedly between 1919 and 1923; at the end
of 1922, the Eliots were still functioning as a team.[56] It seems quite
superfluous to attribute his nervous collapse in the winter of 1921
to some obscure personal crisis when the evidence is plainly in
view; he drove himself to breakdown.

The conquest of literary London was, necessarily, more a matter of image than substance. John Middleton Murry, who despite
Eliot's condescension, had a knack of predicting his next move,
remarked in February 1920 that 'Mr Eliot, who is a connoisseur
in discrepancy between intention and achievement, is likely to be
himself an example of it.'[57] *The Waste Land* secured, for Eliot, the
title of 'best living poet in England', but it also secured, for its
putative author, an image he could neither live up to nor live
down. An ironist's variation on poetic justice, but one he was no
longer disposed to appreciate.

IV

Those reviewers who declared that their response would stand
even if *The Waste Land* turned out to be a hoax wrote more pro-
phetically than they could have known. Many readers will be
familiar with the story of Ern Malley, whose collected poems were
concocted in the space of ten hours on 6 October 1943 by two
young Australian poets, James McAuley and Harold Stewart. Their
intention was to expose the fraudulence of *avant-garde* poetry (as
they saw it) by luring Max Harris, the *enfant terrible* of Adelaide's
minuscule *avant-garde*, into publishing *The Darkening Ecliptic* in
his magazine *Angry Penguins*. (Malley, according to his entirely
convincing sister Ethel, had died of Grave's Disease, unrecognised
and unpublished, at the age of 25.) Ern, with luck, would go on
to acquire an international reputation which they would then
destroy, along with his promoters' credentials, by revealing the
method of composition: more or less metrical lines arbitrarily
assembled with the aid of a stack of reference books, including a

US Army report on mosquito-control. Harris, like his backer John Reed and the painter Sidney Nolan, was enraptured by the poems, and published the entire collection in June 1944. Malley's cover was accidentally blown soon after, sending the Australian press into such a frenzy of philistine glee that his creators were almost as embarrassed as his publisher. In a final oxymoronic twist, the non-existent Ern, in the guise of the all-too-visible Harris, was successfully prosecuted for indecency.

But the hoax did not work out as its perpetrators expected. Ern Malley's admirers (who included Herbert Read, John Ashbery, and – though 'not for publication in any way' – Eliot himself)[58] stuck to their guns, insisting that his creators had produced work of real quality in spite of themselves, a view which has gained adherents as time has passed. Malley is by no means as incoherent as McAuley and Stewart maintained; he remains, as Michael Heyward says, 'an enigma half a century of debate has not solved':

> Had they wished, the hoaxers could have written far more ineptly than Malley does. They did not construct a poet who could not write, or who was a bore, or who had nothing at all to say, but one who writes with panache in a way they thought spurious. . . . Malley's detractors have undervalued his work, and his supporters often overvalued him. . . . As poet and cipher he represents, with whatever perversity or futility, the definitive moment in Australian literary modernism. Malley is the exception that proves the rule: he is the only genuinely avantgarde writer in a country that has never sponsored a literary revolution.[59]

He is, in other words, a true descendant of the early Eliot. *The Darkening Ecliptic* consists of 16 poems, 424 lines in all – just nine lines short of *The Waste Land*. It is a tissue of thefts and borrowings, some straight, some doctored, to the extent that nothing in it cannot be suspected of being stolen; larded with cryptic hints that it is not what it seems; written in a variety of strong but often irregular metres; charged with unexplained menace, constantly teetering on or over the brink of melodrama. Malley is self-parodic in something very like Eliot's fashion, uninterpretably equivocal, and he is not simply pastiche. At his uneven best, he is remarkably like the real thing; as, for example, in the opening lines of 'Culture as Exhibit':

'Swamps, marshes, borrow-pits and other
Areas of stagnant water serve
As breeding-grounds . . .'

which are also the opening words of the swamp-draining manual.[60]
Eliot would not, perhaps, have left 'and other' hanging, but he
would surely have appropriated 'borrow-pits.'

Steeped in traditional forms and metres, McAuley and Stewart
had, as they thought, discarded all formal and logical constraint;
in fact they had loosened up to just the extent needed to sum-
mon the authentic air of spuriousness. In making Ern such a thiev-
ing poet ('an interloper, robber of dead men's dreams'), they were
setting him up to fail the test of originality, as conventionally
understood, but for that very reason he passes the Eliotic version
with flying colours: 'poetic originality is largely an original way
of assembling the most disparate and unlikely material to make
a new whole'.[61] The same applies to their use of 'unpoetic' material.
Intended flaws constantly mutate into Eliotic virtues. In the opening
poem, 'Durer: Innsbruck, 1495', Ern declares himself '[t]he black
swan of trespass on alien waters'. This was meant as blatant
self-contradiction (the black swan is native to Australia) but Malley
wins again, backing his poetic judgement against ornithological
correctness, and leaving open his allegiance in the matter of hemi-
spheres.

'Durer: Innsbruck, 1495' is a 'real' McAuley poem, only slightly
modified for the occasion. It is also, in my judgement, better than
anything he wrote before *Surprises of the Sun* (1967), and the stark,
minimalist lyrics of his last years. McAuley, in the late 1930s,
was steeped in the French Symbolists, an admirer of *Hugh Selwyn
Mauberley* and, in his own phrase, a 'convinced disciple' of the
early Eliot, 'fascinated . . . by the way he superimposed images
of "tradition" and "modernity"', though he thought *The Waste
Land*

carried the method of 'disconnectedness' too far. In his later
poetry Eliot had lost his 'blinding eloquence' and 'macabre wit'.
'It is a melancholy reflection,' McAuley wrote, not able to fore-
see his own conversion, 'but in the main a true one, that the
more a poet becomes reconciled with his Catholicism the more
his art suffers.'[62]

According to Heyward, McAuley had lost his Anglican faith in adolescence after reading Frazer's *The Golden Bough*. He was also a gifted musician, 'a natural parodist', fond of practical jokes, and politically radical; he was pianist and musical director in an anti-war revue, *I'd Rather be Left*, which ran for six months in Sydney in 1941. 'Its target was not the massing armies of Hitler but capitalists profiting from the war, and local politicians out to sell the country short.'[63] But by the winter of 1943, a few months before the Malley poems were written, he had abandoned his pacificism, his radicalism, and – consciously at least – his 'Eliotism', in favour of an equally thoroughgoing traditionalism. In 1952, he joined the Catholic Church, to the dismay of some old friends from his radical days, and began, like the later Eliot, to insist that 'society recover spiritual traditions he believed it had not properly observed since the middle ages'.[64] For the radicals of the next generation he was, as poet, cold warrior, and self-declared political manipulator, a right-wing bogeyman – an image he relished, and cultivated at every opportunity.

Though the two poets always insisted that *The Darkening Ecliptic* had been an even-handed affair, McAuley was, I think, the dominant partner; the best of Ern is closer to McAuley than Stewart. Yet if they had deliberately set out to tune Malley on to Eliot's wavelength, they would probably have failed; their belief that they were perpetrating a hoax was an essential ingredient. Their method, aimed at constructing a parody of bad modern poetry, was hijacked by the parodic voice of the early Eliot. And it could only have been done from the traditionalist side of the fence. Malley's supporters sometimes argue that his creators became successful avant-gardists in spite of themselves, but the point is quite the reverse. They remained traditionalists in spite of themselves; the fact that much of Ern Malley's 'tradition' is spurious only heightens the Eliotic effect. A formless Ern would have been just another free verse poet. Their reverence for tradition, a limiting factor in their own work, turned out to be Malley's trump card; it gave him something to play off against. They had, unwittingly, more or less replicated the process which produced *The Waste Land*. Even the death they chose for Malley heightens the coincidence, for the drowned Bleistein, in a rejected portion of Eliot's manuscript, was also afflicted by Grave's Disease.

Whether or not they thought they had Eliot in their sights, the gun was pointing the other way. In setting Ern Malley before an *avant-garde* audience in 1944, they were also selecting the readers most likely to have had their expectations of poetry transformed by the experience of 'Prufrock' and *The Waste Land*. Eliot has been an academic institution for so long that the exhilaration of first-generation readers, especially young readers, tends to be forgotten. He was admired for his irreverence, not as a champion of high culture; and Ern Malley is nothing if not irreverent. But that same group of readers included some of those most dismayed by *For Lancelot Andrewes* and the religious poems, and by the time *The Darkening Ecliptic* appeared, Eliot was, in the most advanced circles, officially passé. Ern Malley's debut was perfectly timed; far enough away from the early Eliot to cover his tracks, and close enough for the haunting resemblance to work to maximum effect. He survived the discovery of his non-existence because, for some of the readers McAuley and Stewart had hoped to deceive, Eliot had so changed their response to poetry that the hoax turned out to be more authentic than the real McAuley.

5

The Quest for the One True Meaning

Six Hours a-Day the young Students were employed in this Labour; and the Professor shewed me several Volumes in large Folio already collected, of broken Sentences, which he intended to piece together; and out of these rich materials to give the World a compleat Body of all Arts and Sciences . . .

Swift, 'A Voyage to Laputa'

I always said no good would come of poetry.

Sir Walter Raleigh (1913)

I

Gerald Graff suggests 1937–41 as 'the turning-point for the consolidation of criticism' in the American university system – the point, that is, at which the proponents of the old Gradgrindian 'scholarship' had effectively lost their long battle to exclude criticism from the academy, thus enabling the emerging New Critics to reinforce their position.[1] Fifteen years later, it was as if the old battles had never been fought, whereas in England, there had never been quite the same intensity of conflict between scholars and critics; literary criticism was gradually, if grudgingly, accepted into the academy, without, until the rise of I. A. Richards and the Cambridge school in the 1920s, any serious internal challenge to its predominantly amateur ethos. By the late 1930s, the diverse histories had begun to converge: close reading had become a primary tool of advanced professional criticism on both sides of the Atlantic. But it was in the United States, where the research imperative was already well-established, and the demand for coherent theories and methodologies far more pressing, that the problems of institutionalisation first became apparent.

140

The strain was evident even at the theoretical level; the New Critics, as Graff puts it, 'would vacillate between the effort to purge literature of social and moral impurities and to promote it as a form of knowledge that could save the world from science and industrialism'.[2] But in practice, the dilemma was immediate and inescapable. Many critics were committed to the ideal of poetic language as unique and unparaphraseable, but when they stood up in a classroom, or sat down to write a critical essay, found themselves somehow condemned to focus on paraphraseable content, and thus to sprinkle their commentary with disclaimers to the effect that all this should not be confused with 'the real meaning'. The poet had sent an urgent message to the modern world, but the critic was not permitted to deliver it.

For mid-century critics seeking a secure home in the academy, the response to this dilemma was institutionally determined: they could not afford to let go of either horn. 'The autonomy of poetic language', as Graff says, 'demanded the autonomy of departments to teach it as a matter of territorial rights.'[3] If literature was simply a quarry to be mined for great thoughts, then it didn't require a specialist team to do the mining; the job might as well be contracted out to historians, philosophers, and indeed just about anyone working in the discursive disciplines. This was precisely the ground on which the recent battles with the scholars had been fought, and it could not be surrendered. To secure their territory, the critics, as René Wellek declared in 1953, would have to develop 'a technique and methodology teachable and transmissible and applicable to any and all works of literature'[4] – and clearly distinct from the methods of neighbouring disciplines.

Literature could not, therefore, be seen to speak directly to untrained readers. But on the other hand, its message had to be delivered, and here again the position was institutionally determined. For if literature was indeed a unique mode of discourse, but of no practical use, there was again no place for it in the academy. Certainly a poem should not mean, but be – but once it entered a classroom or a learned journal it could not simply exist: it had to do something educative, admirable, and conducive to further research. Throughout the long battle between scholars, critics, and proponents of general education, the one proposition that none of the combatants had challenged, at least in public, was that the academic study of literature was A Good Thing. The good was variously defined: literature instilled respect for our democratic values; it made you a better, or a more sensitive, or a more cultivated person; it offered special insight into the past; it showed you why the modern world was on the road to ruin, and what you should be doing to rescue it. Whatever the variant, literature did you good – but it needed professional assistance.

One can only admire the elegance of the institutional knot into which the critics had tied themselves. Graff has a delightful illustration:

> [P]ostwar textbooks modelled on *Understanding Poetry* sometimes prescribed tactically evasive formulations for students. They point out that terms like 'theme' and 'persona' would help one avoid getting caught making the claim that a poet or poem actually says something. One text warned against attributing a bald assertion to Wordsworth's 'Composed upon Westminster Bridge' such as 'The city is as beautiful a place to live as the country,' which 'comes perilously close to giving advice.' Instead, the shrewd student was advised to speak of the theme of 'the natural beauty of the city,' as if such a circumlocution kept the integrity of poetry intact. As the editors put it, 'the danger of regarding theme as message or moral decreases when a noun with appropriate modifiers replaces the complete sentence.'[5]

But if, as such transparent strategies were bound to suggest, poets really were in the business of giving advice, why couldn't Patience Strong do the job as effectively as Wordsworth or T. S. Eliot? – who often ended up sounding remarkably like Patience Strong by the time the critics had finished with them:

> The hero of 'A Cooking Egg' has confined his social life to mild afternoons with Pipit, to whom he gives what attention he can. . . . But she offers a pallid kind of entertainment, and the hero is understandably distracted with thoughts of a better and more exciting world.[6]

Considering the quality of the advice actually extracted from Eliot's poems in hundreds of interpretive essays, the most obvious difference seemed to be that whereas Patience Strong delivered her message for free, you had to dig deep for Eliot's, and then pretend you hadn't quite heard it – always assuming you hadn't struck rock instead of gold, like the student who, confronting the epigraph to 'Prufrock', complained to Northrop Frye:

> The book I read says this stuff here's the key to the whole thing, but what the hell good's that when you don't know what it says?[7]

Two conflicting claims – for the autonomy of poetic language, and for the efficacy of literature's civilising or redemptive influence – had to be presented in ways that demonstrated the need for systematically trained professional interpreters. Despite continuing efforts to reconcile the first two elements on the level of theory, the characteristic response in practice was to shuttle between them, with each hand striving to distract attention from what the other was doing. Symptoms of internal conflict were everywhere apparent, notably in the clashes between precept and practice generated by 'the heresy of paraphrase' and the 'intentional fallacy', and in the constant tension between the urge to broadcast the moral significance of literary works, and the countervailing insistence that there could be no substitute for 'the work itself'. There was, equally, a general reluctance on the part of academic critics to probe too deeply into the foundations of the business, perhaps because of an uneasy awareness that their house was built upon sand.

II

The current uproar over the politics of criticism conceals how much the warring factions have in common – not only with one another, but with their despised precursors. Afrocentricists, radical feminists, cultural materialists and diehard defenders of the great tradition are poles apart politically, but all insist that literature – however they define it – can usefully be enlisted in their campaigns. The traditionalist who claims that study of the canon will instil respect for democratic (or Republican) values is, in his way, the mirror-image of the radical feminist who believes that close scrutiny of the same canon will prove it to be a powerful instrument for the oppression of women by white European males, and of the Afrocentricist convinced that the study of Afro-American literature will advance the liberation of Afro-Americans. All factions attribute immense political power to literature, or literary and cultural studies, or literary theory, while complaining that the power has somehow been neglected, or suppressed by the opposition, or otherwise prevented from transforming civilisation as we know it.

A further shared characteristic of these claims is that virtually no one apart from the combatants believes a word of them. Yet, looking at the escalation of the political rhetoric, not just over the last five years but since the late 1960s, it is clear that repeated exposure of these absurdities has had no effect whatever. And in this regard, the story of radical theory over the last two decades is a cacophonic replay of the tale of orthodox explication, *c.* 1940–60, at much higher decibel-levels. The mid-century pseudo-science of interpretation was subjected to constant and cogent attack, but the interpreters carried on regardless. New-wave theorists have simply extended Wellek's formula to embrace (in many of the competing versions) 'a methodology applicable to any and all *texts.*' The interpreters of the 1950s claimed that literature could not properly be read without professional assistance; radical theorists in the 1990s insist that nothing can safely be read, nor a TV set watched, nor even a Madonna concert attended, without intensive theoretical care.

Hyperinflation is a clear indication of vulnerability. Academic respectability is again at issue: no development in the modern university since the Second World War has provoked more widespread derision than radical theory, from within as well as from without. Historically speaking, it is, nevertheless, a fascinating development, a *reductio ad absurdum* of the contradictory premises on which mainstream academic criticism was founded. In 1976, for example, Richard Ohmann delivered an impassioned indictment of his profession, of the academy's complicity with 'the military-industrial complex', and of the (to him) consequent failure of literature and humanities departments to exert a transforming influence upon American politics and culture. Much of his critique of what had gone wrong with academic literary studies – as opposed to his solutions – remains cogent. But in an 'imagined chapter',

I *prove* what in actuality I can but state: that there are complex causal relationships among the university teaching of composition, social class, and the management of our society. Since Chapter $6\frac{1}{2}$ would take ten or fifteen years to write, I leave it unwritten.[8]

The sincerity of his conviction that a radical overhaul of English 101 could help to overthrow the capitalist system shines in every chapter that he *did* write, and in his peroration: 'I think we can work with where we are and with what we know to oppose the tyrannies of this culture and lay the groundwork for the next.'[9] Ohmann, deeply committed to political activism and to literary studies, seems not to have questioned his conviction that the two could – and therefore should – be combined. His complaint against the New Critics, for example, was that they saw 'poetry as serving the individual reader, and only very indirectly as amending a flawed society'.[10] Despite all the evidence he had marshalled to the contrary, he remained convinced that the proper study of poetry could play a leading role in the amendment.

The prototype here is not Che Guevara, but Matthew Arnold, as reconstituted by I. A. Richards and the Leavises. Ohmann's book included one approving reference to *Fiction and the Reading Public*, but he was not apparently aware that his prescription was straight Leavis, with a twist of socialism. In *For Continuity* (1933), F. R. Leavis advanced precisely the same argument: who controls Rhetoric and Composition 101 (or its English equivalent) can sway the fate of nations:

> Whether or not we are 'playing the capitalist game' should soon be apparent, for a serious effort in education involves the fostering of a critical attitude towards civilisation as it is. Perhaps there will be no great public outcry when it is proposed to introduce into schools a training in resistance to publicity and in criticism of newspapers – for this is the least opposable way of presenting the start in a real modern education. . . .
>
> The teaching profession is peculiarly in a position to do revolutionary things. . . .[11]

In *The Social Mission of English Criticism* (1983), Chris Baldick places the Leavises in a direct line running from Matthew Arnold, through subsequent advocates of literary education as a means of social control, to I. A. Richards, who radically altered the emphasis without questioning the assumption that literature *could* be made to do the work of individual, and, by extension, social redemption. The one serious flaw in Baldick's analysis is that he himself treats that assumption too seriously. He demonstrates the hold of the social-control hypothesis on the imaginations of conservative educators from the 1860s to the publication of the Newbolt Report, *The Teaching of English in England*, in 1921, and beyond. It was – so the stereotype ran – far too late to prevent the working classes from reading altogether, but the soothing influence of English literature, properly taught, could quell social unrest, nurture patriotic sentiment, and stem the rising tide of communism. As George Sampson put it in 1921:

> A humane [i.e. literary] education is a possession in which rich and poor can be equal without any disturbance to their material possessions. In a sense it means the abolition of poverty, for can a man be poor who possesses so much?[12]

Such proposals rested on condescending fantasies about the character, culture, and aspirations of the working classes which no serious social historian has entertained since the publication of E. P. Thompson's *The Making of the English Working Class* in 1963, but which still thrive among literary intellectuals, on the left as well as the right. Baldick's desire to establish, at least by implication, the malign consequences of social-control theory is such that he neither acknowledges its full absurdity, nor pauses to ask what the intended recipients might have made of it. Almost all of his evidence comes from the proponents; the one significant exception is the following passage from the autobiography of the Chartist Thomas Cooper (1805–92), published in 1872:

> All this practice seemed to destroy the desire of composing poetry of my own. Milton's verse seemed to overawe me, as I committed it to memory, and repeated it daily; and the perfection of his music, as well as the gigantic stature of his intellect, were fully perceived by my mind. The wondrous knowledge of the heart unfolded by Shakespeare, made me shrink into insignificance; while the sweetness, the marvellous power of expression and grandeur of his poetry, seemed to transport me, at times, out of the vulgar world of circumstances in which I lived bodily.[13]

Baldick cites this extract not from the original, but from D. J. Palmer's *The Rise of English Studies* (1965), in order to illustrate the theory of H. G. Robinson, a teacher at York Training College, who had claimed, in 1860, that 'the dangerous and extravagant imaginations of young people could be cured by literary study as a kind of "homeopathic treatment" preferable to surgery':[14]

> Although Robinson would not have known it, his theory had already been confirmed by the experience of the Chartist agitator Thomas Cooper, whose memoirs testify to the sobering effects of literary self-education upon the working-class reader. . . . It was in this way, ideally, that the humanising power of literature operated to counteract anarchy. If the savage Chartist could be soothed so easily, what wonders could literature not perform in the world? Nearly every theorist of popular literary education in this period attempts to show that great literature is capable of breaking down class differences and showing how unimportant they are.[15]

'Confirmed' pretty much cancels any intended irony, which is unfortunate, since the career of Thomas Cooper confirms the exact opposite of the point intended. The passage in question comes from Chapter Five ('Shoemaker Life: Early Friendships; 1820–24'), and it concludes: 'I said to myself, daily – "I am educating my ear and my mind, and I shall be ripe for my true work in time." '[16] Appalled by the grinding poverty of the Leicester handloom weavers, Cooper became, in the early 1840s, a leading and quarrelsome figure in the Chartist movement, editing and publishing one Chartist paper after another: *The Midland Counties Illuminator*, *The Chartist Rushlight*, *The Extinguisher*, *The Commonwealthman*, and more, and addressing public meetings attended by up to ten thousand people. In 1843 he was convicted of sedition and conspiracy, and sentenced to two years in Stafford Gaol. During his time in prison he composed *The Purgatory of Suicides: A Prison-Rhyme: In Ten Books* (in Spenserian stanzas), which 'received quite a warm welcome from Cooper's contemporaries – among them Carlyle and Dickens – and . . . sold well for many years.'[17] Towards the end of his sentence, the prison chaplain offered to get him a place in Cambridge University:

'Go to Cambridge, from this gaol!' I repeated in wonder.

'Yes: all your wants will be provided for. You will have no trouble about anything – only – ' and he stopped and smiled.

'Only I must give up politics?' said I: 'I see what you mean.'

'That's it,' said he, 'that's all.'

'I would not degrade or falsify myself by making such a promise,' I replied, 'if you could ensure all the honours the University could bestow, although it has been one of the great yearnings of my heart – from a boy, I might say – to go to a University.'[18]

So much for 'the sobering effects of literary self-education upon the working-class reader'. Cooper's radicalism was eventually subdued, not by literature, but by a reconversion to fundamentalist Christianity in the 1850s. As for the notion that class-consciousness is soluble in poetry, Dorothy Thompson had shown, ten years before Baldick's study appeared, that Chartism

> was pervaded by a sense of class – both a positive sense of identification and a negative hostility to superior classes – which was stronger than perhaps existed at any other point in the nineteenth century.[19]

A less fortunate illustration could scarcely be imagined. Baldick, without quite realising it, has written a history (from above) of delusions of grandeur among literary critics and educators. Theories of literary education as a means of social control, redemption or improvement were certainly built into the rationale of academic criticism on both sides of the Atlantic. But to ascribe real-world consequences to those theories – and therefore to believe, as Terry Eagleton evidently does, that twentieth-century British or American society might have developed along different lines if literary education had taken some other form – is to compound the delusion. There is a further problem, elegantly if unwittingly identified by Baldick himself. F. R. Leavis's campaign against what he saw as the 'terrifying' power of advertising over 'the herd' was propelled by a truly embarrassing error:

> It never seems to occur to Leavis that advertising is a trade which thrives by advertising *itself*. He thus falls for the biggest advertising 'con' of them all, taking as good coin agency boasts designed to attract investment in publicity whose value has never

been conclusively proved. While appearing to challenge and to scrutinise the output of the advertising business with the utmost vigilance, Leavis's literary/psychological method is in fact grounded on a fathomless gullibility,[20]

and on the extraordinary presumption that he and his fellow Scrutineers were among the few people in the English-speaking world capable of resisting the advertisers' blandishments.

Advertising, however, is not the only trade which thrives by advertising itself. Baldick cites, among others, this passage from the Newbolt Report:

> The interim, we feel, belongs chiefly to the professors of English literature. The rise of modern Universities has accredited an ambassador of poetry to every important capital of industrialism in the country, and upon his shoulders rests a responsibility greater we think than is yet generally recognised. The Professor of Literature in a University should be – and sometimes is, as we gladly recognise – a missionary in a more real and active sense than any of his colleagues.[21]

Though he notes in passing that this has the 'appearance of professional pleading', his commentary is otherwise focused on the political implications. Yet he has already told us that the authorial committee had 'a built-in majority of English Association members'.[22] One can only ask: what conclusion would you expect from a public inquiry dominated by professors of English if not: give us more money and higher status, or the roof of civilisation will fall in? It *is* professional pleading, and the social-control component must be heavily discounted, first because it's hard to imagine what else the professors, regardless of their actual beliefs, would have wanted to say to the coalition government of 1921, and second because no one has ever produced a shred of evidence to suggest that it is anything other than fantasy.

This is not to say that literary education has no social consequences whatever. But few people outside the profession would need convincing that its effects, as compared to those of large-scale economic and political forces, are at best minimal. Second, whatever the influence upon individual students, the overall effect is likely to be self-cancelling rather than cumulative. Third, it is impossible to isolate the literary component from either the impact of the teacher's own political views, or the influence of university life upon students, even ignoring the wider social context. The small minority of students who are strongly influenced by university English studies are, obviously, those most likely to join the profession – which is partly why the belief that the business *must* have larger social consequences endures in the professional imagination.

The Newbolt Committee's insistence that 'a responsibility greater . . . than is yet generally recognised' rested upon the literature professor's shoulders was, equally, F. R Leavis's, who remains, according to a recent survey, the second most popular critic in British colleges and polytechnics.[23] Baldick, in summing up a devastating critique of Leavis's social theories, again sees half of the matter very clearly:

> Wild though Leavis's inaccuracies are, they serve their purpose admirably: to enhance enormously the social importance of literary critics and of English teachers, beyond even the heights at which Arnold and Richards had pitched their claims.[24]

Those 'inaccuracies' were essential to Leavis's influence, and as John Carey has recently shown, his contempt for 'the herd' was directly in line with mainstream intellectual attitudes to 'the masses'.[25] Who would want to confine their teaching to – as Kingsley Amis once put it – discussing not so much the niceties of Pope's use of the caesura as the niceties of who Pope was, if they could be in the vanguard of a movement dedicated to cultural renovation? And what professional body, lobbying for expansion, would stake its claim on the former activity if it could make the latter sound even remotely plausible?

The antitype in all of this is perhaps Sir Walter Raleigh, Merton Professor of English Literature at Oxford from 1904 to 1922:

> Dissatisfied with the lack of heroism involved in professing literature, Raleigh was attempting, as [Virginia] Woolf put it, to become a Professor of Life. His cynicism about teaching literature was not so much a question of gross professional misconduct (as Q. D. Leavis sees it), but arose from a very clear-headed understanding of the ridiculousness of literary culture's ambitions for bringing about social change.[26]

This, I think, is the point at which Baldick is closest to a clear view of his subject. What he underestimates, for the most part, is the strength, among many academic critics, of the will to believe in any programme which presents literary criticism as a force in the affairs of nations. And in this regard, I. A. Richards was arguably an even more potent influence on the profession than Leavis, since it was Richards, in the 1920s, who first attempted to put the redemptive mission of Anglo-American criticism on a sound scientific footing.

It is illuminating to focus on Richards' notorious declaration, in *Science and Poetry* (1926), that 'poetry . . . is capable of saving us' (a claim derided by T. S. Eliot, whose poetry, according to Richards, was supposed to do much of the saving), and to consider which of the arts could have been substituted for 'poetry' without rendering it palpably absurd. 'Ballet is capable of saving us?' Painting? Classical music? Sculpture? Or, for that matter, the novel? Given Richards' own strictures on the pernicious effects of indiscriminate novel-reading, this would scarcely have done. The only other possibility is 'literature', in this context effectively a synonym for 'poetry'.

Richards' accompanying gesture towards Arnold's 'The Study of Poetry' ('[t]he strongest part of our religion today is its unconscious poetry') exploits the analogy with sacred texts common to the promotional rhetoric of the day. Eliot's dismissal of the project as 'a rear-guard religious action'[27] served, however, to muddle the issue. Poetry, in Richards' scheme, is a vehicle for personal, and, by extension, social therapy, hedged with the peculiar qualification that the therapy – a soothing dose of 'pseudo-statement' – only works for a superior minority said to be least in need of it. As Baldick observes:

> His real object of attention in the construction of the theory of value is the systematic establishment of relative merits not for poems but for minds or personalities. . . . The well-balanced mind to which poetry is witness is taken as a touchstone against which different readers may be assessed in terms of relative mental health.[28]

What Richards would evidently have liked to say is that literary criticism is capable of saving us: 'The critic, as we have said, is as much concerned with the health of the mind as any doctor with the health of the body.'[29] Left-wing critics, notably Raymond Williams, Terry Eagleton, John Fekete, Francis Mulhern and Baldick himself, have attacked Richards for seeking to inculcate passivity rather than critical activism, but again without sufficiently questioning the theory's plausibility.[30] Richards believed that he had dispelled the need for 'a Rock to shelter under' by inventing an 'efficient aeroplane in which to ride' the 'tempestuous turmoil' of modern existence.[31] It is unfortunate, in view of his campaign against stereotypes and stock responses, that his invention was assembled from precisely the stereotypes invoked by the Newbolt Committee: the artist as morally superior being, the literature professor as predestined guardian of the masses, and poetry as a prime mover in the work of social renovation. The real question, yet again, is why anybody believed that this Heath Robinson flying machine could ever leave the hangar. Among Richards's precursors, indeed, is the H. G. Robinson who thought that youthful radicalism could be subdued with 'homeopathic' doses of literature, and that the same treatment would expand middle-class minds: 'They are generally *honest* in their opinions, but in too many cases they are *narrow*.'[32]

III

As is often remarked, the adoption of close reading as a central teaching device enabled literary education to assume and update the 'mental discipline' function previously ascribed to the study of Greek and Latin.[33] John Crowe Ransom declared in 1941 that the 'new criticism very nearly began with [Richards]', and went on to describe *Practical Criticism* as 'one of the documents of major influence upon the thinking of our age'.[34] The age aside, *Practical Criticism* is arguably the most influential work – with the single exception of Eliot's *Selected Essays* – in the history of academic criticism.

Yet the method of *Practical Criticism* was, as many critics would now concede, fatally flawed. Ransom, like Richards, thought that 'the protocols revealed dismal deficiencies in the power of supposedly trained students to cope with poetry'.[35] What they actually revealed were the dismal deficiencies of the method. A crude test of contextual knowledge, artificially withheld from the students (sometimes to the extent of altering the texts), was promoted by Richards as a precise instrument for assessing textual insight –

and therefore 'sensibility'. Most of the students inevitably failed the test, thereby confirming the theory around which it had been constructed: that only the superior few possess the mental equipment to cope with the complexities of modern life.[36] It also ensured that the teacher, without having to do much work, would always be among the superior few, thereby setting up, as Gerald Graff observes,

> another excuse for formulary lamentations – themselves a kind of stock response – about how dreadfully ill prepared and inattentive the students are.[37]

Though Eliot provided (or rather, was co-opted to provide) theoretical support for the anti-historical, anti-intentionalist emphasis of mainstream New Critical practice, Richards supplied the method, which the New Critics elaborated into a full-scale methodology. As Richards's 'protocols' abundantly demonstrated, ruthlessly decontextualised close reading did not and could not work, but he and his supporters in the Cambridge English Faculty had convinced themselves that it did, and should. After all, *they* could do it. In their enthusiasm, they attributed their success to trained or superior 'sensibility', rather than to their superior knowledge of contexts.[38] 'If properly set it cannot be faked', said E. M. W. Tillyard of the Cambridge examination in practical criticism,[39] but it was the examiners who were doing the faking.

Richards' original error was compounded by the New Critics as close reading became rapidly more sophisticated. Ransom and his allies, like the Cambridge Ricardians, sincerely believed that they were refining techniques for dealing with 'poetry as poetry, and not another thing', which would at last put an end to reductive moralising and chatter about Shelley. But in order to secure their territory against a rearguard action from the scholars, the New Critics *had* to emphasise method over context; which they could well afford to do, because contextual knowledge was the concealed (and largely unacknowledged) premise upon which the method depended. Richards' work provided a model, not only for classroom teaching, but for competitive reading among professional critics, as Ransom saw very clearly:

> His most incontestable contribution to poetic discussion, in my opinion, is in developing the ideal or exemplary readings, and in provoking such readings from other scholars.[40]

Yet by the early 1950s, as William Cain notes, the founding fathers

> were not only pointing (along with their foes) to the narrow
> canon touted by the New Criticism and bemoaning its failure
> to invoke 'history,' but ... were also scrutinising a defect in
> the very procedures of New Critical close reading,

namely, 'endless explication' which was neither purposeful nor
coherent.[41] But it was already too late to stop the machine. Academic criticism had moved on to an industrial footing, and the
contradiction at the heart of institutionalised competitive reading
was becoming apparent.

The official convention was that 'we' were refining our understanding of canonical texts by a process akin to successive approximation. 'In each poem', said W. K. Wimsatt,

> there is something ... which can never be expressed in other
> terms ... like the square root of two, or like pi, which cannot
> be expressed by rational numbers, but only as their *limit*. Criti-
> cism of poetry is like 1.414 ... or 3.1416 .., not all it would be,
> yet all that can be had and very useful.[42]

Such was the faith that sustained the quest for the One True
Meaning. As an image of what individual critics thought they
were doing in contesting rival interpretations and refining their
own readings, the analogy seemed plausible enough. As an account of collective practice, it was untenable. Competitive interpretation thrived – and could only survive – on disagreement,
but to qualify as 'research', it had to be represented as in some
sense progressive and cumulative.

The One True Meaning, or Single Correct Interpretation, was
paradoxically both an ideal of, and a profound threat to, mid-
century exegesis. The notion is quite implausible in hindsight,
and yet it didn't seem so at the time, or even to P. D. Juhl in
1981.[43] It was an ideal which the profession could neither afford
to abandon, nor subject to rigorous scrutiny. Interpreters tended
to treat each others' readings as sighting shots at an invisible target whose location could nevertheless be inferred from the text.
There had to *be* a target, for if the purpose of interpretation was
not to develop 'ideal or exemplary readings', what was the point?
Yet, however good the individual aim, someone else would always

be able to show that it was slightly off-centre. In principle – though most preferred not to dwell on the point – there were as many exemplary readings as there were readers, but if some were not more exemplary than others, then what, again, was the point of debating them?

To confuse matters further, many interpreters willingly conceded that they were using the wrong equipment. Paraphrase, as almost everybody agreed, could never capture the true significance of a poem, and yet close reading was founded on extended paraphrase, buttressed by technical comment, the pursuit of allusions, and excursions into sources and influences. But if the One True Meaning of a poem was, in effect, the closest possible paraphrase, did it not follow that the best guide to the 'real meaning' was – the poem? Why be content with 1.414, or even 1.4142135, if you could go straight to the square root of two? Wimsatt's analogy cut both ways: however close the approximation, the categorical distinction between surd and integer would remain. Exegesis was supposed to be a kind of scaffolding, to be knocked away once the reader had ascended to 'the poem itself'. Given the countervailing emphasis on the autonomy of poetic language, the analogy was again self-defeating. The supposed beneficiaries – especially those who actually liked poetry – seemed in any case remarkably unappreciative. As the commentaries accumulated, the effect, according to disillusioned observers, was of a comparatively modest dwelling enclosed by a ramshackle structure the size of the Empire State Building. The fuller the treatment, the more it was apt to be condemned as a leaden travesty of what it purported to explain: not 1.414, but 0.001 – not all that could be had, and not in the least useful.

Northrop Frye's distinction, in the 'Polemical Introduction' to *Anatomy of Criticism* (1957) was to describe the chaotic state of academic criticism more accurately than any of his contemporaries, and then reach a conclusion wholly incompatible with the evidence he had canvassed. The historical significance of the *Anatomy* has less to do with Frye's system of archetypal criticism than with the assertion that a Grand Unified Theory of Literature was not only possible but essential if criticism were ever to assume its rightful place in the world:

Mr Eliot's essay *The Function of Criticism* begins by laying down the principle that the existing monuments of literature form an ideal order among themselves, and are not simply collections of the writings of individuals. This is criticism, and very fundamental criticism. Much of this book attempts to annotate it.[44]

Frye cites 'The Function of Criticism' rather than 'Tradition and the Individual Talent' because he needs to dispose of the ensuing 'rhetorical debate' between Classicism and Romanticism in the later essay:

> This is the sort of thing that makes for confusion until we realise how easy it is to snip it off and throw it away.

In setting out to rescue Eliot's 'tradition' from its polemical origins in the defence of 'the sort of poetry that I and my friends wrote',[45] Frye was bent on preserving, and radically expanding, what he called 'the assumption of total coherence'. The polemical thrust of Eliot's definition is contained in the passage not quoted by Frye: that the existing order 'is modified by the introduction of the new (the really new) work of art' – i.e. *Prufrock and Other Observations, Tarr, Cathay, A Portrait of the Artist as a Young Man.* Eliot, as Louis Menand remarks,

> is so automatically associated with the defence of the traditional canon that it has become difficult for some readers to see exactly what he is saying here. The term 'ideal order' is the crux of the misreading: it is clearly intended philosophically, not prescriptively. Our perception of the new work of art depends on our perception of the history of art, which takes a certain shape – is idealised – in our minds. But once we have encountered the new work, that idea of tradition is modified in turn. Value – and, by implication, meaning – are functions of relation; hence the tradition cannot be monolithic.[46]

In the next sentence of 'Tradition and the Individual Talent', Eliot goes on to remark that for 'order to persist after the supervention of novelty, the whole existing order must be, if ever so slightly, altered'.[47] The qualification is only apparent, as witness, again, his conviction that *Ulysses* had

> destroyed the whole of the 19th century. It left Joyce with nothing to write another book on. It showed up the futility of all the English styles. . . .[48]

'Mr Joyce's work', he added a few months later, 'puts an end to the tradition of Walter Pater, as it puts an end to a great many other things.'[49] Which was pretty much what F. R. Leavis and Cleanth Brooks argued, in the 1930s, that Eliot had done to 'the whole of the nineteenth century'. The difference, however, is that Brooks and Leavis, and many who followed their lead, thought that Eliot had recast the tradition into a new and stable form, whereas the implication of 'Tradition and the Individual Talent' is that 'tradition' is always *un*stable, and that there are as many 'traditions' as there are readers, a conclusion wholly unpalatable to anyone seeking to develop a coherent methodology applicable to all works of literature.

Frye, in rejecting Eliot's selective tradition, thought that he had discovered the critical equivalent of Archimedes' lever. It is clear from the outset that he is bent on proving that criticism ought to be, and must become, a science,

> [n]ot a 'pure' or 'exact' science, of course, but these phrases belong to a nineteenth-century cosmology which is no longer with us. The writing of history is an art, but no one doubts that scientific principles are involved in the historian's treatment of evidence, and that the presence of this scientific element is what distinguishes history from legend. . . . However, if there are any readers for whom the word 'scientific' conveys emotional overtones of unimaginative barbarism, they may substitute 'systematic' or 'progressive' instead.[50]

The rhetorical thrust is to claim that 'systematic', 'progressive' and 'scientific' are synonymous, so as to claim, for criticism, all the qualities that *distinguish* 'scientific' from 'systematic' method in the ensuing exposition. This is backed by the routine appeals to relativity theory, quantum mechanics, and Heisenberg's uncertainty principle, endlessly invoked by literary theorists to claim scientific status for the truism that literary works are susceptible to more than one interpretation. Once 'systematic' replaces 'scientific', the predictive capacity which distinguishes the kind of science covertly invoked to underwrite the argument disappears, and the force of the assertion diminishes sharply. Many people, for example, doubt that 'scientific principles are involved in the historian's treatment of evidence'. Systematic, rational, informed – but not scientific. Yet

[i]t seems absurd to say that there *may* be a scientific element in criticism when there are dozens of learned journals based on the assumption that there is, and hundreds of scholars engaged in a scientific procedure related to literary criticism. Evidence is examined scientifically; previous authorities are used scientifically; fields are investigated scientifically; texts are edited scientifically. Prosody is scientific in structure; so is phonetics; so is philology. Either literary criticism is scientific, or all these highly trained and intelligent scholars are wasting their time on some kind of pseudo-science like phrenology.

There are indeed hundreds of scholars engaged in systematic activities apparently related to literary criticism, but this proves nothing about criticism (interpretation and classification of literary works), as Frye immediately concedes:

In the growing complication of secondary sources one misses that sense of consolidating progress which belongs to a science. Research begins in what is known as 'background' and one would expect it, as it goes on, to start organising the foreground as well. Telling us what we should know about literature ought to fulfil itself in telling us something about what it is. As soon as it comes to this point, scholarship seems to be dammed by some kind of barrier, and washes back into further research projects.[51]

The obvious conclusion suggested by the ensuing twenty-page account of critical chaos, is that 'one misses that sense of consolidating progress' precisely because criticism is not a science. Because that conclusion is repugnant to Frye, he has to invent a 'barrier' to explain why criticism has failed to be the science he insists it must be. His 'barrier' is the equivalent of phlogiston, or ectoplasm. His own scheme – so dazzling as to distract attention from the evident contradictions of the introduction – is in no sense 'scientific'; it is one of a range of possible descriptive schemes, underpinned not by scientific principles but by the range of his reading, the quality of his perceptions, and the elegance of his style. An analogous scheme, propounded by someone lacking these qualifications, would have been merely a footnote to the history of eccentricity. Frye, in effect, had been intimidated by the positivism he was bent on displacing. If criticism was not a science, he argued, it was condemned to the status of 'a pseudo-science like phrenology', which was no choice at all. But the attempt to establish criticism as a science turns on 'an inductive leap' to 'the assumption of total coherence': a reified literature 'spread out in conceptual space from some kind of centre that criticism could locate'.[52]

Frye's evidence, coupled with the voluminous testimony of the recent critical past, pointed equally to a very different conclusion: that the effort to isolate literature from its surroundings, coupled to the injunction to publish or perish applied to an exponentially increasing number of players, and to the belief that literary theory and close textual analysis were the central business of criticism, would prove to be a deadly combination in the ensuing decades.

6

'Regret Impossible Stop Writing': The Labyrinth of Theory

I have one Word to say upon the Subject of *Profound Writers*, who are grown very numerous of late; And, I know very well, the judicious World is resolved to list me in that Number. I conceive, therefore, as to the Business of being *Profound*, that it is with *Writers*, as with *Wells*; A Person with good Eyes may see to the Bottom of the deepest, provided any *Water* be there; and, that often, when there is nothing in the World at the Bottom, besides *Dryness* and *Dirt*, tho' it be but a Yard and half under Ground, it shall pass, however, for wondrous *Deep*, upon no wiser a Reason than because it is wondrous *Dark*.

Swift, A Tale of a Tub

I

Ford Madox Ford, it is said, could detect the quality of a manuscript almost by its smell: 'I don't read manuscripts; I know what's in 'em.'[1] An editor in the 1990s, sorting a hundred recent critical books according to their allegiance to theory, could proceed as swiftly as Ford is supposed to have edited *The English Review* from his box at the music-hall. The 'argument against theory', as Frank Kermode observed in 1989, 'is by now a genre in its own right, and so is the counter-genre of defense'.[2] This, however, is a contest in which the two teams are willing to play only on their home grounds, so that Kermode (who, more than anyone, has attempted to referee the series) has had to spend a good deal of his time commuting between the two camps. The fissiparous history of theory since the mid-1960s appears to have been determined almost entirely by forces internal to the movement, coupled

160

with external pressures which have little or nothing to do with the 'argument against theory' – despite the fact that the leading theorists seldom suffer criticism in silence.

Derrida's celebrated reply to John Searle in 1977, for example, concluded 'by voicing doubts as to whether this presumed "encounter" between traditions can really have taken place'.[3] A considerable literature has now been devoted to that exchange alone, and yet one feels that much of the argument, in this as in analogous disputes (like that initiated by Steven Knapp and Walter Benn Michaels in *Critical Inquiry* in 1982), is beside the point.[4] Both sides complain that their opponents refuse to come out and fight fair; thus Walter A. Davis, responding to Stanley Fish's reply to his original attack on Fish, begins by telling us that his first impulse

> was to reply that I see no need to meet any of Fish's arguments since he has not bothered to meet any of mine,[5]

which is followed by a further twenty pages of strenuous argument with (or rather, at) Fish. Though this is a standard tactic in academic disputes, the combatants in the war over theory are separated by an expanse of dead ground which no one, it seems, can cross.

'Theory', in the sense I want to pursue here, includes all of the new critical projects aimed at displacing or 'decentring' traditional modes of discourse. Deconstruction is the best-known, but by no means the only form: Richard Rorty's 'new pragmatism' qualifies because, as Christopher Norris observes, it centres on the view that philosophy at large has 'missed its true vocation'

> through mistaking metaphors for concepts, believing itself firmly on the track of clear and distinct ideas when in fact it was simply devising new tricks to keep the same old debate turning over.[6]

Stanley Fish, though he styles himself an anti-theorist (or 'anti-foundationalist'), belongs, at least in some of his incarnations, with the theorists; his anti-foundationalism, like Rorty's pragmatism, involves a universalist critique of his opponents. There is, so to speak, nothing outside 'the profession', or the 'interpretive community':

> I define antiprofessionalism as any attitude or argument that enforces a distinction between professional labours on the one hand and the identification and promotion of what is true or valuable on the other.[7]

The same goes for the varieties of ideological critique which assert that before Foucault, or Lacan, or Lyotard, or whoever, all is mystification, or that all white male discourse is inherently defective.

Common to all of these approaches is a reversal of the traditional relationship between critic and subject. In J. Hillis Miller's approving formulation, literary works now 'tend to be redefined as "examples" demonstrating the productive effectiveness of this or that theory'.[8] Even to speak of a reversal is misleading, according to Paul de Man, who saw the difference between literature and criticism as 'delusive',[9] just as Richard Rorty is concerned to demolish the distinction between philosophy and other forms of discourse. The standard claim, nevertheless, is that theory transcends or displaces all rival forms of discourse by virtue of its unprecedented insight into the delusions inherent in traditional modes of argument; this is as true of de Man as it is of Derrida or Rorty. The claim to unique insight is characteristically underwritten by the genealogy in which 'modernism' figures as the precursor of theory. The orthodox academic elaboration of 'modernism' as a decisive break with the literary and philosophical past is reiterated and compounded, in this model, by the advent of theory as an absolute break with the mystified past from which the early modernists had struggled unsuccessfully to free themselves.

There are, however, distinctions to be drawn between new pragmatists, new ideologues, and deconstructionists. These may be plotted along a rough axis, depending on the degree to which the project is defined as self-subversive. In so far as the claim is that we alone have the correct political line, whereas everyone else is either evil or deluded, there is obviously nothing new about it, though the absence of novelty is often obscured by recourse to the vocabulary of poststructuralism. Deconstruction in its most rigorous form, in which any 'truth' claimed by the deconstructionist survives only 'at the margin', or 'under erasure', marks the opposite end of the spectrum, with the new pragmatism, as expounded by Rorty or Fish, somewhere between the two. 'Pragmatists and Derridareans', according to Rorty, are 'natural allies',[10] but he does not see the need for all the Derridarean fuss about 'the meta-

physics of presence', *differance*, and so on. Philosophy, according
to Rorty, is best understood as 'a matter of telling stories',[11] so
that what we think of as 'knowledge' is simply the story that
happens to be popular at the moment. This can be made to sound
plausible if confined to metaphysics, but since it effectively re-
duces all critical argument to the level of story-telling, it apparently disqualifies any ethical or political critique not grounded in
the prevailing consensus. Furthermore, Rorty maintains that pain
and humiliation are always bad, which effectively restores much
of what he has tried to banish from the domain of critical and
philosophical activity. Fish's pragmatism runs into similar problems whenever he brings out his knock-down argument that 'theory
has no consequences' – which must also apply to the theory that
theory has no consequences, leaving us exactly where we started.

Alliances notwithstanding, new pragmatists and deconstructionists are at opposite ends of the spectrum so far as their characteristic modes of argument are concerned. For Rorty and Fish,
whatever you can get away with is, by definition, a successful
argument, whereas the hard-line deconstructionist position is that
you can never get away with anything – though neither can anyone else. Derrida's standard response to questions about his 'urgent and interminable' project is to put the question in question,
to say

> That is not what I meant, at all,
> That is not it, at all.

His response, in 1967, to the question, 'which of your works
should one begin with?' ('where is one to make the first incision
into such a reading?'), provides a striking illustration. It is, characteristically, too long to quote in full, but it suggests that any of
his texts could be 'inserted' into any of the others. One thinks of
Finnegans Wake, which Joyce would have liked to see in a circular
binding, but things are clearly more complex in the Derridean
universe:

> In any case, that two 'volumes' are to be inscribed one in the
> middle of the other [and vice-versa] is due, you will agree, to
> a strange geometry, of which these texts are doubtless the con-
> temporaries.

'I asked you where to begin,' replied the bewildered Henri Ronse, 'and you have led me into a labyrinth':

> Derrida: All these texts, which are doubtless the interminable preface to another text that one day I would like to have the force to write, or still the epigraph to another that I would never have the audacity to write, are only the commentary on the sentence about a labyrinth of ciphers that is the epigraph to *Speech and Phenomena.* . . .[12]

A strange geometry indeed. Argument by deferral and complication is the characteristic Derridarean mode, 'interminable', as he repeatedly insists, haunted by infinite regress and yet insisting on the ethical imperative to proceed in no other way.

There is a parable which describes the situation very well. The Emperor, so it runs, has sent a message to you alone:

> The messenger immediately sets out on his journey; a powerful, an indefatigable man; now pushing with his right arm, now with his left, he cleaves a way through the throng; if he encounters resistance he points to his breast, where the symbol of the sun glitters; the way, too, is made easier for him than it would be for any other man. But the multitudes are so vast; their numbers have no end. If he could reach the open fields how fast he would fly, and soon no doubt you would hear the welcome hammering of his fists on your door. But instead how vainly does he wear out his strength: still he is only making his way through the chambers of the innermost palace; never will he get to the end of them; and if he succeeded in that nothing would be gained; he must fight his way next down the stairs; and if he succeeded in that nothing would be gained; the courts would still have to be crossed; and after the courts the second outer palace; and once more stairs and courts; and once more another palace; and so on for thousands of years; and if at last he should burst through the outermost gate – but never, never can that happen – the imperial capital would lie before him, the centre of the world, crammed to bursting with its own refuse. Nobody could fight his way through here even with a message from a dead man. – But you sit at your window when evening falls and dream it to yourself.[13]

'If from such appearances any one should draw the conclusion that in reality we have no Emperor, he would not be far from the truth.'[14] 'Deconstruction' is something that writers have always done, far more skilfully and subtly than its supposed inventor or his disciples. In the form perfected by Kafka, it anticipates and surpasses every move in the Derridarean game. The labyrinth is the governing figure in both: the goal of the urgent, interminable, and impossible quest is an illumination which must and cannot be found until it is too late, like the radiance that streams from the doorway of the Law towards the dying 'man from the country', or that which illuminates the faces of the victims of the punishment machine, the dawn light shining upon Gregor Samsa in his last moments, or the lighted window glimpsed by Joseph K. as his executioners prepare to strike.

But whereas a Kafka parable conveys the experience of interminability and labyrinthine complication in plain, seemingly transparent prose, Derrida's style is itself impenetrable and interminable, so that the reader is placed in the position of Joseph K. in the stifling chambers of the Law, or Land Surveyor K. falling asleep just as Burgel begins to tell him what he most wants to know.[15] T. S. Eliot once replied to an invitation to lecture with a cable which read REGRET IMPOSSIBLE STOP WRITING, a motto invisibly inscribed above the entrance to the Derridarean labyrinth. In 'Biodegradables', Derrida's second contribution to the de Man controversy in *Critical Inquiry*, his inability to stop writing is enacted and reenacted throughout this labyrinthine defence of a defence:

> Will I have been right to respond? Would it not have been better to put my trust in honest and intelligent readers? One will never know: the calculation will be, by definition, impossible. Ought I respond briefly? At length? In the one case I will be accused of being too 'elliptic' . . . forgetting that I myself began by excusing myself for this ellipsis on the fifteenth page of my article: 'Permit me an ellipsis here since I do not have much more time or space. . . .'[16]

'And would it have been worth it, after all?' Kafka, until the onset of his fatal illness, was at times driven almost to suicide by the impossibility of ever finding the time he needed to write, whereas Derrida, paid only to write, is haunted by the impossibility of ceasing.

Talk of an 'entrance' to the Derridarean labyrinth is in any case delusive, for it suggests a geography that could be mapped, a thread that one could follow, whereas there is, he insists, no entrance (and certainly no exit); or perhaps the entrance is wherever you enter, or would enter if you could ever get past the doorkeeper, who is not, in this case, a huge man with a furred robe and a Tartar beard, but the Cretan Liar, who says: if everything is in question, nothing is in question. He is not only the doorkeeper but the planning authority of the Derridarean labyrinth. 'Whatever can be said, can be said clearly', according to Wittgenstein, but within the Derridarean labyrinth nothing can be 'said' clearly – or indeed at all, except 'at the margin' or 'under erasure'. Deconstruction exists 'at the margin' for two reasons: first because it can only occur in the interstices of another text, and second because as soon as the deconstructionist claims to have uttered a 'truth', that statement is in turn subject to further deconstruction, and so on, endlessly deferring 'closure'. In J. Hillis Miller's (1976) formulation:

> the interpretation or solving of puzzles of the textual web only adds more filaments to the web. One can never escape from the labyrinth because the activity of escaping makes more labyrinth, the thread of a linear narrative or story. Criticism is the production of more thread to embroider the texture or textile already there. This thread is like the filament of ink which keeps flowing from the pen of the writer, keeping him in the web but suspending him also over the chasm, the blank page that thin line hides. In one version of Ariadne's story she is said to have hanged herself with her thread in despair after being abandoned by Theseus.[17]

There is no Ariadne in the Derridarean labyrinth: one's 'thread' is simply the 'trace' of where one has been, a path which can never be retraced except by repeating one's exact words and hence returning to the point at which one became lost.

Once inside the labyrinth, there is apparently no way out; equally, the way in appears to be barred by the doorkeeper. In *The Trial*, however, the parable of the doorkeeper is offered by the priest as the description of a 'particular delusion' about the Law. K. never learns what the delusion is; the priest leads him from one interpretation to another until the 'simple story' loses its 'clear outline'. Along the way, the priest offers him a saying from 'the commentators':

> The right perception of any matter and a misunderstanding of the same matter do not wholly exclude each other.[18]

Barbara Johnson, one of Derrida's translators, is unable to match Kafka's concision:

> Consider the following passage from Derrida's *Dissemination*: 'It is thus not simply false to say that Mallarmé is a Platonist or a Hegelian. But it is above all not true. And vice versa.' Instead of a simple either/or structure, deconstruction attempts to elaborate a discourse that says neither 'either/or', nor 'both/ and' nor even 'either/nor', while at the same time not totally abandoning these logics either.[19]

The priest's commentary on the parable is, equally, a 'deconstructive' reading of unsurpassed elegance, with Joseph K. playing the part of the naive reader whose logocentric delusions are to be dispelled:

> They were both silent for a little while. Then K. said: 'So you think the man was not deluded?' 'Don't misunderstand me,' said the priest, 'I am only showing you the various opinions concerning that point. You must not pay too much attention to them. The scriptures are unalterable and the comments often enough merely express the commentator's bewilderment.'[20]

One possibility that is never seriously considered by either K. or the priest is that the man from the country could simply get up and walk away from the door, into the wide world beyond. Yet the priest insists that the man remains

> of his own free will; in the story there is no mention of any compulsion. But the doorkeeper is bound to his post by his very office, he does not dare strike out into the country, nor apparently may he go into the interior of the Law, even should he wish to. Besides, although he is in the service of the Law, his service is confined to this one entrance; that is to say, he serves only this man for whom alone the entrance is intended....

> One must assume that for many years . . . his service was in a
> sense an empty formality, since he had to wait for a man to
> come . . . But the termination of his service also depends on the
> man's term of life, so that to the very end he is subject to the
> man. And it is emphasised throughout that the doorkeeper re-
> alises nothing of this.[21]

In this reading of the parable, Derrida-as-writer becomes the doorkeeper, since the Derridarean labyrinth exists only 'at the margin'. Like the doorkeeper, he must wait 'at the margin' for a 'man
from the country', a reader like Joyce's ideal insomniac, prepared
to spend a lifetime contemplating the deferral of meaning until
death, the final 'closure', intervenes. The parable, like the project
of deconstruction, turns on the illusion that the doorkeeper is
immortal – and deluded 'in a much more important issue, affecting his very office'.

Though Derrida has not lacked readers, his characteristic response
to them betrays an obsession with control of his text, an obsession curiously at odds with his insistence that authors can never
control, or 'authorise', their texts. As Robert Scholes remarks,

> All of Derrida's jokes about copyright and property in 'Lim-
> ited Inc' are an index of his own investment in the takeover of
> the Communications Corp. (or core or corps or corpus or corpse)
> by Writing Unlimited, J. Derrida, Prop.[22]

In the course of the de Man controversy, W. Wolfgang Holdheim
accused Derrida of producing, in his first defence, something like
'a straightforward exposition' of de Man's wartime writings, 'radically at odds with the usual Derridarean practice'.[23] Derrida, with
the exasperation of a man who has made his meaning plain beyond doubt, calls this an 'ignorant and aberrant reading of
"Deconstruction"':

> When he believes that I am faithful to what he *believes* or wants
> others to believe deconstruction means to say or do, then I am
> reproached for decontextualizing, making meaning indetermi-
> nate and neglecting history. I will not respond on these points;
> I have done so a thousand times over the last twenty-five years,
> and once again just a few pages ago. Faced with those who do
> not want or do not know how to read, I confess I am powerless.[24]

He proceeds to the thousand-and-second response. Yet throughout those twenty-five years he has routinely contested any attempt to define 'deconstruction' in terms accessible to the uninitiated. The thousand-and-one reproaches suggest that every reading of his text is 'aberrant', yet he insists that his meaning is plain – except to those 'who do not want or do not know how to read':[25]

> And at this very moment the verger began to put out the candles on the high altar, one after another. 'Are you angry with me?' asked K. of the priest. 'It may be that you don't know the nature of the Court you are serving.' He got no answer. 'These are only personal experiences,' said K. There was still no answer from above. 'I wasn't trying to insult you', said K. And at that the priest shrieked from the pulpit: 'Can't you see anything at all?'[26]

K's struggle for enlightenment takes place in the near-impenetrable darkness of the cathedral. During the exposition of the parable, the priest gives K. his lamp to hold, but by the time the exposition is over, the lamp has 'long since gone out'. To readers lost in the darkness of his text, Derrida can only say, like the priest, 'it is not necessary to accept everything as true, one must only accept it as a necessary'.

> 'A melancholy conclusion', said K. 'It turns lying into a universal principle',[27]

which is also the melancholy conclusion of deconstruction. As Frank Kermode observes of Paul de Man:

> blindness and impossibilism, a love of the aporetic, seem, among initiates, to promote not silence but endless linguistic fluency. This is in a way strange, for the prevalent deManian tone might be called depressed: every critical victory, to be recognised as a victory, must be a defeat.

Like Eliot defending *The Waste Land*, however, the initiate replies, 'there is nothing melancholy about it!'. Kermode continues:

> a definition of reading which claims that hitherto it has never been attempted, and now that it has turns out to be impossible,

might well have seemed dispiriting, but it turns out to be positively exhilarating. One might compare these writers to the early Christians, who thought they were the first people ever to read the Jewish Bible properly, were caught in the end-time of an aporia that could not end, and managed to feel pretty exhilarated about it.[28]

(Kafka, it is said, reading the first chapter of *The Trial* to his friends, was so overcome by laughter that he was unable to continue.) There is, obviously, something very exhilarating about belonging to an embattled minority (even a minority of one) – especially a minority convinced it has found the one true Way to enlightenment, or, in this case, to the impossibility of enlightenment.

Deconstruction is often condemned as nihilistic; John Sutherland, commenting on J. Hillis Miller's labyrinthine analogy, protests:

> Surely this harping on abysses, inescapable labyrinths, chasms and suicide invokes a wholly nihilistic view of the critical enterprise?[29]

The encounter with the (textual) void is, however, the goal of the *via negativa* of deconstruction. Strenuous contemplation of the fissures in the textual surface allows the initiate to pass 'through' the gaps and into the 'blissful' confrontation with the aporia, the heart of light (or darkness) 'down the labyrinthine ways' of deconstruction:[30]

> I shall find the dark grow luminous, the void fruitful, when I understand that I have nothing, that the ringers in the tower have appointed for the hymen of the soul a passing bell.[31]

Literary religion, it would seem, dies hard. The kingdom of *differance* is a kingdom not of this world, accessible only through a doctrine whose terms must never, on pain of immediate deconstruction, be defined in the idiom of the profane. Though the goal can never be attained in this life, there are glimpses along the way, moments of bliss as the mind is stopped by an aporia. Narrow is the way: caught in the toils of logocentricism, beset by the temptations of 'totalisation' and 'closure', the initiate has at least the consolation of knowing, like the early Christians in Kermode's comparison, that he or she is marching in the right direction.

Derrida's urgent, interminable and impossible project is, in other words, a displaced religious quest. The religion is antinomian, in that believers are above the law of binary logic; the theology is negative, in its resistance to definition and to any of the traditional consolations of belief. This, I think, goes far towards explaining why Anglo-American philosophers have had such difficulty in coping with Derrida; he belongs in a rival European tradition centred on Nietzsche and his rival Heidegger (and including Derrida's despised predecessor, Sartre), which has never really accepted the death of God, or which, to put it another way, is so obsessed with the death of God that it is compelled to reinvent him in a series of strenuously displaced forms.

Derrida admits to being much influenced by Sartre in his youth, but, according to Christopher Norris, was later

> puzzled to explain how anyone so *wrong* on so many issues . . . could nonetheless achieve such extraordinary prominence as the intellectual conscience of his age.[32]

Writers who claim (or are claimed) to be doing something unprecedented are usually anxious to direct attention away from their immediate precursors. Eliot's success in distracting his critics from his Victorian and Nineties precursors for over half a century is a classic instance. Derrida, likewise, is keen to direct attention towards Heidegger, Husserl, Hegel and Nietzsche, and away from Sartre. Yet there is a striking resemblance between the Sartrean quest for 'authenticity' and the Derridean struggle to escape from the toils of logocentricism (the analogue of 'bad faith' in his lexicon), into the authenticity of the deconstructive stance. Both of these 'interminable' writers (witness Sartre's monstrous biography of Flaubert)[33] are obsessed with the loss or absence of absolute values. Both, in their philosophical writings, share the compulsion of their immediate predecessors to make things as difficult as possible for themselves – and hence for their readers. Difficulty, in this tradition, is a moral as well as an intellectual virtue, so that the Anglocentric formulation, 'making things as difficult as possible', is from the European perspective a sign of failure to grasp the necessity of difficulty – or, in Derrida's case, of the impossibility either of proceeding in the old philosophical way, or of dispensing with it altogether.

Derrida, of course, has seldom been read as a theologian. Given the impenetrability of his texts, his refusal to accept any outsider's definition of his project, and the apparently self-defeating nature of the procedures he employs, it is at first sight remarkable that he has acquired so many disciples. Christopher Norris is very clear about the difficulty of entering the kingdom of Derrida. *Differance*, he tells us

> should function not as a concept, not as a word whose meaning could be finally 'booked into the present', but as one set of marks in a signifying chain which exceeds and disturbs the classical economy of language and representation. . . .

> In short, *differance* is the upshot of a long and meticulous process of argument, such that it cannot (or should not) be wrenched out of context for the purposes of ad hoc definition. That is why Derrida insists that there is no substitute for the hard work of reading and re-reading texts (his own texts included); that it is pointless to ask what *differance* means, or indeed what 'deconstruction' amounts to, unless one is prepared (in every sense of the phrase) to find out the difficult way. On the one hand this involves an adequate grasp of the philosophical background to Derrida's writings. On the other it demands that his texts be read with uncommon attentiveness to those features – too loosely termed 'stylistic' or 'literary' – that mark their distance from received philosophical tradition.[34]

This, as Australian cricket commentators like to say, is a big ask. Nothing less than the equivalent of the Holy Grail, one feels, could justify such an excursion; especially since the neophyte is compelled by the nature of the quest to travel blind, without knowing whether the guide is King Arthur or Monty Python. Yet when Norris, an expert, lucid and sympathetic expositor, sums up the reward, it comes to this:

> What Derrida is suggesting – in short – is that we read the great texts of Western tradition ('from Socrates to Freud and beyond') as so many messages that circulate without any absolutely authorised source or destination.[35]

The implication is that until the advent of Derrida, the streets were packed with card-carrying Platonists, Kantians and Hegelians, all of whom must now be made to see the error of their ways.

Here one glimpses the archetypal straw person, or reader as mug punter, on whom the rhetoric of deconstruction – and of theory at large – depends.

Derrida, as John Ellis observes, makes 'the dismantling of worn-out theories' the focal point of deconstruction, 'so much so that this will become its interminable work; the next step will, in this formulation, never be reached'.[36] Richard Rorty is engagingly direct in this regard. Jonathan Culler, he says, is right to argue[37] that deconstruction, viewed as a method of reading texts, 'needs a clear distinction between philosophy and literature':

> For the kind of reading which has come to be called 'deconstruc-tionist' requires two different straight persons: a macho pro-fessional philosopher who is insulted by the suggestion that he has submitted to a textual exigency, and a naive producer of literature whose jaw drops when she learns that her work has been supported by philosophical oppositions.[38]

There is, Rorty continues, 'something suspiciously old-fashioned about this way of setting up one's subjects':

> Still, the quest for philosophical machismo is not nearly as hope-less as that for literary naivete. You can still find philosophy professors who will solemnly tell you that they are seeking the *truth*, not just a story or a consensus but an honest-to-God, down-home, accurate representation of the way the world is. A few of them will even claim to write in a transparently straightfor-ward way, priding themselves on manly straightforwardness, on abjuring 'literary' devices.
>
> Lovably old-fashioned prigs of this sort may provide the only excuses which either Culler or I have for staying in business. Still *pace* Culler, I think that all of us – Derridareans and prag-matists alike – should try to work ourselves out of our jobs by conscientiously blurring the literature–philosophy distinction and promoting the idea of a seamless, undifferentiated 'general text.'[39]

Derrida, one feels, may well have muttered, 'with friends like this . . . ' There is a good deal of Rortian machismo at work in the heads-or-tails choice between honest-to-God truth and 'a story or a consensus'. He is right to draw attention to the 'suspiciously old-fashioned' need for straw persons common to both projects, and yet his tone also illustrates the cultural misprisions on which the fortunes of deconstruction have turned. Rorty approves of Derrida's assault on the authority of the European philosophical tradition, but considers the major premise outdated:

> Much of Derrida's account of what he is up to depends ... on the idea that literature, science and politics have been forbidden to do various things by 'the history of metaphysics.' This idea repeats Heidegger's claim that the history of the genre which has sought a total, unique, and closed language is central to the entire range of human possibilities in the contemporary West. This claim seems very implausible.[40]

From his robust pragmatist perspective, the tradition is no more than a hangover left by ancient superstitions:

> Concepts like causality, originality, intelligibility, literalness and the like are no more dangerous, and no more suicidal, than sunsets and blackbirds. It is not their fault that in another country, long ago, they were believed to have magical powers,[41]

long since dispelled, he argues, in the post-bourgeois world of liberal America. Yet *pace* Rorty, literary, or rather literary-critical naïveté, is in no danger of extinction.

II

From the point of view of mainstream Anglo-American language philosophy in the late 1960s, Derrida's project was very much behind the times, an attack on metaphysical certainties which the philosophers had, in their view, demolished half-a-century earlier. But for American literary critics in 1966, nurtured by the old New Critical dispensation and seeking a new approach, the perspective was very different. New Critical analysis, according to its founding fathers, had become a dull routine; the problem of overproduction was pressing; the student rebellion of the Sixties was well under way. J. Hillis Miller's remark that 'if you wanted to make your way, you had to do something different from Eliot'[42] is worth recalling in this context. Doing something different required a complete break – or at least the appearance of a complete break – with the orthodox critical procedures of the 1950s, in which Eliot's influence was still omnipresent. Anglo-American language philosophy, however, offered no acceptable alternative; part of the impetus behind the New Criticism had been to rescue litera-ture not only from reductive 'scholarship', but from the depreda-tions of logical positivism. Hence, in part, the New Critical emphasis on the uniqueness of literary language, the stress on irony, para-dox, and 'the heresy of paraphrase' – a heresy honoured largely in the observance, but nonetheless an article of faith.

Derrida, along with Barthes and Lacan, arrived at the legen-dary Johns Hopkins conference on 'The Languages of Criticism and the Sciences of Man' in October 1966, just as the power-vacuum in American criticism was becoming apparent to the more am-bitious players. Derrida's writing not only promoted but exemp-lified all of the qualities which the most strenuous of the New Critics had been pursuing since the 1940s: difficulty, irony, para-dox, resistance to paraphrase, while going far beyond the wildest New Critical dreams by standing the traditional hierarchy of philosophy, literature and criticism on its head. John Sutherland describes the result of the Johns Hopkins conference as 'a violent spasm in the American academy'.[43] This is true in a sense, and yet Yale's transition from the 'Anglo-Catholic nightmare' of the late 1950s to the Derridarean *rêve* of the 1980s has a certain logic to it.

If all that had been required was a warrant for greater inter-pretive licence, this could have been derived much more easily from the American pragmatist tradition exemplified by James, Peirce and Dewey, anticipating Rorty by turning criticism into a story-telling contest with no rules other than making the stories per-suasive. But, as we have seen, a characteristic complaint in the late 1950s was that interpretive criticism had *degenerated* into a story-telling contest, entirely lacking in rigour, and condemned by the prevailing conventions of exegesis to tell the same dull stories over and over again with minor variations. Derrida pos-sessed all the right qualifications for the time. Structuralism had arrived before him but, as a method of literary criticism, it was unwieldy, and it did not offer any compelling reason for preferring it above all other alternatives, whereas deconstruction, according to its inventor, was the method to end all methods. The Ameri-can dream of turning criticism into a science had at last arrived, promising to put the critic in charge, not only of literature, but of

'discourse' at large. The old subservience of criticism to literature, as Jonathan Culler tirelessly reminds us, was at an end.

The apparent paradox of Derrida's reputation is that while the
handful of professional philosophers who admire his project have
construed it as a roadblock – no philosophy beyond this point,
but no exit from philosophy either – he is hailed (or damned) by
the bulk of his vast literary-critical audience as the prophet of
interpretive liberation (after Derrida, anything goes). His few
philosophical admirers are characteristically scathing about what
they regard as the literary misuse of deconstruction. 'The professors of literature', according to John Sturrock, have

> made it less a recognisable way of doing philosophy than a
> peculiarly narcissistic fashion in the study of far-from-philo-
> sophical texts. Derrida is on record as having disowned most
> of what has been done in the name of Deconstruction. . . . This
> disavowal may have been tactful, offered as it was to a jury of
> French academic philosophers, but it was surely sincere as well,
> since the chances of Deconstruction being understood, let alone
> appreciated, daily grow thinner as the number of deconstructive
> essays in literary criticism increases. Deconstruction has to do
> with the close, inward examination of philosophical arguments
> and with their logical deficiencies or tacit a-prioris: it can have
> little to do with specific works of literature which contain nothing
> resembling a philosophical argument.[44]

He admits, however, that Derrida's later writing (which he dubs
'Derri-Dada') is itself increasingly narcissistic: 'there is a strong
risk that he will now become too literally promiscuous for his
own good':

> The literary Derrida is for most of us parasitical on the philo-
> sophical one; thought is what we demand of him, not flighty
> approximations to fiction.

'Most of us', ironically, refers to the small band of philosophers
bent on 'recaptur[ing] Derrida for philosophy', and 'giving
Deconstruction back its good name'. Sturrock's comments are
reminiscent of the calls for more waste land and less Anglo-
Catholicism from Eliot's admirers in the early 1930s; but in Derrida's
case, he was 'captured' by his critical admirers in 1966, before

he had even published the first of his canonical works. It has been an uphill battle for the philosophers ever since.

'No philosopher', according to Christopher Norris,

> has done more to disown the idea that his writings embody some kind of masterly or authoritative wisdom. And the irony is compounded by the fact that Derrida goes out of his way to resist any kind of adequate treatment in a book like this.[45]

Norris, like Sturrock, is concerned to rescue him from his literary admirers, and in particular from 'those zealots of a limitless textual "freeplay" who reject the very notions of rigorous thinking or conceptual critique':[46]

> To treat deconstruction as an open invitation to new and more adventurous forms of interpretative criticism is clearly to mistake whatever is most distinctive and demanding in Derrida's texts.[47]

Yet he admits that this response

> cannot be written off simply as a case of wilful misappropriation, since there are indeed texts of Derrida – mainly those written with a view to translation for American readers – which exploit such a rhetoric of 'freeplay' and limitless interpretive licence.[48]

It would be truer to say that no philosopher has done more to encourage the idea that his writings embody 'some kind of masterly or authoritative wisdom'. Derrida's 'resistance' to 'adequate treatment' inheres largely in his refusal to accept any restatement of his terms or procedures; his standard response to the question, what do you mean by this?, is either to say 're-read my collected works', or to launch into an aria questioning the terms of the question. The implication is that his writings are of such unparalleled significance and precision that any paraphrase is necessarily a travesty. This – presented as an analytic technique of unprecedented power, and coupled with a body of very dark doctrine which could be taken to 'prove' that criticism had not only assumed the power formerly attributed to philosophy, but had become the most powerful of all discursive disciplines – was more or less guaranteed to appeal to ambitious critics seeking to enhance their prestige at the end of the age of Eliot.

It was, in Norris's formulation, precisely those features of Derrida's style – 'too loosely termed "stylistic" or "literary" – that mark their distance from received philosophical tradition'[49] that ensured his appeal to literary critics. Derrida, by insisting on the uniqueness and unparaphrasability of his text, was claiming for it precisely the qualities around which the New Critical distinction between literature and other forms of discourse had revolved. By dissolving – or being taken to have dissolved – the distinction between literature, philosophy and criticism he had also opened the way for critics to assume the status formerly reserved for poets. Eliot was dead: long live Derrida and de Man – and anyone else who could command the idiom of deconstruction.

In 'Mnemosyne' (1986), the first of his memorial lectures for Paul de Man, Derrida devotes several pages to explaining why he is not going to talk about deconstruction:

> Were I not so frequently associated with this adventure of deconstruction, I would risk, with a smile, the following hypothesis: America *is* deconstruction (L'Amerique, mais *c'est* la deconstruction'). *In this hypothesis*, America would be the proper name of deconstruction in progress, its family name, its toponymy, its language and its place, its principal residence. And how could we define the United States *today* without integrating the following into the description: It is that historical space which today, in all its dimensions and through all its power plays, reveals itself as being undeniably the most sensitive, receptive or responsive space of all to the themes and effects of deconstruction. ... In this fiction of truth, 'America' would be the title of a new novel on the history of deconstruction and the deconstruction of history.[50]

L'Amérique, c'est moi.

III

Deconstructionists often condemn the old New Criticism as a repressive, formalist ideology which inhibited the free play of reading, whereas in fact mainstream New Critical theory exerted virtually no constraint upon interpretation; the agreed constraints had to be smuggled in from outside. All that the most thoroughgoing contextual criticism can do is set some broad and hazy boundaries around the reading of literary works – and then only on the premise that the task is to try to locate the work in its historical and biographical context. Once that premise is discarded, texts become mirrors in which interpreters see their own reflections plain. A compelling dramatisation of the power of obsessive reading occurs in Russell Hoban's *Riddley Walker*, in which Abel Goodparley, the 'Pry Mincer' of a devastated 'Inland' thousands of years after a nuclear war, recovers the formula for gunpowder from a twentieth-century description of a lost fifteenth-century wall-painting, *The Legend of Saint Eustace*:

> Any how I wer reading over this here Legend like I use to do some times and I come to '*the figure of the crucified Saviour*'. Number of the crucified Saviour and wunnering how that be come the Littl Shyning Man the Addom. Suddn it jumpt in to my mynd 'A littl salting and no saver'. I dint have no idear what *crucified* myt be nor up to then I hadn't give Saviour much thot I thot it myt mean some 1 as saves only that dint connect with nothing. Id never put it to gether with saver like in *savery*. Not sweet. Salty. A salt crucified. I gone to the chemistery working I askit 1 Stoan Phist that were Belnots dad what *crucified* myt be nor he wernt cern but he thot itwd be some thing you done in a cruciboal. 1st time Id heard the word. That's a hard firet boal they use it doing a chemistery try out which you cud call that crucifrying or crucifying. Which that crucified Saviour or crucifryd salt thats our Littl Shyning Man him as got pult in 2 by Eusa. So the '*the figure of the crucified Saviour*' is the number of the salt de vydit in 2 parts in the cruciboal and radiating lite coming acrost on it. The salt and the saver. 1ce youve got that salt youre on your way to the woal chemistery and fizzics of it.[51]

Every detail of the *Legend* conspires with Goodparley's 'juicying for Power' to deliver, not the '1 Big 1', but an explosive within reach of his 'tecker knowledging'. Seek, and ye shall find: 'Words! Theywl move things you know theywl do things. Theywl fetch.'

Interpretive ingenuity is in one sense limitless, and yet obsessive readers are doomed to meet their own reflections wherever they look. 'Once the context goes, anything goes' is a standard complaint about deconstruction, but the record of deconstructive practice is quite the reverse: as in a glass darkly, the method discovers itself in every text it scrutinises. New Critics hungered for paradox and irony, and found that even the despised Tennyson would, in the end, yield up those qualities. Deconstructionists seek indeterminacy, self-subversion, transgression, vertigo and aporia, and find them everywhere. Postmodern theorists fascinated by 'textual reflexivity' display, unwittingly, a fascination with their own mental processes. The real 'problem of interpretation' is not to prevent it from being arbitrary, but to restrain the power of obsessive or reflexive reading. Theorists of several current persuasions would argue, inconsistency notwithstanding, that any such restraint is (a) impossible, (b) repressive, and (c) politically motivated. Obsessive reading, however, is closely related to fundamentalist reading, which is by no means the exclusive property of the far religious right. Teachers who believe that they are radicalising their students by demanding that they uncover a politically correct message in every text are, like their apparent opposites in clean-cut Bible colleges, giving instruction in fundamentalist reading, which is not something that should be taught, however ineptly, in universities.

As for the argument that all we can ever see are our own reflections, it is routinely disingenuous: the real thrust is that all *you* can see in a text is your own mystified reflection (or that of the ideology which has 'constructed' you), whereas *we*, possessed of theoretical insight, can see through it. A moderated version tries to establish the impossibility of disinterested reading by exploiting the same either/or rhetoric to insist, as Louis Menand puts it,

> that one speck ruins the whole fruit, that a blurry distinction must be a false distinction. Because no interpretation is free of political implications, this way of reasoning seems to run, all interpretations must be political; because our beliefs are only our own creations, they must always be meanly self-serving; because language is never entirely transparent, it is never transparent enough.[52]

Even the most rigorous contextual investigation is necessarily a personal venture. No one can set out, or would want to set out, without a stock of hypotheses, prejudices examined and unexamined, and assumptions about where the question might lead and how it might be pursued. But the hallmark of genuine investigation is a willingness to discard some of this baggage *en route*. At the other extreme, criticism degenerates into self-fulfilling prophecy, driven by what John Ellis calls single-factor analysis:

> When it comes to literary analysis – the ostensible reason for RLT's [radical literary theory's] existence, after all – the nature of literature itself almost guarantees that single-factor analysis will be disastrous. The diversity of literary texts has no limit: they are written by all kinds of people and about every conceivable aspect of human life and experience. This enormous diversity of theme is in practice reduced by RLT to one of two results: either a particular text shared in the prejudices of its age in matters of class, race or gender, or it deviated from them. Even that is further reduced: there is either repression or resistance. But how many times does one need to look at different texts just to denounce racism and chauvinism?[53]

Why bother with literature at all? Whether the aim is to liberate the oppressed or keep them down, literary criticism – even when comprehensible to outsiders – is about the most ineffectual tool imaginable. The same applies to reflexive reading at large: if interpretation is a form of ventriloquism, why not simply say what you want to say instead of going the long way round? Terry Eagleton made the point neatly, if inadvertently, in *Criticism and Ideology* (1976):

> Criticism is not a passage from text to reader: its task is not to redouble the text's self-understanding, to collude with its object in a conspiracy of eloquence. Its task is to show the text as it cannot know itself, to manifest those conditions of its making (inscribed in its very letter) about which it is necessarily silent. It is not just that the text knows some things and not others; it is rather that its very self-knowledge is the construction of a self-oblivion. To achieve such a showing, criticism must break with its ideological prehistory, situating itself outside the space of the text on the alternative terrain of scientific knowledge.[54]

His determination not to acknowledge the existence of authors sparks a wonderful display of Hegelian grammar ('the text has gone home for an aspirin and a good lie down').[55] If the business of criticism is to work 'outside the space of the text', and to deal with issues about which the text is 'necessarily silent', then the text is plainly an encumbrance, and literary criticism superfluous. The 'scientific knowledge' that counts is not to be found in literature, but in Althusserian Marxism (which unfortunately proved rather less scientific than phrenology). Since the verdict is already in, there is no point in hauling the text down to the station for yet another round of questioning.

Eagleton has since abandoned Althusser, but his conviction that literary criticism can play a useful role in the class struggle remains unaltered.[56] Humanities departments are, and always have been, well-supplied with people struggling to adapt literary criticism to purposes for which it is plainly unsuited. The same problem arises in cultural studies: much of the culture ostensibly studied is superfluous to the political rhetoric imposed upon it. There is no compelling institutional reason why such people shouldn't discard the encumbrance of literary theory and criticism, and set up on their own as moralists, political activists, or whatever; universities accommodate numerous academics working officially in one field while successfully publishing, and to a considerable extent teaching, in another.

To do so, however, they would have to contend on equal terms with people far better informed about the history of capitalism, slavery, female suffrage and so forth. Menand, again, makes the point concisely:

> English professors ... are taught how to identify tropes, not how to eliminate racist attitudes. To turn their courses into classes on (say) Post-Colonial Literature with the idea of addressing with some degree of insight the problem of ethnocentrism is to ask someone equipped to catch butterflies to trap an elephant.
>   This is done, usually, by pretending that the butterfly *is* an elephant – by loading up a poem with so much ideological baggage that it can pass for an instrument of oppression. Poems won't bear the weight; most works of literature are designed to deflect exactly this kind of attention and to confute efforts to assign them specific political force.[57]

The critic as self-appointed moralist is unlikely to get much of a hearing. But if the message can be attributed to Shakespeare, it

will sound much more authoritative; or so the Critic as Ventrilo-
quist evidently assumes. The assumption is largely unconscious;
the more reflexive the reading, the more persuaded, as a rule,
the reader. If the supporters of all contending party-political
Shakespeares could agree to put the plays back on the shelf and
fight it out among themselves, a great deal of misplaced effort
could be spared. As witness the record of Shakespearean interpretation and production, there is virtually no political cause in
which Shakespeare cannot be enlisted. He is the worst possible
ally, because he can be made to fight for any side, confuting, as
it were, every effort to assign him specific political force.

In politically correct, theory-driven criticism, the authority formerly attributed to canonical white male authors is characteristically reinvested in master-theorists – a nice illustration of the law
of diminishing returns. But the unmasking of the ideological sins
inscribed in literary texts depends, for its effect, on the reputation of those texts, which the theorist must somehow maintain in
order to stay in the business of demolition. Though the author is
officially dead, he lives on in the guise of corrupter of public
morals; the more insidiously powerful his influence, the greater
the need for theorists. Which is, in its parodic way, an exact in-
version of the dilemma faced by the previous generation of explicators.

7

The Law and the Prophets

Now the method of growing Wise, Learned, and *Sublime*, having become so regular an Affair, and so established in all its Forms; the Number of Writers must needs have encreased accordingly, and to a Pitch that has made it of absolute Necessity for them to interfere continually with each other. Besides, it is reckoned, that there is not at this present, a sufficient Quantity of new Matter left in Nature, to furnish and adorn any one particular Subject to the Extent of a Volume.

Swift, *A Tale of a Tub*

I

Whereas critics like Blackmur had seen themselves as high priests at the altar of literature, the religious (or religiose) attitude to writers characteristic of the 1950s faded rapidly from the work of the newly-converted theorists in the late 1960s and early 1970s. Criticism could now become as difficult and unparaphraseable as the texts it had formerly served; theory was subordinate only to the master theorists. The old author-worship was apparently dead; religion, according to many theorists, is simply another form of establishment mystification, waiting in line for deconstruction. In reality, the mantle had passed from the poets to the theorists; the high priests of the old dispensation had become the gods of the new one.

'Theory', according to Jonathan Culler,

should be understood not as a prescription of methods of interpretation but as the discourse that results when conceptions of the nature and meaning of texts and their relations to other discourses, social practices and human subjects become the object of general reflection.[1]

184

One might as well argue that F. Scott Fitzgerald should be regarded as a secret teetotaller who only drank to keep up the appearance of alcoholism. Given the aggressively prescriptive claims scattered throughout *Framing the Sign*, Culler's remark is plainly disingenuous. Argument by prescription, as Frederick Crews observes, is a defining characteric of the genre:

> In the human studies today, it is widely assumed that the positions declared by structuralism and post-structuralism are permanently valuable discoveries that require no further interrogation. Thus one frequently comes upon statements of the type: 'Deconstruction has shown us that we can never exit from the play of signifiers'; 'Lacan demonstrated that the unconscious is structured like a language'; 'After Althusser, we all understand that the most ideological stance is the one that tries to fix limits beyond which ideology does not apply'; 'There can be no turning back to naive pre-Foucauldian distinctions between truth and power.' Such servility constitutes an ironic counterpart of positivism – a heaping up, not of factual nuggets, but of movement slogans that are treated as fact.[2]

The effect of asserting that such prescriptions override any empirical investigation is to reduce criticism to a power-game conducted by way of obfuscation coupled with appeals to authority. Hence, in part, the politicised rhetoric of theory. Another reason for the ubiqituous appeal to authority is that many of the disciples evidently do not understand the doctrines of their masters, and are thus compelled to treat doctrine as revelation.

Jonathan Culler, like Stanley Fish, charts the success of theory by way of its supposed colonisation of neighbouring fields:

> 'Theory', as we call it ... is anti-disciplinary, challenging not only the boundaries of disciplines ... but also these disciplines' claims to judge writing that touches their concerns. In practice, 'theory' contests the right of psychology departments to control Freud's texts, of philosophy departments to control Kant, Hegel and Heidegger.[3]

This tells us less about the peculiar assumption that psychology departments can be said to control Freud's texts, than about the theorist's longing to assume control of them – and of the psychology department. A 'major goal of the humanities', according to Culler, 'ought to be the elimination of the social sciences, which consume valuable resources to little purpose.'[4] Stanley Fish, off duty, is disarmingly frank about the function of criticism at the present time:

> I want to walk into any first-rate faculty anywhere and domi-nate it, shape it to my will. I'm fascinated by my own will.[5]

But when accused of *Wille zur Macht* in professional debate, he blandly denies the charge.[6] One of his standard tactics is to ac-cuse his opponents (or the opponents of theory) of paranoia and will-to-power, as in his characterisation of Walter Jackson Bate's 'The Crisis in English Studies' (1982) as 'the attempt of a dispos-sessed monopolist to regain the professional power and control that he and his colleagues have long since lost'.[7] Yet Fish's advo-cacy of 'professionalism' turns on aspirations to power and con-trol far beyond those he attributes to Bate:

> If there is anything like a 'crisis in English studies, it is a crisis in confidence, and one that we have in part created by taking ourselves too seriously as the priesthood of a culture already made, and not seriously enough as professionals whose business is to make and remake that culture, even as we celebrate it.[8]

As if the notion that literary theorists can 'make and remake' an entire culture is insufficiently grandiose, Fish, in a recent critique of the 'new historicism', inflates the claim still further:

> One can imagine general political conditions such that the ap-pearance on Monday of a new reading of *The Scarlet Letter* would be the occasion on Tuesday of discussion, debate, and proposed legislation on the floor of Congress; but before that can hap-pen (if we really want it to happen) there will have to be a general restructuring of the lines of influence and power in our culture; and while such a restructuring is not unthinkable, it will not be brought about by declarations of revolutionary in-tent by New Historicists or materialists or anyone else.[9]

It is hard to detect any irony in context. W. J. T. Mitchell, editor of *Critical Inquiry*, joins the chorus:

The relation between cultural achievements and colonialism is one that was nearly invisible to the traditional humanistic scholar, much less the 'man of letters'. Both these venerable figures had a role to play in the theatre of imperialism: namely to re-affirm the eternal value of Western civilisation and its masterpieces, while studiously ignoring the devastation that this civilisation was imposing on the rest of the planet in the name of 'progress' and 'enlightenment'. If post-imperial criticism and post-colonial literature have a relationship, then we have grounds, perhaps, to hope that it is not simply a repetition of this sordid history, but a new intellectual collaboration that seeks to build a new, more equitable civilisation out of the ruins of empire.[10]

This sits rather uneasily with J. Hillis Miller's presentation of theory as the ultimate weapon in his presidential address to the MLA in 1986. Literary theory, he said, might have its origins in Europe, but the United States was now exporting it in a new form, 'as we do many of our scientific and technological inventions, for example, the atom bomb'.[11]

'However large the political claim', as Frank Kermode remarks,

it can in practice only be expressed as opposition to a limited number of rival academic disciplines (none of them regarded as of vast importance by the regnant knowledge generators) and to an image of them that is in any case distorted. . . . That opposition to these disciplines by yet another discipline of very little interest to the bosses can be represented as having potentially a 'crucial' influence on the academy, indeed on politics more generally, is a claim so fantastically inflated that it belongs not to the real world but to carnival.[12]

This is all the more compelling in view of the incomprehensibility of the average theorist's prose, not only to non-academic readers, but to neighbouring professionals. It is essential to theory's self-image that the product should be regarded as radical, threatening and subversive but, outside the ranks of the theorists, this is a view shared only by conservative academics who, along with sensation-seeking journalists and right-wing political hangers-on, are in a sense the mainstay of the movement.

'Deconstructive logic', as John Ellis observes,

makes its way not by any genuine logical means but, instead, by its psychological appeal. Deconstruction offers its followers much psychological satisfaction. Essential to its logic – not a by-product, as is the case where substantial intellectual inno- vation really has taken place – is the sense of belonging to an intellectual elite, of having left behind the naivete of the crowd, of operating on a more sophisticated intellectual plane than that of the crowd. I say essential, because the naivete of the crowd is deconstruction's very starting point, and its subsequent move is as much an emotional as an intellectual leap to a position that *feels* different as much in the one way as the other.... Curiously enough, while the deconstructionist feels rebellious, iconoclastic, and nonconformist, what strikes the outsider is the standardised, routine quality of the performance.[13]

The war-cry of theorists, namely that everyone else has been mystified by language, surely betrays the uneasy suspicion that they are the deluded 'crowd' – with Derrida as mystifier-in-chief. By the same token, the insistence that theory is radical, subver- sive and dangerous betrays the fear that it may be reactionary and futile. Deconstruction, on Derrida's own showing, exists only 'at the margin', dismantling outworn theories and traditional read- ings upon whose far from obviously malevolent qualities it must endlessly insist in order to justify the procedure. This, as Gerald Graff and others have observed, highlights the essential conserva- tism of theory, which obstructs any genuine inquiry by stalling all investigations at the point where the issue is revealed to be 'problematic'.[14]

To make matters worse, the bulk of theoretical discourse con- sists, not of analysis, but of prophecies about what will happen when the project finally gets under way. The intricate machine is wheeled out; the theorist solemnly announces that here is an in- terpretive engine of unimaginable power:

> I will do such things –
> What they are yet I know not, – but they shall be
> The terrors of the earth.

More often than not, the contraption is then wheeled offstage without anything having happened. When a demonstration is provided, the machine is inclined to dismantle itself, injuring only those who, like the officer in Kafka's penal settlement, insist on strapping themselves to the mechanism. Thus, confronting a celebrated passage in *A Farewell to Arms* ('I was always embarrassed by the words sacred, glorious, and sacrifice, and the expression in vain . . .'), the hapless theorist in the 1990s is reduced to the assertion that

> Hemingway's character is embarrassed by the collapse of any representative function on the part of some of his signifiers,[15]

which might be enough to drive an author-function to drink, but seems unlikely to start a revolution.

Theory amounts to a self-defeating system, one of whose central purposes is to ensure the failure of its political objectives. Radical theorists are haunted by the fear that the project will be 'institutionalised' or 'co-opted by the establishment'; an irony compounded by the fact that the funding for the 1966 conference which made Derrida an institution in his own right was provided by Henry Ford II, thus, as John Sutherland notes, 'establishing American capitalism as the sugar-daddy of Deconstruction'.[16] Theory at large is hobbled by the fact that, on the theorists' own showing, it can retain its radical credentials only by losing every battle with the establishment.

Theorists tend to respond to such observations, not with reasoned argument but with vitriolic attacks on the observer, which suggests that the case is unanswerable.[17] When all else fails, the critic may be accused of promoting what Jonathan Culler calls 'an ideology of lucidity'.[18] Ironically, Culler himself has been reproached by Mas'd Zavarzadeh for 'his unproblematic prose and the clarity of his presentation, which are the conceptual tools of conservatism'.[19] Considering the obfuscatory jargon and fractured syntax (to say nothing of old-fashioned lying) universally deployed by presidents and White House spokespersons, this amounts to an oxymoron to rival 'White House intelligence'.

According to the most politicised theorists, all criticism of the movement is part of a right-wing conspiracy to repress the new intellectual freedoms. Yet, if the far right had indeed set out to disable the radical left in the academy, they could hardly have found a better vehicle for the purpose than theory. Henry Ford II, as it were, sits down with his co-conspirators in 1965 and decides to bring over a team of radical French theorists whose

projects are more or less guaranteed to keep the radical professors off the streets for decades, and to ensure that whatever
they write will be incomprehensible to anyone *on* the streets.

Given the eagerness with which the self-styled radical left has
embraced theory, such implausible machinations would have been,
in any case, redundant. Theory's faltering self-image as the epi-
centre of political radicalism has been revived by a series of attacks in the conservative press, following on the popular success
of Allan Bloom's jeremiad.[20] There is not much theory involved
in the new sectarianism of 'political correctness', but since its
exponents have retained the terminology, the style, and many of
the gurus of poststructuralism, the distinction is somewhat blurred.
Ironically, the journalists, along with the New McCarthyists, have
taken the promotional rhetoric of theory at face-value.

As more detached observers have noted, radical theorists have
set out to provoke a response of this order. It is as if the British
Government, confronted with *Blast*'s announcement of the END
OF THE CHRISTIAN ERA in 1914, had decided that Lewis and
Pound constituted a serious threat to the stability of the nation.
The analogy with the tactics employed by Pound and Lewis to
promote 'the movement' is striking: Pound, while he never tired
of complaining about establishment plots against him, went to
considerable effort to stir up opposition where none had existed,
a strategy which required increasingly provocative measures.

Though New Sectarians and New McCarthyists locate themselves at opposite ends of the political spectrum, their rhetorical
strategies are virtually indistinguishable. Roger Kimball says of
the 'Afrocentric curriculum':

A swamp opens before us, ready to devour everything. The
best response to all of this is . . . not to enter these murky waters
in the first place. As Nietzsche observed, we do not refute a
disease. We resist it.[21]

His peroration implicitly equates multiculturalism with Nazism,
deploying a string of metaphors used by Nazis to characterise
Jews: swamp, disease, devouring waters, aliens in our midst. The
year, according to Kimball, is 1938, and the barbarians are at the
gate; with which compare the response from 'a professor of philosophy at Scranton' to John Sturrock's 'griping' review of *Glas*:

The signs of the Holocaust were all around but only the Madman saw them. And no one listened to the Madman. It is 1939 with regard to the world of letters, and Derrida is telling us to wake up. But we don't listen.[22]

The extremists on both sides advocate book-banning (or burning), and, metaphorically at least, the annihilation of their opponents, as the solution to the problem, alternatively defined as the end of western civilisation, and as an establishment conspiracy to disempower or enslave all non-WASP persons.

Deconstruction, in its crudest form, amounts to a linguistic conspiracy theory which asserts that before Derrida, everyone was deluded by logocentricism. The rhetoric of theory is strewn with one-line explanations of this kind: before Foucault, everyone was deluded about the nature of power; before Lyotard, everyone was in thrall to totalisation, and so on. The claim that the rest of humanity is in thrall to a delusion to which we, by virtue of our leader's unparalleled insight, are not subject, is an obvious manifestation of full-blown political paranoia: the Masons, or the Catholics, or the Jews, are running the world, and the proof is that they have managed to cover up every trace of the conspiracy. In the case of theory, the paradigm also derives from antinomian religion: our reading of the sacred texts puts us above the laws to which everyone else is subject – because nobody else knows how to read. 'Faced with those who do not want or do not know how to read, I confess I am powerless', says Derrida.[23] 'How are literary studies ever to get started,' asked de Man, 'when every proposed method seems based on a misreading and a misconceived preconception about the nature of literary language?':

> The systematic avoidance of the problem of reading . . . is a general symptom shared by all methods of literary analysis. . . . It is as if an organised conspiracy made it anathema to raise the question, perhaps because the vested interests in literary studies as a respectable intellectual discipline are at stake or perhaps for more ominous reasons.[24]

Academic critics have ignored 'the problem of reading' – hardly a convincing diagnosis, for a start – therefore it is 'as if' there is a conspiracy of silence; the simile then dissolves into the assertion that the conspirators cannot be identified, which makes it all the more 'ominous'. 'It is 1939 with regard to the world of letters . . . .

Ironically, one of the central principles of deconstruction is that texts have a tendency to betray (or 'reinscribe') precisely the convictions that their authors are most concerned to exclude. The greater the effort of concealment, the more radical the self-betrayal, in the deManian formulation. Equally, devotees of closed or paranoid belief-systems, in attempting to characterise their opponents, are generally depicting themselves, a principle evident in the rhetoric of theory at large. Opponents of theory are characteristically depicted as deluded, mystified, reactionary, authoritarian, repressive, hungry for power and control over texts and canons, determined to impose their interpretations on other readers, intolerant, inflexible, and unyielding. The accuracy of this unwitting self-portrait is all too apparent.

This is not intended *ad hominem*, but as a description of the rhetorical stance forced upon theorists by the extremities of theory. I noted earlier that twenty years of damaging, not to say devastating criticism of theory appear to have had little or no effect. John Ellis is puzzled and exasperated by this phenomenon:

> Any sense of a continuing dialogue and interchange between the two sides is completely lacking. . . . Deconstructionists have generally reacted with hostility and even outrage to any serious criticism of deconstruction and thus to any possibility of an exchange with their intellectual opponents.[25]

But no criticism, however cogent, will discourage the antinomian reader persuaded that he or she is already in possession of the only valid reading of the sacred texts – or that only the elect know how to read at all.

II

From this perspective, aspects of theory that have puzzled informed observers like John Ellis become more intelligible. The refusal to spell out the doctrine in ordinary language, indeed the insistence that there is no 'doctrine' in any sense that the profane can apprehend; the need to hold everything 'in question'; the attacks on the 'old' logic; the claim to unique insight accessible only to the devout; the attack on clarity itself; the contempt for em-

pirical investigation and ordinary standards of proof; the attack
on profane ('bourgeois') conceptions of individuality and the in-
tegrity of the self; the insistence on absolute purity ('political correctness') within the fold – these are the hallmarks of antinomian
conviction. Religion, supposedly excluded from the house of theory,
has got in by the back door in a displaced, but historically familiar
form invoked by Kermode's comparison with the early Christians.

The comparison extends to the apocalyptic strain at the heart
of theory, the reiterated conviction that the last days of the Post-
Everything era are at hand. The rhetoric of theory is doubly apocalyptic, in that it proclaims itself as an absolute break with the
mystified past, such that we are now (in 1994) living in the year
32 AD (After Derrida), and projects this schismatic conception
outwards through the proliferation of 'post-' formations routinely
deployed by theorists to stress the discontinuities. Peter Collier
and Helga Geyer-Ryan, introducing *Literary Theory Today*, provide an excellent illustration:

> Literary and cultural theory are in ferment today because litera-
> ture and culture themselves appear threatened in our 'post-
> modern' age, a post-industrial age of instantaneous electronic
> communications, where the privileged status of the text and
> the coherence of cultural activity are increasingly destabilised.
> Jean-François Lyotard has described this world (too indulgently,
> perhaps) in *The Postmodern Condition*. But although it could be
> argued that this 'postmodern' ideology is itself a product of
> the anarchic liberalism of the new right, disguising prescrip-
> tion as description when it declares modernism to be played
> out and artistic experimentation and ideological critique out-
> dated, one has to admit that there is little virtue in trying to
> revive an idealised past.[26]

This (reiterated in dozens of similar introductions) is pretty much
the standard inside view.

The routine appeal to French authority is followed by an assertion so bizarre that even the authors feel impelled to distance
themselves with 'it could be argued'. One would have thought
that the new right were too busy lobbying for more tax exemptions,
welfare cuts and police powers to worry about modernism. Who
are these 'anarchic liberals'? What 'idealised past'? It becomes
apparent, as one reads on, that the claims are self-referential. One

of the central goals of literary and cultural theory is the 'de-stabilizing' of what theorists call 'the privileged status of the text'. One of its articles of faith is that 'modernism' is 'played out' (as it must be to make room for 'postmodernism'). The anarchic liberal-ism is that of M. Lyotard himself.

The occasion for this cloudy soul-searching is in fact a 'cata-strophic' event in the world of theory: the crisis provoked by Victor Farias's exposure, in 1987, of Heidegger's 'deep and long-lasting commitment to National Socialism', and 'blatant anti-Semitism',[27] closely followed by Paul de Man's posthumous fall from grace after the discovery that he had written some 170 articles for *Le Soir*, a Nazi-controlled Belgian newspaper in 1940–42.[28] The aim of the introduction is not to convey information, but to reaffirm the faith in a time of tribulation:

> a series of articles and books has revealed the cruel paradox which lies at the heart of . . . deconstructive purism. The pro-Nazi stances of Heidegger and de Man, both writers who had seemed dauntingly, quintessentially independent, have been experienced retrospectively as catastrophic. Whereas the right-wing politics of Yeats, Pound, Eliot and Lewis, not to mention Marinetti, Céline or Gottfried Benn, have long been the subject of critical discrimination between degrees and kinds of com-mitment in expression and action, Heidegger and de Man were somehow assumed to have deactivated the crude relation of philosophy and literature to personality and society, making their play of argument sublimely inclusive of, yet untouched by, contingency.[29]

'Somehow assumed' is poignant, invoking as it does a method credited with the power to uncover the ideological substrata of every text it scrutinised. As with Althusser, the search for an historical rationale reverts to the fallen fathers, whose sins are visited upon the sons and daughters, so that the entire 'history of modern literary theory' must now be reconsidered, though 'cri-tique is still possible despite the crisis'. One can only hope, for the sake of the sons and daughters, that Derrida has lived an exemplary life.

Barbara Johnson's account of her reaction to the news is, to use her own word, symptomatic:

my first impulse was a desire to rename my dogs (Nietzsche and Wagner). That is, my reaction was symptomatic of a logic of purification, expulsion, the vomiting of the name. It was as though the milk of de Man's writing, which I had already drunk, had turned to poison. Yet the logic of contamination and puri-fication is the very logic of Nazism. Surely this 'good breast/ bad breast' split was too simplistic a way a way of dealing with what amounted to an urgent imperative to historicise? De Man's later writings had to be re-read in the light of their own history.[30]

If Paul de Man had been a television repairman, his customers, though they might have wished they had taken their business elsewhere, would hardly have had their sets checked to ensure that he had not installed a fascist picture-tube. Nor, had he been mathematician, would his readers have accused him of smuggling a Nazi calculus into his equations. The point of the episode is not, as conservative opponents triumphantly declared, that deconstruction is inherently fascist, but that theory is sustained by faith in deified authorities whose Word is inscrutable even to their disciples. Howard Felperin, writing before de Man's past was uncovered, suggested that

[t]he authority that such figures as Barthes, de Man, Derrida, Foucault, *et al.* have exercised over literary studies in the past decade . . . may itself be charismatic, authorial, quasi-religious *even as they argue for the compelling power of an impersonal textuality.*[31]

'May'? Or, with a few substitutions:

The authority that Eliot exercised over literary studies in the years 1940–1965 was itself charismatic, authorial, quasi-religious even as he argued for the compelling power of an impersonal poetry.

As a number of commentators have noted, the furore over the award of the Bollingen Prize to Pound's *Pisan Cantos* in 1949 closely anticipated the de Man controversy.[32] The defence of Pound, then and since, characteristically fuses two incompatible arguments: first, that the value of the poetry is not affected by the evil acts of its creator, and second, that Pound was not as fascist, or as anti-Semitic, as the Rome broadcasts, or the *Cantos*, suggest (he was insane at the time; this was not the 'real' Pound; the broadcasts are not as bad as they sound, etc.). The same pattern appears in the defence of de Man: first, in the insistence that the value, or validity, or purity of deconstruction (which is what much of the argument is about) is not affected by the wartime writings, and second, in repeated attempts to rescue his reputation by minimising the offensiveness of those writings. Yet the defence is haunted by the fear that his later writings are somehow contaminated – a fear betrayed by the stridency of the assertions, as opposed to demonstrations, of their ideological purity.

The standard defence, adopted by Jonathan Culler, Christopher Norris, Barbara Johnson, J. Hillis Miller and Derrida himself, is that de Man's later writings, in Culler's formulation, 'offer some of the most powerful tools for combating ideologies with which he had earlier been complicitous'[33] – though Derrida goes further in trying to acquit de Man of complicity. Culler, however, is merely repeating de Man's own assertion that deconstruction (i.e. his own work) is

> more than any other mode of inquiry ... a powerful and indispensible tool in the unmasking of ideological abberations, as well as a determining factor in accounting for their occurrence.[34]

Much of the defence of de Man proceeds by appeal to the authority of de Man's own writings, an authority founded upon his reiterated conviction that he, almost alone, has grasped 'the problem of reading' while everyone else remains deluded. Anyone who opposes the authority of de Man, or of theory, is characterised as totalitarian. Miller, for example, compares the 'unreasoning hostility' of 'recent attacks on de Man, on "deconstruction" and on theory generally' to 'well known totalitarian procedures of vilification'.[35] De Man, for him, is above criticism, a transcendent authority whose 'austere rigour' sometimes makes his essays

> sound as if they were written by some impersonal intelligence or by language itself, not by somebody to whom the laws of blindness and impossibility also apply, as they do to the rest of us.[36]

Here again the authority is de Man himself – not only the de Man of *Blindness and Insight*, but the de Man of 1942:

the development [of literary style] does not depend on arbitrary personal decisions but is connected to forces which perform their relentless operations across the doings of individuals.[37]

It is the following manifestation of that 'impersonal intelligence', published in 1941, which has aroused what Miller calls 'unreasoning hostility':

> If our civilisation had let itself be invaded by a foreign force, then we would have to give up much hope for its future. By keeping, in spite of semitic interference in all aspects of European life, an intact originality and character, it has shown that its basic nature is healthy. What is more, one sees that a solution of the Jewish problem that would aim at the creation of a Jewish colony isolated from Europe would not entail, for the literary life of the West, deplorable consequences. The latter would lose, in all, a few personalities of mediocre value and would continue, as in the past, to develop according to its great evolutive laws.[38]

This, Miller concedes, is 'appalling',

> but it must be recognised that this is not the same thing as saying that the Jews are a pollution of Western culture.[39]

It is in fact a repetition of precisely that point: the reason, according to de Man, that 'all of contemporary production' is not 'polluted and harmful' is that 'the Jewish takeover' of literature has not (yet) succeeded.

Miller then pleads that this is 'the kind of double-talk one learns to practice under a totalitarian regime'. De Man, he says, praises Gide, Kafka, D. H. Lawrence, and Hemingway in the same essay. 'Did de Man not know that Kafka was a Jew?' Possibly not: 'Kafka' is misspelled 'Kafha', and De Man's list (with the omission of Proust) appears to have been copied from Aldous Huxley's *Music at Night*.[40] The same applies to an earlier approving reference (in May 1941) to Peguy's defence of Dreyfus; de Man, it seems, may not have known that Dreyfus was Jewish, and as Kermode notes,

> is seemingly at a loss to understand why such a straightforward case of an officer wrongly accused and reinstated by due course of law should have caused such a furore.[41]

Yet, according to Miller, 'the evidence'

> suggests that he stupidly wrote the deplorable essay in order to please his employers and keep his job, putting in as much double-talk as he dared,

and in the next sentence he tells us that de Man left *Le Soir* five months later

> when 'Nazi thought control' made it impossible for him *any longer* to express himself freely [emphasis added].

It would be futile to labour the point that Miller's defence of the indefensible is itself indefensible. Other commentators have wondered if the later work is a form of confession, de Man cryptically 'unmasking' the evil of his collaborationist youth.[42] Like Stanley Corngold, I see de Man's critical career as a displaced re-enactment, rather than a critique, of his complicity with totalitarian notions of 'purity'.[43] The tenor of his later work suggests to me that de Man, rather than brooding on his past, had recoiled from it, embarking instead upon a quest for an impossible clarity of vision which became a symbolic re-enactment of the ideology with which he had formerly collaborated. His 'final solution' to 'the problem of reading' was, in any ordinary sense, totalitarian. He sought to displace all other readers by becoming the ultimate authority on the impossibility of reading. In speaking of 'the madness of words' he spoke, unknowingly, of the madness of his project, embodied in his conviction that he, almost alone, possessed the secret of reading. Even the title of his last book, *The Resistance to Theory*, unwittingly characterises theory as totalitarian.

De Man's apologists, in accusing his critics of totalitarianism, or of a desire to 'silence' deconstruction, are similarly trapped into unwitting self-accusation. Miller's 1988 apologia concludes, like Jonathan Culler's, by citing de Man on the power of theory:

> Those who reproach literary theory for being oblivious to social and historical (that is to say ideological) reality are merely stating their fear at having their own ideological mystifications exposed by the tool they are trying to discredit.[44]

Fear of this power, says Miller, accounts for the 'unreasoning hostility' to de Man, and to theory at large. Yet Miller's presidential address to the MLA in 1986, as John Sutherland observes, displayed an unreasoning hostility to every form of literary study except theory:

> He denounced the upstart New Historicists, thus alienating most of the young scholars in his audience. He asserted the 'triumph of theory', achieved principally by him and by de Man (whose *Resistance to Theory*, 1979, was proclaimed 'already a classic'). Theory had won. Not even bibliography could now be done outside 'the context of the triumph of theory'. More significantly, perhaps, it was American theory. Miller had at last freed himself from any sense of national inferiority.[45]

Miller's defence of de Man, however, seems a picture of restraint beside Derrida's 'Paul de Man's War', which covers much the same ground at much greater length, and with recourse to every conceivable (and inconceivable) variety of special pleading. Confronting de Man's remarks about 'vulgar antisemitism', Derrida dwells on the supposed ambiguity of the passage, admitting that this 'may leave one to understand that there is a distinguished antisemitism in whose name the vulgar variety is put down', and then argues that

> to condemn 'vulgar antisemitism,' especially if one makes no mention of the other kind, is to condemn antisemitism itself inasmuch as it is vulgar, always and essentially vulgar. De Man does not say that either. If that is what he thought, a possibility I will never exclude, he could not say so clearly in this context. One will say at this point: his fault was to have accepted the context. Certainly, but what is that, to accept a context?[46]

'To accept a context' was for de Man to argue, of his own free will, in a special anti-Semitic number of a Nazi-controlled paper, in March 1941, that Europe would be better off without its Jewish population. According to Derrida, the final paragraph of the essay, advocating 'the creation of a Jewish colony isolated from Europe', is 'in fact the only one that can be suspected of antisemitism'.[47] He concludes by hinting that the article may be a forgery.[48]

The experience of reading Derrida is often described as 'vertiginous'. 'Paul de Man's War' is no exception:

> Having just re-read my text, I imagine that for some it will seem I have tried, when all is said and done and despite all the protests or precautions, to protect, save, justify what does not deserve to be saved. I ask these readers, if they still have some concern for justice and rigor, to take the time to reread, as closely as possible.[49]

'Paul de Man's War' is about as rigorous as a party political broadcast, but it nevertheless reads like a model of rational debate alongside 'Biodegradables', Derrida's reply to five essays critical of his defence of de Man (and to a supportive response from Jonathan Culler).[50] As the tantrum rages on, one can only murmur, like Umberto Eco's William of Baskerville listening to Jorge's sermon on the Antichrist: 'It seems his own portrait.' Derrida is convinced that the 'venom' is directed less against de Man than against him, and

> less against me, in truth, than against 'Deconstruction' (which at the time was a year minus twenty-five of its calendar! This suffices to shed light on this whole scene and its actual workings).[51]

The essays do indeed include several complaints that deconstructors tend to decontextualise the texts they confront, but Derrida's tirade betrays a paranoid identification with deconstruction – and de Man. The fear that haunts both 'Paul de Man's War' and 'Biodegradables' is that if de Man is posthumously convicted of war crimes, so to speak, deconstruction will fall: therefore de Man must be innocent because deconstruction must be saved.

Derrida might reply that his opponents have identified de Man's fall with that of deconstruction, but that is not the point. If, as he claims, deconstruction is the 'necessary condition for identifying and combating the totalitarian risk in all the forms already mentioned', and if 'a vigilant political practice' could not survive without it,[52] then Derrida, as the inventor and leading practitioner of deconstruction, should have been able to defend the project calmly and conclusively. All he needed to say, indeed, was 'what does deconstruction (in the singular) have to do with what was written in 1940–42 by a very young man in a Belgian newspaper?'[53]

But he could not leave it at that. Instead he responded, as Claude Rawson justly remarks, with what

> must be the most voluminous mixture of Shandean self-exhibition and vulgar abuse ever to have been allowed into a journal professedly committed to rational discourse,[54]

whereupon the editors of *Critical Inquiry* closed the debate.

'Biodegradables', which begins with a dream and ends in exhaustion, is the logical conclusion of Derrida's twenty-five year refusal to define his project, which is indeed not a method or a philosophy, but a personality cult, a cult of moral and intellectual superiority. This is why de Man's disgrace was 'catastrophic' for the bewildered disciples and for Derrida himself. By vilifying his critics, and embarking upon a futile attempt to salvage the cult by whitewashing de Man, Derrida proved the point more decisively than any outsider could ever have done. He later embarked upon an equally disastrous defence of Heidegger.[55]

Ezra Pound, like Jacques Derrida, was convinced that he had discovered a 'new method of scholarship', and a new logic (the 'ideogramic method') which in his view justified the increasing incoherence of his writings. As with Derrida, the motto invisibly engraved above his study door was REGRET IMPOSSIBLE STOP WRITING:

> 'God I beat this eight hours,' he wrote on his typewriter to James Laughlin in December 1935, 'and forgot what I meant to start the day with.'[56]

Like Derrida, he saw himself as the founder and promoter of a literary and cultural revolution; like Derrida and de Man, he became the object of a personality cult. Pound's inability to explain the rationale of his 'endless poem', as 'urgent and interminable' as Derrida's project, was similarly adopted by his disciples as proof of the importance of the work.

Though Pound's admirers are frequently aligned with the extreme right (Eustace Mullins, one of his first hagiographers, was also the self-styled 'Director of the Aryan League of America'), the defence of de Man recapitulates many of the strategies employed by Pound's apologists. 'Biodegradables' echoes the tone of the Rome broadcasts and of Pound's later correspondence in its hysterical invective, wild punning, and incoherence – the manic pace of Pound in full flight – and of Pound's most fervent disciples defending their master in *Paideuma*.[57] There is, in any case, no real difference between left and right-wing personality cults, which at their respective extremes merge into identity. Tzvetan Todorov, in a strong critique of Heidegger's apologists, analyses a number of standard tactics employed by apologists of either persuasion: denial of the facts; dissociation of the author from his works; the assertion that ideals of truth and justice are merely subjective, or too 'problematic' to be applied to their hero; and the assertion that the offensive component of the work is aberrant or atypical.[58]

These tactics have been deployed in the promotion of theory at large. In the absence of rational underpinnings, it was doomed to evolve as a network of personality cults, and therefore to sanction the authoritarianism it purportedly opposed. Far from being a liberation movement within the academy, theory is 'academic' in the most pejorative sense. As John Ellis notes, French literary theory in the 1960s emerged in reaction to the repressive Lansonist orthodoxy: 'in France, unlike America, there really was a single authoritative traditional opinion on literary texts, and it was administered ruthlessly to all'.[59]

Whereas in the 1920s the United States had exported many of its would-be *avant-garde* artists to Paris, in the 1960s the traffic reversed, ironically importing, by way of the vogue for French theory, a new orthodoxy as repressive as the Lansonism which had prompted the French rebellion in the first place. With the 'death of the author' came the birth of the theorist as guru. Though Ellis is right to describe the American critical tradition as pluralist with regard to the interpretation of individual works, the personality cults of theory could never, I think, have been accepted by so many if Eliot had not been regarded with such reverence by the preceding generation. Equally, the schismatic conception of cultural history at the centre of the orthodox picture of 'modernism' prepared the ground for theorists to proclaim an absolute break with the deluded past. The effect, inside the sheltered workshop of theory, has been to turn criticism into a power game in which personal power is the only thing left to argue about. This, coupled with the highly competitive nature of the American academy, was guaranteed to take the endemic power-struggles chronicled by Graff in *Professing Literature* to their illogical – and ugly – conclusion.

III

We have now reached a point at which two key professional imperatives – the pressure to publish, and the need to present interpretation as theoretically grounded, and therefore underwritten by specialist expertise – are in direct conflict. Too many knights have returned with too many grails for the result to be anything other than Pythonesque. It would take a monograph just to list the procession of grand theories that have been tried and discarded over the last three decades alone, but even to speak of theories is misleading. What we have had, as the de Man affair illustrated all too clearly, is a procession of gurus.

Claude Rawson, in a swashbuckling attack on theory, argues that it is sustained by 'coercive egomania' and 'positions of tribal leadership in a discipline not formerly given to the unquestioning worship of intellectual thuggery'.[60] On the contrary: today's coercive egomania is yesterday's thuggery revisited, as anyone with direct experience of a hard-line Leavisite department will testify. Even the sceptical Frank Kermode, surveying the conflict a decade ago, felt that

> [w]e lack a great man who might, like Eliot, hold together the new and the traditional, catastrophe and continuity; unfortunately we do not lack doctrinaire and unconsidering people on both sides of the argument.[61]

A continuing supply of great men and women is, unfortunately, a professional necessity. 'Mr Eliot' was, for at least three decades, an object of tribal worship because the authority conferred upon him was, to a considerable extent, the glue that held the edifice of New Critical theory together. 'Our field', said Richard Ohmann, addressing the National Council of Teachers of English in 1966, 'is too populous to be organised as it is. . . . we must do something about its organisation or we will choke.'[62] In the same year, Eliot's role as guarantor was transferred, by a new generation of critics, to another outsider, Derrida – an academic this time, but, as a French-language philosopher, twice removed from the Anglo-American critical scene. Observers, including many academic critics, were again bewildered by the speed with which Derrida's 'influence' grew; he had become, by 1979, the most frequently-cited authority in papers submitted to the journal of the Modern

Language Association. One French theorist after another followed in his footsteps in the 1970s and 1980s: Foucault, Althusser, Lacan, Lyotard, Baudrillard; though Derrida remained the pre-eminent authority, the new territory had grown too large and diverse to be ruled by a single figure.

So much energy has been expended on factional brawling that the obvious has largely escaped notice: Derrida and Co. were endowed with immense influence *because* they were outsiders. Just as Richards, Leavis, Brooks, Ransom, *et al.*, had drawn upon Eliot's authority, so J. Hillis Miller, Geoffrey Hartman, and Paul de Man (though in an ambivalent fashion, since he maintained an outsider's stance within the American academy, and therefore acquired something of the outsider's charisma) drew upon Derrida's. They could, as it were, place their hands on their hearts and swear that they had not invented a new methodology just as the old one was collapsing under the weight of overproduction; what they were doing had the backing of another discipline, indeed of a new academic discipline called 'theory' – which, like the New Criticism, had managed to acquire at least one parent (Saussure) before the end of the season. If philosophers attacked Derrida, they were revealing their lack of critical insight; if literary critics attacked him, that showed that they didn't understand philosophy, and *any* attack betrayed ignorance of theory.

Like New Critical exegesis, deconstruction became popular despite the gaping holes in the theory, because it fulfilled all the professional requirements of a successful methodology. Immense critical effort, from the 1920s until well into the 1960s, was invested in the elaboration of a selective tradition, underwritten by Eliot's early valuations and by the theories attributed to him. As is generally acknowledged, his taste for complex, ironic verse coincided admirably with the requirements of sophisticated close reading, and the selective tradition was progressively extended by the New Critics as the demand for raw material increased. The contrast between Cleanth Brooks's *Modern Poetry and the Tradition* (1939) and his *The Well-Wrought Urn* (1947) provides, to adapt a point made by Gerald Graff, an excellent illustration of how 'literature' is homogenised in the service of an expanding methodology. In the first study, Brooks followed Eliot in downgrading poetry from the late seventeenth century until the French Symbolists, whereas in the second, he rehabilitated much of the intervening work, not by embracing its variety, but by 'so widening the categories of "paradox" and "irony" that these poets now fit[ted] them':

> Paradox and irony were suddenly no longer the poetic qual-
> ities admired by a partisan school admittedly promoting one
> kind of poetry over others. They were the defining character-
> istics of poetry in general.
>   The 'tradition' had been stretched to cover almost all the poets
> anyone in the university liked, which is to say, one could now
> accept New Critical poetics without renouncing the poets in
> one's field.[63]

Deconstruction, likewise, began as a mode of analysis applied to
a restricted range of philosophical texts and was rapidly univers-
alised (by 1979 Paul de Man was arguing that 'the whole of literature would respond' to deconstructive techniques)[64] – thereby
'proving' that all literary works, and eventually all texts, were
'problematic' in ways that only deconstruction could unravel.
    Old methodologies don't, of course, die; they remain on the
shelves of the critical hypermarket along with the newer, more
heavily-advertised products, and as each miracle ingredient turns
out to be not quite the elixir that was promised, the theoretical
laboratory churns out yet another: New Historicism will make
your readings sparkle like they've never sparkled before; cultural
materialism brings out the colour in your interpretations. The anti-
capitalist rhetoric of so much recent theory is ironic, given that
the business is such a prime example of the capitalist system at
work. Market forces keep the products moving, and ensure their
rapid obsolescence; thriving secondary industries spring up, offering the bemused undergraduate a choice of seventeen different approaches to try out on Pope, even as he or she is still pondering
the niceties of who Pope was.[65]
    New theories are now appearing as frequently as interpreta-
tions of *The Waste Land* were being published in the 1940s. The
result is a scaled-up equivalent of the problem of endless explication: the One True Theory has gone the way of the One True
Meaning. There is no theoretical solution to 'the quandary suggested by three thousand advanced critics reading each other to
everyone else's unconcern', as Edward Said put it a decade ago.[66]
With each new advance, theory-driven criticism digs itself deeper
into the mire. Thomas Docherty, for example, prescribes a cure

called 'postmarxism', and begins with yet another rendition of the Theorist's Lament:

> While writing the book, my abiding concern was the apparent inefficacy of the theoretical intellectual in terms of social and intellectual practice.[67]

His entire book is one more demonstration of this 'inefficacy'; it would be unintelligible to any lay person, and after two hundred pages of strenuous theorising, his conclusion is as follows:

> Postmarxism asserts that thought is only possible at the very interface between theoretical systems. In other words, it is not so much 'after theory' as 'inter-theoretical', or 'ana-theoretical', if I may coin a phrase. Here the sense of the term 'post-theoretical' becomes more apparent. . . . Postmarxism is like postmodernism in this: it makes thought once more possible by working at the interface of ideologies.[68]

Nothing but the coining of a phrase is left to human agency: as for thinking, postmarxism will do that for us.

Some who were leading the theoretical charge in the 1970s and 1980s now feel that it has all gone too far: Christopher Norris calls for a return to truth; J. Hillis Miller calls for a return to ethics; others are pursuing a return to history, or rather an advance into New Historicism. A. D. Nuttall, reviewing Norris's *Uncritical Theory: Post-Modernism, Intellectuals and the Gulf War*, observes that

> chapter after chapter is devoted to justifying the practice of claiming truth for one's own statements, and to a defence of that most elementary of speech-acts, assertion, while almost no space is given to an argumentative basis for the political thesis itself. How could one begin to explain to a person in the street that Norris is arguing for the right to say, for example, that 'the Post Office is in West Street,' as opposed to 'the cultural construction x is conventionally and rhetorically sited in y'?[69]

How indeed? Among the arguments that Norris feels it necessary to refute are those of Jean Baudrillard, who maintains that 'the Gulf War did not happen'. Why not simply concentrate on the Gulf War? Norris would no doubt reply that postmodernist, relativist nihilism is on the increase in universities, and must be countered with a new theory of truth. Leaving aside his belief that Derrida is an ideal ally in the campaign for truth, this is a classically self-defeating theoretical strategy. Healthy scepticism is one thing; the belief that no angel on a pinhead can ever be left uncounted must lead eventually to a full-scale refutation of the claims of the Flat Earth Society.

One can only assume that the combatants are incapable of imagining the view from outside. 'The writer who drops in on this world', says Robert Hughes,

> is bound to feel like Gulliver visiting the Royal Academy of Lagado, with its solemn 'projectors' laboring to extract sunbeams from cucumbers, build houses from the roof down and restore the nutritive power of human shit, all convinced of the value of their work.[70]

For all the talk of revolutions and paradigm-shifts, the story of institutionalised, theory-driven criticism since the 1930s is largely the story of a retreat from the public domain, and from the editorial standards of the best public criticism, as currently exemplified in *The London Review of Books*, *The New York Review of Books*, *The Nation*, and so forth. Unlike specialist theoretical journals, these reviews assume an audience of equals, informed, exacting, alert to nuance, for whom reading is an end in itself, rather than a problem in search of a theoretical solution. Many of the best public critics are now university-based, but they are also, with few exceptions, at odds with academic orthodoxy. Consequently, when it comes to classifying them according to schools and theoretical allegiances, they won't go through the mesh.[71] But they do have some things in common: independence of mind, elegance of style, breadth of knowledge, and a commitment to the educated, non-specialist reader.

These essential qualities are, as a rule, lacking, or at best diluted, in mainstream academic criticism, not because they are the exclusive possession of a small elite, but because the dominant professional ethos, and the dominant research paradigms ('research performance indicators', in today's jargon) might as well have been designed to exclude them. Even diehard professionals will concede, in private, that a system which rewards people according to the cost and quantity of refereed publication they produce, while actively discouraging communication with the outside world, *belongs* in the Grand Academy of Lagado. The modern university research machine is, in effect, a nineteenth-century invention which turned out to be self-replicating, and is now completely out of control. But to shut it down for an overhaul, even if that were possible, would destroy the system of professional certification on which countless thousands of academic careers depend.

Northrop Frye's gloomy prediction – that if there were no such thing as a coherent and comprehensive theory of literature, the high proportion of futility in all criticism could only increase with its bulk until it became, for academic critics, 'merely an automatic method of acquiring merit, like turning a prayer-wheel' – has been amply fulfilled. Contextual scholarship is, within certain limits, progressive and cumulative, and from time to time it produces definitive results in the form of editions, biographies, and historical studies. But straitjacketing interpretation into a wholly inappropriate research paradigm only ensures that as the number of critics increases, so will the number of interpretations, until the demand for new theories of interpretation becomes so pressing that theorising about theory becomes the object of the exercise.

The quest for a theoretically-guaranteed critical methodology transcending the limits of individual knowledge and judgement has been, to sum up, futile from the outset. To abandon it would mean discarding all of the apparatus which distinguishes academic criticism, in the pejorative sense, from public criticism: the pseudo-scientific stance and style; doctrinaire allegiance to schools and gurus, 'isms' and orthodoxies; and so forth. It would mean, in essence, abandoning the cult of the specialist interpreter. An *Encyclopedia of Pseudo-Sciences*, as Randall Jarrell said forty years ago,

> might define critical method as *the systematic (q.v.) application of foreign substances to literature; any series of devices by which critics may treat different works of art as much alike as possible.*[72]

There's a sense in which no 'substance' is foreign to literature, which deals with every imaginable subject from every imaginable angle, but as soon as the critic begins to flatten out the differences between works of art in order to secure an investment in methodology, he or she has become a psuedo-scientist. Though the Leaning Tower of Theory displays all the signs of a condemned building, the work of demolition has been hampered because so many of those apparently engaged in it are intent on reinforcing their own apartments. Like the cathedral in William Golding's *The Spire*, the building has no foundations; it is sustained by the occupants' yearning for higher authority.

Notes

For repeated citations, the first reference is given in full in each chapter, and thereafter in abbreviated form. The following abbreviations are also employed:

C Ezra Pound, *The Cantos of Ezra Pound* (London: Faber, 1986).
EL1 Valerie Eliot (ed.), *The Letters of T. S. Eliot (Volume I) 1898–1922* (London: Faber, 1988).
OPP T. S. Eliot, *On Poetry and Poets* (London: Faber, 1957).
SE T. S. Eliot, *Selected Essays*, 3rd edn (London: Faber, 1951).
SL *Selected Letters of Ezra Pound*, ed. D. D. Paige (London: Faber, 1951).
SW T. S. Eliot, *The Sacred Wood*, 2nd edition (London: Methuen, 1928).
TCC T. S. Eliot, *To Criticize the Critic* (London: Faber, 1965).
UPUC T. S. Eliot, *The Use of Poetry and the Use of Criticism* (London: Faber, 1933).
WLMS T. S. Eliot, *The Waste Land/ A Facsimile and Transcript of the Original Drafts*, ed. Valerie Eliot (London: Faber, 1971).

Prologue

1. Roger Shattuck, 'The Poverty of Modernism', in *The Innocent Eye* (New York: Farrar, Straus, Giroux, 1984), pp. 338, 340.
2. Gerald Graff, *Professing Literature: An Institutional History* (Chicago: University of Chicago Press, 1987), p. 14.
3. *OPP* 114.
4. See Stephen Stepanchev, 'The Origin of J. Alfred Prufrock', *Modern Language Notes*, 66 (1951), 400–1.
5. J. Isaac, 'Eliot's Friends', *Observer*, 18 June 1967, 19.
6. Robert A. Day, 'The "City Man" in *The Waste Land*: The Geography of Reminiscence', *PMLA*, 80 (1965), 285–91.
7. Randall Jarrell, *Poetry and the Age* (London: Faber, 1955), p. 73.
8. Interview with Frank Kermode, Imre Salinsky, *Criticism in Society* (London: Methuen, 1987), p. 105.
9. Nicolas Tredell, 'Frank Kermode in Conversation', *PN Review*, 16:1 (1990), 9–17; pp. 12–13.
10. Ibid., p. 12.
11. Frank Kermode, 'Theory and Truth', *London Review of Books*, 21 November 1991, 9–10.
12. Frank Kermode, 'The Men on the Dump: A Response', in Margaret Tudeau-Clayton and Martin Warner (eds), *Addressing Frank Kermode: Essays in Criticism and Interpretation* (London: Macmillan, 1991), 89–106; p. 103.
13. Ibid., p. 95.

14. Kermode, 'Theory and Truth', p. 10.
15. Tredell, 'Frank Kermode in Conversation', p. 12.
16. Robert Pirsig, *Zen and the Art of Motorcycle Maintenance* (1974; London: Corgi, 1976), p. 207.
17. Louis Menand, 'Lost Faculties', *The New Republic*, 9 and 16 July 1990, 36–40; p. 38.
18. Graff, *Professing Literature*, p. 228.
19. Ibid., p. 237.
20. See John Sutherland, 'The Annual MLA Disaster', *London Review of Books*, 16 December 1993, 11–12.
21. Frank Kermode, *An Appetite for Poetry* (London: RKP, 1989), p. 8.
22. Northrop Frye, *Anatomy of Criticism* (1957; New York: Atheneum, 1965), p. 4.
23. See Stanley Fish, *Doing What Comes Naturally* (Durham and London: Duke University Press, 1989), esp. pp. 197–246.
24. Page Smith, *Killing the Spirit: Higher Education in America* (New York: Viking, 1990), pp. 110–11.
25. Frank Kermode, 'Theory and Truth', p. 9.
26. Frederick Crews, *Skeptical Engagements* (New York: Oxford University Press, 1986), p. 127.
27. Alexander Nehamas, 'The Postulated Author,' *Critical Inquiry* 8 (1981), 133–49; pp. 133–4.
28. See Mildred Martin, *A Half-Century of Eliot Criticism* (Lewisburg: Bucknell University Press, 1972).
29. Beatrice Ricks, *T. S. Eliot: A Bibliography of Secondary Works* (Scarecrow Bibliographies; London: Methuen, 1980).
30. Volker Bischoff, *Ezra Pound Criticism 1905–1985/ A Chronological History of Publications in English* (Universittsbibliothek: Marburg, 1991).
31. K. P. S. Jochum, *W. B. Yeats: a Classified Bibliography of Criticism* (Urbana: University of Illinois Press, 1978).
32. I am grateful to K. P. S. Jochum for this information.
33. Frye, *Anatomy of Criticism*, p. 11.
34. Frank Kermode, 'Frye Reconsidered', *Continuities* (London: Routledge & Kegan Paul, 1968), p. 116.
35. Jarrell, *Poetry and the Age*, p. 90.
36. Eileen Simpson, in *Poets in Their Youth* (London: Faber, 1982), describes Jarrell as the man 'of whom John [Berryman] said second-class poets were so afraid that they thought twice before rushing into print, the critic who made even first-class poets fear for their skins' (p. 110).
37. Jarrell, *Poetry and the Age*, pp. 82–3.
38. Piere van den Burghe, *Academic Gamesmanship* (New York and London: Abelard Schuman, 1970), p. 102. See also Simon O'Toole (pseud.), *Confessions of an American Scholar* (Minneapolis: University of Minnesota Press, 1970).
39. Page Smith, *Killing the Spirit: Higher Education in America* (New York: Viking, 1990), p. 197.
40. Iain McGilchrist, 'A pessimist's solution', *TLS*, 10 December 1982, p. 1358. Cf. Stefan Collini, 'Interpretation terminable and interminable',

in Umberto Eco, with Richard Rorty, Jonathan Culler, Christina Brooke-Rose, *Interpretation and Overinterpretation*, ed. Stefan Collini (Cambridge: Cambridge University Press, 1992), 1–21:

> Succinctly expressed, the dilemma is that the traditional canonical works of literature have by now been very thoroughly studied. . . . Novelty, or at least apparent novelty, of method and provocativeness of formulation are, therefore, at a premium. . . . (p. 20)

41. John Sutherland, 'The Annual MLA Disaster', p. 11.
42. Peter Keating, *The Haunted Study: A Social History of the English Novel 1875–1914* (1989; Fontana: London, 1991), p. vii.
43. Louis Menand, 'The Politics of Deconstruction', *New York Review of Books*, 21 November 1991, 39–44; p. 44.
44. Roger Poole, 'The Yale School as a Theological Enterprise', *Renaissance and Modern Studies* 27 (1983), 3–29; p. 18.
45. Ibid., p. 17. See also Roger Poole, 'Generating believable entities: post-Marxism as a theological enterprise', *Comparative Criticism* 7 (1985), 49–71.

1. The Invention of Modernism

1. A comment on Madonna's 'eclectic borrowings' quoted by Graham Coster, 'Paradise News', *London Review of Books*, 12 September 1991, p. 14.
2. Frank Kermode, *Continuities* (London: Routledge & Kegan Paul, 1968), p. 28.
3. Ibid., p. 7.
4. See Alan Bullock and Oliver Stallybrass (eds), *The Fontana Dictionary of Modern Thought* (London: Fontana, 1977), pp. 395–6.
5. Cf. Ellery Queen, *The Finishing Stroke* (1958; Harmondsworth: Penguin, 1967), which includes a conversation (set in 1929) about

> the modernist movement in art, led by Picasso, Modigliani, Archipenko, Utrillo, Soutine – Soutine who took a landscape 'and threw it upon the canvas as if it were a dishrag, but one which suddenly caught fire!', as Dan Freeman quoted . . . (p. 137).

6. Matei Calinescu, *Five Faces of Modernity/ Modernism/ Avant-Garde/ Decadence/ Kitsch/ Postmodernism* 2nd edn (Duke University Press: Durham, 1987), p. 81.
7. Ibid. I have not seen a copy of this journal.
8. 'The New Art' (1915), repr. in E.E. Cummings, *A Miscellany*, ed. George J. Firmage (London: Peter Owen, 1966), pp. 5–11.
9. John Crowe Ransom, 'The Future of Poetry', *The Fugitive* 3, No. 1 (February 1924), 2–5.
10. Calinescu, *Five Faces of Modernity*, p. 82.
11. Ibid., p. 85.
12. Ibid., p. 84.

13. In the reading list for his 1916 extension lecture on 'The Return of the Catholic Church', Eliot defined 'modernism' as 'a compromise between the point of view of historical criticism – inherited from Renan – and orthodoxy'. See Ronald Schuchard, 'T. S. Eliot as an Extension Lecturer, 1916–1919,' *Review of English Studies* 25 (1974), 163–73; p. 167.

14. T. S. Eliot, 'Contemporary English Prose', *Vanity Fair* (July 1923), 51. The essay first appeared in French in the *Nouvelle Revue Française*, 19 (1 December 1922), 751–6.

15. *SE* 386. Cf. Eliot, 'A Note on Poetry and Belief', *The Enemy*, 1 (January 1927), 15–17:

    Christianity will probably continue to modify itself, as in the past, into something that can be believed in (I do not mean conscious modifications like modernism, etc., which always have the opposite effect . . .).

16. *SE* 477–8.

17. *SL* 248.

18. Padraic Colum, 'Studies in the Sophisticated', *The New Republic* (8 December 1920), 54.

19. See Pound, 'Prufrock', *Poetry* 10 (August 1917), 264–71.

20. See, for example, Stanley Sultan's chapter, '"Our Modern Experiment"', in *Eliot, Joyce and Company* (New York: Oxford University Press, 1987), pp. 91–133.

21. Janko Lavrin, *Aspects of Modernism: From Wilde to Pirandello* (London: Stanley Nott, 1935), p. 9.

22. The Very Rev W. R. Inge, *Modernism in Literature*, Presidential address to the English Association, November 1937 (Oxford: Oxford University Press, 1937), p. 33. Cf. George Gordon's inaugural address as Professor of Poetry at Oxford: *Poetry and the Moderns* (Oxford: Oxford University Press, 1935), in which he castigated

    that oblique, equivocal, ego-centric, Anglo-American, and wholly unintelligible school of poetry, built in the eclipse, fathered and hatched in the waste lands of these whimpering, inhibited postwar years (pp. 6–7).

23. George Orwell, *Inside the Whale and Other Essays* (1940; Harmondsworth: Penguin, 1957), p. 25.

24. See Herbert Grierson and J. C. Smith, *A Critical History of English Poetry* (1944; Harmondsworth: Peregrine, 1962), pp. 478–84.

25. Joseph Wood Krutch, *'Modernism' in Modern Drama* (Ithaca: Cornell University Press, 1953), p. vii.

26. William Van O'Connor, *The New University Wits* (Carbondale: Southern Illinois University Press, 1963), p. 131.

27. Randall Jarrell, 'The End of the Line' [*Nation*, 21 February 1942], repr. in *Kipling, Auden & Co: Essays and Reviews 1935–1964* (1981; Manchester: Carcanet Press, 1986), 76–83.

28. See 'A Note on Poetry: The Rage for the Lost Penny' (1940); Ibid., 47–8.
29. Randall Jarrell, 'The Obscurity of the Poet', in *Poetry and the Age* (London: Faber, 1955), pp. 17, 23.
30. The phrase 'discrimination of modernisms' also appears in Kermode's obituary essay for Eliot; see 'A Babylonish Dialect' (1965); *Continuities*, pp. 67–77.
31. Leslie A. Fiedler, 'The New Mutants', *Partisan Review* 32 (Fall 1965), 505–25.

> I am not now interested in analysing ... the diction and imagery which have passed from Science Fiction into Post-Modernist literature, but rather in coming to terms with the prophetic content common to both ... the myth of the end of man, of the transcendence or transformation of the human. ... (p. 508)

32. See, for example, Gerald Graff's survey in *Literature Against Itself* (Chicago: Chicago University Press, 1979), Ch. 2, 'The Myth of the Postmodern Breakthrough', pp. 31–62; Andrew Ross, *The Failure of Modernism* (New York: Columbia, 1986); Ronald Bush, 'But is it Modern?: T. S. Eliot in 1988', *Yale Review* 77 (Winter 1988), 193–206.
33. Marshall Berman, *All That is Solid Melts into Air* (1982; London: Verso, 1983), p. 16.
34. Ibid., p. 235.
35. Frank Kermode, 'Modernisms', *London Review of Books* (22 May 1986), 3–6; p. 3.
36. C. K. Stead, *Pound, Yeats, Eliot and the Modernist Movement* (London: Macmillan, 1986), p. 30.
37. Ibid., p. 277.
38. See, in regard to this debate, the essays by Ronald Bush, Thomas Parkinson, Ronald Schuchard and M. J. Sidnell in George Bornstein and Richard J. Finneran (eds), *Yeats: An Annual of Critical and Textual Studies* III (Ithaca and London: Cornell University Press, 1985).
39. See Jeffrey Meyers, *The Enemy: A Biography of Wyndham Lewis* (London: Routledge and Kegan Paul, 1980), pp. 147–8.
40. Ibid., p. 133.
41. William Chace, 'On Lewis's Politics', in Jeffrey Meyers (ed.), *Wyndham Lewis: A Revaluation* (London: Athlone Press, 1980), p. 161; citing Lewis, *Count Your Dead: They Are Alive! or A New War in the Making* (London, 1937), p. 81.
42. Ibid., p. 162.
43. Frederic Jameson, *Fables of Aggression: Wyndham Lewis, The Modernist as Fascist* (Berkeley: University of California Press, 1979), pp. 5, 23.
44. See John Carey, 'Wyndham Lewis and Hitler', *The Intellectuals and the Masses* (London: Faber, 1992), pp. 182–208.
45. See, for example, Timothy Materer, *Vortex: Pound, Eliot and Lewis* (Ithaca: Cornell University Press, 1979); Erik Svarny, 'The Men of 1914': *T. S. Eliot and Early Modernism* (Milton Keynes: Open Univer-

sity Press, 1988), and Dennis Brown, *Intertextual Dynamics within the Literary Group: Joyce, Lewis, Eliot and Pound* (London: Macmillan, 1990).

46. Bonnie Kime Scott (ed.), *The Gender of Modernism: A Critical Anthology* (Bloomington: Indiana University Press, 1990), pp. 2, 4.

47. Ibid., pp. 16–17.

48. Sanford B. Schwarz, *The Matrix of Modernism* (Princeton: Princeton University Press, 1985), pp. 3–4. See also James Longenbach, *Modernist Poetics of History* (Princeton: Princeton University Press, 1987), for a similar style of argument.

49. David Trotter, 'Six hands at an open door', *London Review of Books* (21 March 1991), 11–12.

50. Michael H. Levenson, *A Genealogy of Modernism* (Cambridge: Cambridge University Press, 1984), p. vii.

51. Ibid., p. xi.

52. See Levenson, pp. 210–19.

53. Richard J. Quinones, *Mapping Literary Modernism: Time and Development* (Princeton: Princeton University Press, 1985), pp. 14, 19.

54. Louis Menand, *Discovering Modernism: T. S. Eliot and his Context* (New York: OUP, 1987), pp. 3–4.

55. Jacques Derrida, *Of Grammatology*, tr. Gayatri Chakravorty Spivak (Baltimore: Johns Hopkins University Press, 1974), p. 92.

56. Frank Kermode, *Romantic Image* (London: Routledge and Kegan Paul, 1957), p. 143.

57. Jonathan Culler, *Framing the Sign: Criticism and its Institutions* (Oxford: Basil Blackwell, 1988), p. 39.

58. Paul de Man, *Allegories of Reading* (New Haven, Conn.: Yale University Press, 1979), p. 19.

59. Christopher Butler, 'The Concept of Modernism', in Susan Dick, *et al.* (eds), *Omnium Gatherum: Essays for Richard Ellmann* (Gerrards Cross: Colin Smythe, 1989), 49–59; p. 59.

60. Ibid., p. 58.

61. Ibid., p. 49.

62. Bullock and Stalleybrass, *The Fontana Dictionary of Modern Thought*, pp. 395–6, supplemented by cross-references.

63. Cf. 'Beyond Postmodernism', the introduction to Peter Collier and Helga Geyer-Ryan (eds), *Literary Theory Today* (Ithaca: Cornell University Press, 1990).

64. Frank Kermode, *History and Value* (Oxford; Clarendon Press, 1988), p. 129.

65. Ibid., p. 131.

66. Cf. Bruce Chatwin, *What Am I Doing Here* (London: Picador, 1990): by the early 1920s, Alexander Rodchenko alone had 'tried out and discarded almost every experiment the New York abstract painters tried in the Fifties and Sixties before reaching the present impasse' (p. 166).

67. Robert Hughes, *The Shock of the New*, rev. edn (London: Thames and Hudson, 1991), p. 365.

68. Ibid., p. 393.

69. Ibid., pp. 422, 425.
70. Claude Rawson, 'Old Literature and its Enemies', *London Review of Books*, 25 April 1991, 11–15, p. 12.
71. *SL* 300.
72. W. B. Yeats, *Autobiographies* (London: Macmillan, 1955), p. 315.

2. 'These fragments you have shelved (shored)': Pound, Eliot and *The Waste Land*

1. Wyndham Lewis, *Time and Western Man* (London: Chatto and Windus, 1927), pp. 85–6.
2. *OPP* 109.
3. *SL* 248.
4. *EL1* 530, 596.
5. See *SE* 368, *WLMS* 1, *OPP* 109, and 'T. S. Eliot', in Kay Dick (ed.), *Writers at Work/ The Paris Review Interviews* (Harmondsworth: Penguin, 1972), 114–32; p. 127 (hereafter *PR Interview*).
6. *PR Interview*, p. 127.
7. Helen Gardner, *The Composition of Four Quartets* (London: Faber, 1978), p. 3.
8. 'Mr. T. S. Eliot,' *New Statesman and Nation* (18 April 1936), 603–4.
9. Wallace Fowlie, 'Jorge Guillén, Marianne Moore, T. S. Eliot: Some Encounters,' *Poetry*, 90 (1957), 103–9; p. 107.
10. Peter Ackroyd, *T. S. Eliot* (London: Hamish Hamilton, 1984).
11. Cf. 'Shakespeare and the Stoicism of Seneca' (1927): 'I am used to having cosmic significances, which I never suspected, extracted from my work ... and to having my personal biography reconstructed from passages which I got out of books ... and to having my biography invariably ignored in what I did write from personal experience ...'. (*SE* 127).
12. *EL1* 351.
13. Conrad Aiken, 'An Anatomy of Melancholy', in C. B. Cox and Arnold R. Hinchliffe (eds), *T. S. Eliot/ The Waste Land/ A Casebook* (London: Macmillan, 1968) [hereafter *WLCB*], 91–9; p. 92.
14. *EL1* 251.
15. Anthony Cronin, 'A Conversation with T. S. Eliot About the Connections Between *Ulysses* and *The Waste Land*', *The Irish Times*, 16 June 1971, 10; quoted in Louis Menand, *Discovering Modernism/ T. S. Eliot and His Context* (New York: Oxford University Press, 1987), p. 76 [hereafter *Menand*]. Cf. Eliot to John Quinn, 9 July 1919: 'The part of *Ulysses* in question ['Scylla and Charybdis'] struck me as almost the finest I have read: I have lived on it ever since I read it' (*EL1* 314).
16. 'Ulysses, Order, and Myth', *Selected Prose of T. S. Eliot*, ed. Frank Kermode (London: Faber, 1975), p. 177.
17. Ronald Bush, *T. S. Eliot/ A Study in Character and Style* (New York: OUP, 1984), p. 71.
18. Ibid., p. 69.
19. *SL* 234.

20. Eliot described the manuscript as 'sprawling' and 'chaotic' in 'Ezra Pound', *Poetry*, 68 (September 1946), 326–38; reprinted in Walter Sutton (ed.) *Ezra Pound/ A Collection of Critical Essays* (Englewood Cliffs: Prentice-Hall, 1963), 17–25; hereafter *Sutton*.

21. Cf. Eliot to Daniel H. Woodward, 3 April 1964: 'the poem in the form in which it finally appeared owes more to Pound's surgery than anyone can realise' (*WLCB* 90).

22. *EL1* 280.

23. See Humphrey Carpenter, *A Serious Character/ The Life of Ezra Pound* (London: Faber, 1988), pp. 340–51 [hereafter *Carpenter*]; also *WLMS* 131.

24. *EL1* 496.

25. Valerie Eliot follows D. D. Paige's interpretation of the date, '24 Saturnus An 1', on Pound's first surviving letter about the manuscript (*EL1*, 497–9), as 24 December 1921. Hugh Kenner argues persuasively for 24 January 1922 as the correct date. See Hugh Kenner, 'The Urban Apocalypse', in A. Walton Litz (ed.), *Eliot in His Time* (Princeton: Princeton University Press, 1973), 23–49, p. 44. His argument is accepted by Richard Ellmann in an essay in the same volume, 'The First *Waste Land*' (51–66); see p. 65. See also Lawrence Rainey, 'The price of modernism: reconsidering the publication of *The Waste Land*', *Critical Quarterly*, 31.4 (1989), 21–47; pp. 41–2.

26. *WLMS* 127.

27. 'Reflections on *Vers Libre*' (1917), begins with a portrait of a lady, 'renowned in her small circle for the accuracy of her stop-press information of literature', who sounds very like Ottoline Morrell: '"Since the Russians came in I can read nothing else"' (*TCC* 183). Cf Fresca: 'The Russians thrilled her to hysteric fits' (*WLMS* 27). Ottoline Morrell recommended Dr Roger Vittoz to Eliot, who was given the room at the Hotel Ste Luce in Lausanne that she had occupied when she consulted Vittoz in 1913. See Ackroyd, *T. S. Eliot*, pp. 117–18; also Sandra Darroch, *Ottoline/ The Life of Lady Ottoline Morrell* (New York: Coward, McCann & Geoghegan, 1975), p. 120.

28. See *Ulysses I* (1969 Penguin edition, p. 55).

29. See, for example, David Craig's 'The Defeatism of *The Waste Land*' (1960), *WLCB* 200–15, and Ian Hamilton, '*The Waste Land*', in Graham Martin (ed.), *Eliot in Perspective* (London: Macmillan, 1970), 102–11.

30. Eliot was still referring to: 'a poem of about four hundred and fifty lines in four parts' when writing to Scofield Thayer on 20 January 1922 (*EL1* 502).

31. Valerie Eliot said, in a recent interview: 'I think it was Ezra Pound, if anyone, who gave him the title.' See Blake Morrison, 'The Two Mrs Eliots', *The Independent on Sunday* (24 April 1994), *Sunday Review*, 4–9; p. 7.

32. *EL1* 504.

33. Lyndall Gordon, *Eliot's Early Years* (Oxford: Oxford University Press, 1977), pp. 136–7.

34. Edmund Wilson, 'The First Waste Land – II', *New York Review of Books* (18 November 1971), 16.

35. A criterion which, when Pound was finally offered the (1928) prize in 1927, did not suit him at all. See *Carpenter*, 441, SL 288–9.

36. *WLMS*, xxvi.

37. See *UPUC*, 71; also Hugh Sykes Davies, 'Mr. Kurtz: He Dead', in Allen Tate (ed), *T. S. Eliot: The Man and His Work* (1967; Harmondsworth: Penguin, 1970), 353–61: 'my delight in [Eliot's] poetry was enhanced when my English master picked the book up from my desk one day . . . and handed it back with the advice that I should not waste my time on such "Bolshevik" stuff' (p. 354).

38. *Carpenter*, p. 419.

39. Eliot's printing of Canto VIII (then Canto IX) begins with line five of the final version (C 28). See *The Criterion*, 1:4 (July 1923), p. 363. Canto VIII also includes a transparent allusion to Pound's ill-fated 'Bel Esprit' scheme: 'I want to arrange with him to give him so much per year/ And to assure him that he will get the sum agreed on.'

40. *SE* 30.

41. *SE* 368. Cf 'In Memoriam' (1936): 'It happens now and then that a poet by some strange accident expresses the mood of his generation, at the same time that he is expressing a mood of his own which is quite remote from that of his generation' (*SE* 334). Also TSE to Paul Elmer More, 20 July 1934:

    I was not aware [in *The Waste Land*], and am not aware now, of having drawn a contrast between a contemporary world of slums, hysterics and riverside promiscuity etc. with any visibly more romantically lovely earlier world. I mean there is no nostalgia for the trappings of the past, so far as I can see, and no illusion about the world ever having been a pleasanter place to live in than it is now.

    (Cited by James Longenbach, '*Ara Vos Prec*: Satire and Suffering', in Ronald Bush (ed.), *T. S. Eliot: The Modernist in History* (Cambridge: Cambridge University Press, 1991), 41–66, p. 42).

42. See 'From T. S. Eliot', in Ford Madox Ford, *et al.*, *The Cantos of Ezra Pound: Some Testimonies* (New York: Farrar and Reinhard, 1933), 16–17.

43. 'On a Recent Piece of Criticism', *Purpose*, 10:2 (April–June 1938), 90–4; cited by Helen Gardner, '*The Waste Land*: Paris, 1922' in Litz (ed.), *Eliot in His Time*, 67–94; p. 77.

44. 'Ezra Pound', *Poetry*, 68 (September 1946), 326–38; *Sutton*, pp. 17–25.

45. *PR Interview*, p. 118.

46. Ibid., p. 127.

47. Ibid., p. 119.

48. See, for example, Eliot's reaction to the news that Conrad Aiken's review was to be entitled, 'An Anatomy of Melancholy'; missing the allusion to Burton, Eliot replied, 'with that icy fury of which

he alone was capable . . . "There is nothing melancholy about it!"'
(*WLCB* 92).

49. *Menand*, p. 152.

50. Ibid., pp. 152–3, 162, 163.

51. *SL* 80.

52. Philip Blair Rice, 'Out of the Waste Land,' *Symposium*, 3 (1932),
    422–42; p. 428.

53. 'Mr. Eliot's New Poem', *TLS* (29 May 1930), 452.

54. *UPUC* 144–56. Cf. *UPUC* 69: 'anyone who has ever been visited
    by the Muse is thenceforth haunted'.

55. See Ackroyd, *T. S. Eliot*, p. 196.

56. Rayner Heppenstal, 'The Use of Poetry', *Adelphi* (March 1934),
    460–62.

57. Anon., 'Profiles: T. S. Eliot, O. M.', *Observer*, 7 March 1948.

58. *EL1* 498.

59. *EL1* 499.

60. *EL1* 358.

61. *EL1* 451.

62. *Pound/Ford: The Story of a Literary Friendship*, ed. Brita Lindberg
    Seyersted (London: Faber, 1982), p. 157.

63. Pound, 'Harold Munro', *The Criterion*, 11 (July 1932), p. 590.

64. 'Ezra Pound', *Poetry*, LXVIII (September 1946), 326–38; *Sutton*,
    p. 18.

65. See Christopher Middleton, 'Documents on Imagism from the Papers
    of F. S. Flint' *The Review*, No. 15 (April 1965), 34–51; also Ronald
    Schuchard, '"As Regarding Rhythm": Yeats and the Imagists', in
    Richard Finneran (ed.), *Yeats: An Annual of Critical and Textual Studies*
    (Ithaca: Cornell University Press), Vol. II, 1984, 209–26.

66. *Carpenter*, 37, Cf. Aldington in 1913: 'Ezra Pound actually does
    know more about poetry than any other person in these islands,
    Yeats not excepted' (*Carpenter*, p. 178).

67. *The Collected Letters of W. B. Yeats/ Volume I/ 1865–1895*, ed. John Kelly
    and Guy Domville (Oxford: Oxford University Press, 1986), p. 7.

68. *Carpenter*, 36.

69. George P. Elliott, 'Poet of Many Voices', in J. P. Sullivan (ed.),
    Ezra Pound (Harmondsworth: Penguin, 1970), p. 261.

70. Ezra Pound, *Collected Early Poems*, ed. Michael John King (Lon-
    don: Faber, 1977), p. 71.

71. See Bloom's introduction to Harold Bloom (ed.), *Modern Critical
    Views/ Ezra Pound* (New York: Chelsea House Publishers, 1987),
    pp. 1–8.

72. Cf. Carpenter: '"The River-Merchant's Wife: A Letter", the most
    celebrated piece in *Cathay* – indeed the most appealing poem of
    Ezra's whole career – is a vision through female eyes. For all the
    aggressive masculinity . . . it is the River-Merchant's Wife . . . who
    seems the most convincing' (*Carpenter*, p. 268).

73. Ezra Pound, *Collected Shorter Poems* (London: Faber, 1984), p. 74.

74. *SL* 179; 'Et faim sallier les loups des boys' (1915), *Collected Early
    Poems*, p. 284.

75. *Carpenter*, p. 193.
76. *PR Interview*, p. 118.
77. *Pound/Joyce: The Letters of Ezra Pound to James Joyce*, ed. Forrest Read (London: Faber, 1969), p. 148.
78. Cf. his later tendency to 'hint that Macmillan's rejection [of his proposed ten-volume anthology of world poetry] had marked the start of a conspiracy among British publishers to exclude his work' (See *Carpenter*, pp. 308–9).
79. *Pound/Joyce*, pp. 65–6; *Blast*, No. I (June 1914), p. 45.
80. Pound had initially hoped to take over Lowell: 'When I get through with that girl she'll think she was born in free verse' (*Carpenter*, p. 209).
81. Michael Levenson, *A Genealogy of Modernism* (Cambridge: Cambridge University Press, 1984), p. 148.
82. *EL1* 337.
83. *SL* 191.
84. EP to Simon Guggenheim, 31 March 1925, quoted in Donald Gallup, 'T. S. Eliot and Ezra Pound: Collaborators in Letters', *Poetry Australia*, No. 32 (February 1970), 58–81; p. 76.
85. Cited in Hugh Kenner, *The Invisible Poet*, p. 83.
86. *SL* 256.
87. Levenson, *Genealogy of Modernism*, p. 219.
88. Ibid., pp. 213–20.
89. *Menand*, p. 134.
90. Ibid., p. 151.
91. Eliot, 'Observations', *The Egoist*, May 1918, 69.
92. Cf. Donald Hall, 'The Cantos in England' (1960), reprinted in Eric Homberger (ed.), *Ezra Pound: The Critical Heritage* (London: Routledge & Kegan Paul, 1972) [hereafter PCH], 457–60: 'Eliot has developed and argued Pound's insights so that they are believed by critics and professors' (p. 457).
93. *Menand*, pp. 153, 124.
94. Warwick Gould, 'The Unknown Masterpiece: Yeats and the Design of the Cantos', in Andrew Gibson (ed.), *Pound in Multiple Perspective* (London: Macmillan, 1993), pp. 40–92.
95. Robert Casillo, *The Genealogy of Demons/ Anti-Semitism, Fascism, and Myths of Ezra Pound* (Evanston, Illinois: Northwestern University Press, 1988), p. 332. Hereafter *Casillo*.
96. See Gould, 'The Unknown Masterpiece', pp. 69–77.
97. *PCH* 444.
98. Carol T. Christ, *Victorian and Modern Poetics* (Chicago: University of Chicago Press, 1984), p. 98. See also *Menand*, 27.
99. Ronald Bush, *The Genesis of Pound's Cantos* (Princeton: Princeton University Press, 1976), p. 16.
100. Leon Surette, *A Light From Eleusis/ A Study of Ezra Pound's Cantos* (Oxford: Clarendon Press, 1979), pp. vii–viii.
101. Hugh Kenner, *The Poetry of Ezra Pound* (Norfolk, Conn.: New Directions, 1951), p. 252. Cf. (with very different intent) Yeat's introduction to *The Oxford Book of Modern Verse* (Oxford: Clarendon

Press, 1936): 'Ezra Pound has made flux his theme; plot, charac-
terization, logical discourse, seem to him abstractions unsuitable
to a man of his generation' (pp. xxiii–iv).

102. See *Carpenter*, pp. 169–70, 271–4, for a plain account of these matters.

103. *Carpenter*, p. 273.

104. Casillo's closing attempt to redeem the *Cantos* (pp. 332–6) is at
odds with the entire preceding analysis, which is in turn hampered by overinsistence and a doggedly humourless style. Nevertheless, his central argument remains compelling, as witness the
unease (and dismay) of several hostile reviewers. See, for example,
Bruce Fogelman in *American Literature*, 61 (May 1989), 308–9; Lawrence S. Rainey in *JEGP*, 88 (October 1989), 559–63; and Denis
Donoghue, 'Pound's Book of Beasts', *New York Review of Books*, 2
June 1988, 14–16.

105. *Casillo*, p. 16.

106. Martin A. Kayman, *The Modernism of Ezra Pound* (London: Macmillan,
1986). See his 'Introduction: Some of our Best Poets are Fascists',
especially pp. 24–32.

107. *Casillo*, pp. 157, 115.

108. See, for example, *Menand*, pp. 115–16, on Eliot's 'rhetoric of hy-
giene'.

109. *Carpenter*, p. 393.

110. *SL* 287–8.

111. *SL* 248.

112. Note to *Personae* (1926); cited in *Carpenter*, p. 368.

113. *Carpenter*, p. 422.

114. *SL* 320.

115. Quoted by Donald Gallup, 'T. S. Eliot and Ezra Pound: Collaborators in Letters', p. 77.

116. *PR Interview*, p. 118.

117. See *Carpenter*, p. 912.

118. *C*, CX 781.

3. Death by Exegesis

1. Inaugural lecture, University of Sheffield; cited in Martin Rowson,
The Waste Land (Harmondsworth: Penguin, 1990), p. [74].

2. [G. S. Fraser], 'The Waste Land Revisited', *TLS* (28 August 1953),
viii–x. I am grateful to Nick Mays for assistance with this and other
identifications of *TLS* contributors.

3. [G. S. Fraser], 'The Waste Land Forty Years On', *TLS* (28 September
1962), 670.

4. I. A. Richards, *Principles of Literary Criticism*, 2nd impression (London: RKP, 1926), p. 291. Thence to F. R. Leavis: 'By means of such
references and quotations, Mr Eliot attains a compression, otherwise unattainable . . .' (*New Bearings in English Poetry* [1932;
Harmondsworth: Peregrine, 1960], p. 90), whereafter the idea becomes commonplace in mainstream Eliot criticism.

5. Richard Poirier, 'The Literature of Waste: Eliot, Joyce, and Others'

(1967); in *The Performing Self* (London: Chatto & Windus, 1971), p. 45.

6. Arthur Waugh, 'The New Poetry', *Quarterly Review* (October 1916), 365–86; p. 386. Conrad Aiken's 'Esoteric Catholicity' (*Poetry Journal* 5 [April 1916], 127–9) is too much an inside view to qualify as a *critical* notice.

7. Ezra Pound, 'Drunken Helots and Mr. Eliot', *The Egoist*, 4 (June 1917), 72–4.

8. [Frederick Thomas Dalton], untitled, *TLS* (21 June 1917), 299. Dalton (1872–1927) was assistant editor of the *TLS* from 1902 to 1923. John Gross remarks that Bruce Richmond, the *TLS* editor who commissioned Eliot as a leader-writer and reviewer for the paper in 1919, 'is said to have deeply regretted' the derogatory notices of Eliot's first two volumes, and yet 'subsequent coverage of his poetry during Richmond's time, while it was always respectful, tended to be guarded and rather meagre'. See John Gross (ed.), *The Modern Movement* (London: Harvill, 1992), introduction, pp. xvi–xviii.

9. Anon., 'Shorter Notices', *New Statesman* (18 August 1917), 477.

10. Anon., untitled, *Southport Guardian* (18 August 1917).

11. R[obert] L[ynd], untitled, *Daily News* (18 August 1917).

12. Anon., untitled, *Athenaeum* (December 1917), 667. Two years later, Eliot was reviewing Lynd for the *Athenaeum* – 'Lynd's collected papers stuck in my throat . . . and in revenge he shan't go in this week' (TSE to Mary Hutchinson, 1 June 1919, *EL1* 298).

13. Anon., 'Recent Verse', *Literary World (and Reader)*, 83, 5 July 1917, 107.

14. B[abette] D[eutsch], 'Another Impressionist', *New Republic* (16 February 1918), 89.

15. May Sinclair, '"Prufrock: And Other Observations": A Criticism', *Little Review* (December 1917), 8–14. Pound had known her since 1909; Eliot had invited her to contribute to the *Egoist* two months before the review appeared. See *EL1* 205, 218.

16. Edgar Jepson, 'Recent United States Poetry', *English Review*, 26 May, 1918, 419–28.

17. Edgar Jepson, 'The Western School', *Little Review* (September 1918), 4–9. See Harriet Monroe, 'An International Episode', *Poetry*, 13 (November 1918), 94–5; *SL* 194–5; *EL1* 275.

18. William Carlos Williams, 'Prologue', *Little Review* (May 1919), 74–80; p. 76.

19. Anon. [Leonard and Virginia Woolf], 'Is This Poetry?', *Athenaeum*, 20 June 1919, 491.

20. See Louis Menand, *Discovering Modernism: T. S. Eliot and his Context* (New York: Oxford University Press, 1987), p. 176. (Hereafter *Menand*).

21. Arthur Clutton-Brock, in the *TLS*, 20 December 1920, 795, praised the book very highly, as did the *New Statesman*, 26 March, 733–4. Leonard Woolf, *Athenaeum*, 17 December 1920, 834–5, and Richard Aldington, *Poetry*, March 1921, 345–8, were equally – and not surprisingly – enthusiastic, as was Marianne Moore in the *Dial* (March 1921), 336–9. 'E.S.' [Edward Shanks] in the *London Mercury* (Febru-

ary 1921), 447–50, though not wholly in agreement, spoke of Eliot the critic with respect and evident familiarity.

22. Desmond MacCarthy, 'New Poets III: T. S. Eliot', *New Statesman*, 8 January 1921, 418–20. MacCarthy was literary editor of the *New Statesman*. See *EL1* 375, 440, 464. Cf. Robert Nichols, 'An Ironist' [review of *Ara Vos Prec*], *Observer*, 18 April 1920: 'The irony of things-as-they-are haunts the poet as it haunted his forerunner Laforgue.' Eliot had written to Nichols on 8 August 1917: 'I do feel more grateful to [Laforgue] than to anyone else' (*EL1* 191).

23. Richard Aldington, 'The Poetry of T. S. Eliot', *Outlook*, 49, 7 January 1922, 12–13; *New York Evening Post Literary Review*, 14 January 1922, 350; cited from Leonard Unger (ed.), *T. S. Eliot: A Selected Critique* (New York: Russell and Russell, 1948), pp. 4–10. See 'Mr Eliot at Austin', *TLS*, 11 August 1961, 539; Eliot to Aldington, 16 September 1921 (*EL1* 469–70).

24. [Arthur Clutton-Brock], 'Not Here, O Apollo', *TLS* 12 June 1919, 322.

25. *EL1* 363.

26. W[illiam] S[tanley] B[raithewaite], 'A Scorner of the Ordinary Substance of Human Nature', *Boston Evening Transcript*, 14 April 1920, 2:6.

27. R. M. Weaver, 'What Ails Pegasus', *Bookman* (New York) 52 (September 1920), 59.

28. Louis Untermeyer, 'Irony De Luxe', *The Freeman*, 1, 30 July 1920, 382. Cf. Harriet Monroe on the 'loud protests from shocked critics' following the first appearance of 'Prufrock' in *Poetry*:

> The most violent of them all came from Louis Untermeyer.... He wrote to me that the 'Long Song' was 'the first piece of the English language that utterly stumped me ... the muse in a psychopathic ward drinking the stale dregs of revolt. And he told of reading the poem 'quite seriously' to a 'not too arts-and-crafty group – a few poets, a lawyer, a couple of musicians and one psychoanalyst'. Of these 'no one could keep a straight face ... except the psychoanalyst, who said "I think a lot could be done for him – it's a muddled case of infantile repressions and inhibitions."'
>
> *A Poet's Life* (New York: Macmillan, 1938), pp. 394–5.

29. 'M.V.D.', *Nation*, [New York] 26 June 1920, 856. BRD. Padraic Colum (see p. 34 above) took a very similar line; see also E. E. Cummings, 'T. S. Eliot', *The Dial* (June 1920), 781–4; reprinted in *E. E. Cummings: A Miscellany*, ed. George Firmage (London: Peter Owen, 1966), pp. 25–9.

30. See Mildred Martin, *A Half-Century of Eliot Criticism* (Lewisburg: Bucknell University Press, 1972), pp. 266–9, for a full bibliography of the hoax rumours; also C. B. Cox and Arnold R. Hinchliffe (eds), *T. S. Eliot/ The Waste Land/ A Casebook* (London: Macmillan, 1968) [hereafter *WLCB*], p. 11. The story was still running a decade later;

see Herbert E. Palmer, 'The Hoax and Earnest of *The Waste Land*', *Dublin Magazine*, 8 (1933), 11–19. Cf. Karl Shapiro (1960):

> [*The Waste Land*'s] critical success was, I dare say, carefully planned and executed, and it was not beyond the realm of possibility that the poem was originally a hoax, as some of its first readers insisted (*WLCB* 63).

31. Elinor Wylie, 'Mr. Eliot's Slug Horn', *New York Evening Post Literary Review*, 20 January 1923, 396. Cf. F. Van De Water, 'Books and So Forth', *New York Tribune*, 28 January 1923, 19, who also wondered whether the poem was a hoax, but concluded: 'We're almost tempted to fall on our knees and call T. S. Eliot great' (cited by Martin, *Eliot Criticism*, p. 269).

32. Burton Rascoe, 'A Bookman's Day Book', *New York Tribune*, 5 November 1922, 5:8. After lunching with Gilbert Seldes and Edmund Wilson early in January 1923, Rascoe changed his tune, and set about quelling the hoax rumours. On 28 January 1923 he published, in the *Tribune*, an anonymous letter he had received, 'stating that Eliot told the writer *The Waste Land* was a hoax', followed by his own defence of Eliot and an exchange of letters between himself and Louis Untermeyer. He returned to the question in the *Tribune* on 1 and 22 April, reporting, in the latter issue, that Eliot had 'denied saying that *The Waste Land* was a hoax, in letters to the *Chicago Daily News* and the *New York Globe*'. See Martin, *Eliot Criticism*, pp. 268–9. See also Donald Gallup, *T. S. Eliot: A Bibliography* 2nd edn (London: Faber, 1969), item C138a, p. 209: a letter from Eliot published in the New York *Globe and Commercial Advertiser*, 17 April 1923, concerning 'a statement attributed (in [N. P.] Dawson's column of 6 March) to Ben Hecht that *The Waste Land* was planned as a hoax on the American public'.

33. *OPP* 109.

34. F. L. Lucas, 'The Waste Land', *New Statesman and Nation*, 6 November 1922, 116–18; *WLCB* 37. Cf. Edmund Wilson: 'it is true that, in reading Eliot and Pound, we are sometimes visited by uneasy recollections of Ausonius, in the fourth century, composing Greek-and-Latin macaronics and piecing together poetic mosaics out of verses from Virgil' (*Axel's Castle*, [1931; London: Collins, 1961], p. 94).

35. Gilbert Seldes, 'T. S. Eliot', *Nation* [New York] (6 December 1922), 614–16; *WLCB* 38–44.

36. Wilson's 'The Poetry of Drouth', (*The Dial* 73 [November 1922], 611–16) was commissioned by Seldes as part of the promotional campaign. See *WLCB* 75, 87–8.

37. John Drury, 'World's Greatest Poem', *Chicago Daily News* (14 February 1922), 15; Harriet Monroe, 'A Contrast', *Poetry* (March 1923), 325–30; C[harles] P[owell], *Manchester Guardian*, 31 October 1923, 7; *WLCB*, 29–30.

38. John Crowe Ransom, 'Waste Lands', *New York Literary Review*, 14 July 1923, 825–6.

39. Louis Untermeyer, 'Disillusion as Dogma', *The Freeman*, 17 January 1923, 453.

40. Cf Swift, *A Tale of a Tub*, Sect. VII: 'I have sometimes heard of an *Iliad* in a *Nut-shell*; but it hath been my Fortune to have much oftner *seen* a *Nut-shell* in an *Iliad*.'

41. Conrad Aiken, 'An Anatomy of Melancholy', *The New Republic*, 7 February 1922, 294–5; *WLCB* 93–9.

42. E. M. Forster, 'T. S. Eliot and His Difficulties', *Life and Letters*, June 1929, 417–25.

43. Patric Dickinson's account of his first encounter with Eliot in 1929 is characteristic: 'Though I had read poetry at school for some time, and also tried to write it, this was wholly different. It was an awakening to a new life' (*The Good Minute* [London: Gollancz, 1965], pp. 95–6).

44. Edwin Muir, 'T. S. Eliot', *Nation*, 121 (5 August 1925), 162–4; repr. in *Transition* (London: L & V. Woolf, 1926), p. 142.

45. H. S. Davies, 'Mistah Kurtz: He Dead', in Allen Tate (ed.), *T. S. Eliot: The Man and His Work* (1967; Harmondsworth: Penguin, 1970), pp. 353–61; 354–5.

46. Ibid., p. 359.

47. Richard Church, 'Mr T. S. Eliot', *Spectator*, 2 August 1930, 169–70.

48. See 'G. W. R.', untitled, *Cambridge Review*, 29 April 1932, 353; Geoffrey Grigson, 'Latter Day Poetry,' *Saturday Review*, 30 April 1932, 448–49; 'New Bearings', *TLS*, 21 April 1932, 286; Richard Church 'The Labyrinthine Way', *Spectator*, 26 March 1932, 453–4.

49. Cf. Dorothy Shakespear to Pound, 27 September, 1911: 'You are in this week's "Punch": they love you!' (*Ezra Pound and Dorothy Shakespear: Their Letters 1909–1914*, ed. Omar Pound and A. Walton Litz [London: Faber, 1985], p. 67). Hereafter *EDL*.

50. Barbara Everett, 'Impersonality', *London Review of Books*, 10 November 1988, 8–10; p. 10.

51. Donald Davie, The Universe of Ezra Pound', *Critical Quarterly*, 15 (1972), 50–7; p. 50.

52. Cf. Pound to Dorothy Shakespear, 16 July 1911: 'when my biographers unearth this missive [the original table of contents for *Canzoni*] it will be recorded as an astounding proof of my genius' (*EDL* 38). Sure enough, James Longenbach, in *Modernist Poetics of History* (Princeton: Princeton University Press, 1987) declares the document 'an astounding proof of the tenacity of Pound's genius' (p. 66).

53. Louis Menand, 'T. S. Eliot', in *Modernism and New Criticism, The Cambridge History of Literary Criticism*, Vol. 7 ed. A. Walton Litz, Louis Menand and Lawrence Rainey (Cambridge University Press: forthcoming). I am grateful to Louis Menand for permission to quote from this chapter.

54. Ibid.

55. [J. C. Smith], 'An Exploration with Mr. T. S. Eliot', *TLS*, 16 November 1935, 741.

56. See, for example, Mark Reinsberg, 'A Footnote to *Four Quartets*', *American Literature*, 21, (1948), 342–44.

57. Norman Nathan, 'Eliot's Incorrect Note on "C.i.f. London', *Notes and Queries*, 203 (1958), 262.
58. Malcolm Cowley, *The Literary Situation* (New York: Random House, 1955), p. 19.
59. Allen Tate, 'Reflections on American Poetry; 1900–1950', *Sewanee Review*, 64 (1956), 59–70; p. 61.
60. H. S. Gorman, 'The Waste Land of the Younger Generation', *Literary Digest International Book Review*, 1 (April 1923), 46.
61. [G. S. Fraser], 'Mr. Eliot Expounded', *TLS* (5 July 1957), 414.
62. Staffan Bergsten, 'Illusive Allusions', *Orbis Litterarum*, 14 (1959), 9–18.
63. See Cleanth Brooks, *Modern Poetry and the Tradition* (1939; London: Poetry London, 1948), 137–70.
64. Henry Reed, 'If and Perhaps and But', *Listener*, 18 June 1953, 1017–18.
65. See Gerald Graff, *Professing Literature: An Institutional History* (Chicago: University of Chicago Press, 1987), pp. 227–32, citation p. 231.
66. Imre Salinsky, *Criticism in Society* (London: Methuen, 1987), p. 61.
67. Ibid., pp. 238–9.
68. See John C. Pope, 'Prufrock and Raskolnikov', *American Literature*, 17 (1945), 213–30, and 'Prufrock and Raskolnikov Again', ibid., 18 (1947), 319–21; also T. S. Eliot, 'Author and Critic' (1955; unpublished, John Hayward Collection, Kings College Library, Cambridge), p. 7.
69. See, for example, Jonathan Culler, 'Political Criticism: Confronting Religion', in *Framing the Sign* (Oxford: Basil Blackwell, 1988), pp. 71–82.
70. R. P. Blackmur, *Annis Mirabiles 1921–1925* (Washington: Library of Congress, 1956), p. 39.
71. R. P. Blackmur, 'The Enabling Act of Criticism', in R. W. Stallman (ed.), *Critiques and Essays in Criticism*, 1920–1948 (New York: Ronald Press, 1949), 412–17; p. 413.
72. *Some Winchester Letters of Lionel Johnson* (London: Allen and Unwin, 1919), p. 111.
73. See, for example, the essays by Ian Hamilton, Gabriel Pearson and Graham Martin in Graham Martin (ed.), *Eliot in Perspective* (London: Macmillan, 1970).
74. Peter Ackroyd, *T. S. Eliot* (London: Hamish Hamilton, 1984), p. 317.
75. See *OPP* 113, 118.
76. See, for example, F. W. Bateson, 'Dissociation of Sensibility', *Essays in Criticism*, 1 (1951), 302–12; Victor Brombert, 'T. S. Eliot and the Romantic Heresy', *Yale French Studies*, 13 (1954), 3–16. See also G. M. Turnell, 'The Poetry of Jules Laforgue', *Scrutiny*, 5 (1936), 128–49.

4. The Case of the Missing Subject

1. Hugh Kenner, *The Invisible Poet* (1959; London: Methuen, 1965), p. 50.
2. Christopher Ricks, *T. S. Eliot and Prejudice* (London: Faber, 1988), pp. 18, 15.
3. Louis Menand, 'T. S. Eliot', in *Modernism and New Criticism*, *The Cambridge History of Literary Criticism*, Vol. 7, ed. A. Walton Litz,

Louis Menand and Lawrence Rainey (Cambridge: Cambridge University Press, forthcoming).

4. Ricks, however, overplays his hand by attempting to disarm almost every manifestation of prejudice he can discover in Eliot, from the early poems through to the later prose. Cf. Hugh Haughton, 'The Pent and its Venting,' *TLS* (17–23 March 1989), 285–6: Ricks's 'case about Eliot's simultaneous distrust of prejudice and "distrust of the distrust of prejudice" often has the effect of making him sound like a brilliant connoisseur of prejudice and turns Eliot into a poet engaged in exploring the prejudices of other people (Gerontion's or his readers') rather than his own'.

5. See Kenner, *The Invisible Poet*, p. 6.

6. Richard Poirier, *The Renewal of Literature* (London: Faber, 1987), p. 108.

7. See Louis Menand, *Discovering Modernism: T. S. Eliot and his Context* (New York: Oxford University Press, 1987), pp. 21–2. (Hereafter *Menand.*)

8. *UPUC* 151.

9. Peter Beagle, *I See By My Outfit* (New York: Ballantine, 1966), p. 125.

10. *Menand*, p. 19.

11. Ibid., p. 55.

12. Ibid., pp. 3, 4.

13. Ibid., p. 61.

14. Ibid., p. 51.

15. Ibid., pp. 22, 18, 27.

16. Ibid., p. 27.

17. T. S. Eliot, 'Reflections on Contemporary Poetry – IV', *The Egoist* 6 (July 1919), 39. Cf. *UPUC* 35: 'the development of genuine taste, founded on genuine feeling, is inextricable from the development of personality and character'.

18. *Menand*, pp. 70–1.

19. Cf. Eliot, 'The Perfect Critic':

> if we can recall the time when we were ignorant of the French symbolists, and met with *The Symbolist Movement in Literature*, we remember that book as an introduction to wholly new feelings, as a revelation. . . . The book has not, perhaps, a permanent value for the one reader, but it has led to results of permanent importance for him. (*SW* 5)

20. *Menand*, p. 143.

21. See, for example, Maud Ellmann, *The Poetics of Impersonality* (Brighton: Harvester, 1987).

22. Keats to Richard Woodhouse, 27 October 1818.

23. Cited in *UPUC* 101.

24. *Menand*, p. 141.

25. *Menand*, pp. 145, 143.

26. *Menand*, p. 143.

27. *The Diaries of Franz Kafka 1910–23*, ed. Max Brod (1948; Harmondsworth: Peregrine, 1964), pp. 212–13.

28. Jorge Luis Borges, *Labyrinths* (Harmondsworth: Penguin, 1970), pp. 234, 236.
29. See Donald Davie, 'T. S. Eliot: The End of an Era' (1956; in Bernard Bergonzi (ed.), *Four Quartets: A Casebook* (London: Macmillan, 1969), 153–67.
30. See *EL1* 45–7.
31. To Conrad Aiken, 30 September 1914, *EL1* 58.
32. 'Reflections on Contemporary Poetry – IV', p. 39.
33. To Robert Nichols, 8 August 1917, *EL1* 191.
34. *UPUC* 34.
35. *The Letters of W. B. Yeats*, ed. Allan Wade (London: Rupert Hart-Davis, 1954), p. 780.
36. 'Professional, Or . . .', *The Egoist* 5 (April 1918), 61.
37. Cf. *Ezra Pound: His Metric and Poetry*: 'Any poet, if he is to survive beyond his twenty-fifth year, must alter . . .' (*TCC* 177).
38. Eliot, 'Observations', *The Egoist* 5 (March 1918), 69.
39. Cf. Karl Shapiro in 1960 (from the other side of the fence): 'The proof of the failure of the "form" of this poem is that no one has ever been able to proceed from it, including Eliot himself. It is, in fact, not a form at all but a negative version of form' (*WLCB* 63).
40. Frank Kermode, 'A Babylonish Dialect' (1965), *WLCB* 234.
41. A. Walton Litz (ed.), *Eliot in His Time* (Princeton: Princeton University Press, 1973), p. 6.
42. Martin Rowson, *The Waste Land* (London: Penguin, 1990).
43. *Menand*, 91–2. See *The Diary of Virginia Woolf*, Vol. II: 1920–1924, ed. Anne Olivier Bell (London: Hogarth Press, 1978), pp. 202–3.
44. Richard Poirier, *The Renewal of Literature* (London: Faber, 1987), p.6.
45. In a letter to Bertrand Russell in October 1923, Eliot described 'What the Thunder Said' as 'not only the best part, but the only part that justifies the whole, at all'. See *The Autobiography of Bertrand Russell 1914-1944*, Vol. II (London: George Allen and Unwin, 1968), p. 174.
46. See *EL1* 313, 363.
47. See Ricks, *Eliot and Prejudice*, pp. 33–6.
48. T. S. E[liot], 'The Poetic Drama', *Athenaeum* 4698, 14 May 1920, 635–6.
49. Ricks, *Eliot and Prejudice*, p. 29.
50. See *EL1* 504–5.
51. Quoted by Woodward, in C. B. Cox and Arnold R. Hinchliffe (eds), *T. S. Eliot/ The Waste Land/ A Casebook* (London: Macmillan, 1968), p. 85.
52. *EL1* 596.
53. *EL1* 280. Cf. *Menand* (p. 154): 'even before the appearance of *The Sacred Wood* in December 1920, we find his name in a survey of the important contemporary critics [Douglas Goldring, 'Modern Critical Prose', *The Chapbook*, 2 (February 1920), pp. 11–12] – with the suggestion that he is already one of a small group of "star" critics who "control . . . England's literary output"'.
54. Vivien Eliot suggested the title in June 1922; but Eliot accepted it without demur. See *EL1* 534.
55. *Menand*, p. 153.

56. As they were in July 1923; see *The Diary of Virginia Woolf*, Vol. II, pp. 256–7.
57. John Middleton Murry, 'The Eternal Footman', *The Athenaeum*, 20 February 1920, 239.
58. Michael Heyward, *The Ern Malley Affair* (St Lucia: Queensland University Press, 1993), p. 156.
59. Ibid., pp. 235–6.
60. The poet Elisabeth Lambert though that the author of the drainage report 'might be a suppressed poet'; one wonders if the opening lines of 'Gerontion' had stuck in his mind. See Heyward, p. 96.
61. *OPP* 108.
62. Heyward, pp. 34–5.
63. Ibid., p. 40.
64. Ibid., p. 222.

5. The Quest for the One True Meaning

1. See Gerald Graff, *Professing Literature: An Institutional History* (Chicago: University of Chicago Press, 1987), (citation p. 152), Chs 8, 9 and 11.
2. Ibid., p. 128. See also his *Literature Against Itself* (Chicago: University of Chicago Press, 1979), pp. 129–49.
3. Ibid., p. 148.
4. Cited in Graff, *Professing Literature*, p. 161.
5. Graff, *Professing Literature*, p. 230.
6. Jane Worthington, 'The Epigraphs to the Poetry of T. S. Eliot', *American Literature* 21 (1949), 1–17; p. 9.
7. Northrop Frye, *T. S. Eliot* (Edinburgh: Oliver and Boyd, 1963), p. 6.
8. Richard Ohmann, *English in America: A Radical View of the Profession* (New York: Oxford University Press, 1976), p. 173.
9. Ibid., p. 335.
10. Ibid., p. 77.
11. F. R. Leavis, *For Continuity* (Cambridge: Minority Press, 1933), pp. 188–9, cited by Chris Baldick, *The Social Mission of English Criticism* (Oxford: Clarendon Press, 1983), p. 169.
12. George Sampson, *English for the English* (1921), p. 141; cited in Baldick, *Social Mission*, pp. 101–2.
13. *The Life of Thomas Cooper/Written by Himself* (London: Hodder and Stoughton, 1872; repr. Leicester University Press, 1971 with intro. by John Saville), pp. 63–4; cited in Baldick, p. 66.
14. Baldick, *Social Mission*, p. 65.
15. Ibid., pp. 65–6.
16. *The Life of Thomas Cooper*, p. 64.
17. John Saville, introduction to *Life of Thomas Cooper*, p. 22; Thomas Cooper, *The Purgatory of Suicides: A Prison-Rhyme*, 3rd edn (London: Chapman and Hall, 1853).
18. *The Life of Thomas Cooper*, pp. 256–7.
19. Dorothy Thompson, *The Early Chartists* (London: Macmillan, 1971), p. 13.

20. Baldick, *Social Mission*, pp. 189–90.
21. Cited in Baldick, *Social Mission*, p. 97.
22. Ibid., p. 94.
23. *THES*, 7 February 1992, p. 2: 'Critical Mass':

> The most popular literary critic on Engl.lit. courses in polytechnics and colleges, according to an on-going survey, is Roland Barthes who currently leads by a short head from F. R. Leavis. Hard on his heels come the Marxist professor of English at Oxford, Terry Eagleton, and the Russian formalists. But, warns the survey's author Dr Tim Cook of Kingston Poly, incoming entries could yet change the leaders' position.

24. Baldick, *Social Mission*, p. 192.
25. See John Carey, *The Intellectuals and the Masses* (London: Faber, 1992), p. 93.
26. Baldick, *Social Mission*, p. 79.
27. *UPUC*, p. 135.
28. Baldick, *Social Mission*, pp. 151–2.
29. I. A. Richards, *Principles of Literary Criticism* 2nd edn, (London: Routledge & Kegan Paul, 1926), p. 35.
30. These arguments are conveniently, if defensively reviewed by John Paul Russo in *I. A. Richards: His Life and Work* (London: Routledge, 1989), pp. 166–9.
31. Richards, *Principles of Literary Criticism*, p. 57.
32. H. G. Robinson, 'On the Use of English Classical Literature in the Work of Education', *Macmillan's Magazine*, II (1860), p. 427; cited in Baldick, p. 60. (Italics Robinson's.)
33. See, for example, D. J. Palmer, *The Rise of English Studies* (University of Hull Publications; London: Oxford University Press, 1965), p. 153.
34. John Crowe Ransom, *The New Criticism* (Norfolk, Conn.: New Directions, 1941), pp. 3, 44.
35. Ibid., p. 45.
36. See Baldick, *Social Mission*, pp. 149–55, on the links between Richards' theory of value and the method of *Practical Criticism*.
37. Graff, *Professing Literature*, p. 176.
38. Gerald Graff makes the point concisely:

> hindsight suggests that the conclusions he drew from his data were the very opposite from the ones he should have drawn. For what Richards' experiment unwittingly showed was that though students may have needed more 'direct' contact with literature, if one's way of providing that contact is to withhold information from them about a poem's period, authorship and circumstances of composition, they will not be able to grasp the poem successfully. (*Professing Literature*, p. 174)

39. E. M. W. Tillyard, *The Muse Unchained* (1958); cited in Baldick, *Social Mission*, p. 156.

40. Ransom, *The New Criticism*, p. 45.
41. William E. Cain, 'Towards a History of Anti-Criticism', *New Literary History*, 28 (Autumn 1988), 33–48; p. 43.
42. Cited by Frank Kermode in *Romantic Image* (London: Routledge & Kegan Paul, 1957), p. 159.
43. See Kermode's critique of P. D. Juhl, and Juhl's response: 'The Single Correct Interpretation', in *Essays on Fiction* (London: Routledge & Kegan Paul, 1983), pp. 201–20.
44. Northrop Frye, *Anatomy of Criticism* (1957; New York: Athenaeum, 1965), p. 18.
45. TCC 16.
46. Louis Menand, 'T. S. Eliot', in *Modernism and the New Criticism: The Cambridge History of Literary Criticism*, Vol. 7, ed A. Walton Litz, Louis Menand and Lawrence Rainey (Cambridge: Cambridge University Press, forthcoming).
47. SE 15.
48. *The Diary of Virginia Woolf, Vol II, 1920–1924*, ed. Anne Olivier Bell (London: Hogarth Press, 1978), p. 203.
49. T. S. Eliot, 'Contemporary English Prose', *Vanity Fair* (July 1923), p. 51.
50. Frye, *Anatomy*, pp. 7–8.
51. Ibid., p. 8.
52. Ibid., pp. 16–17.

6. 'Regret Impossible Stop Writing': The Labyrinth of Theory

1. Cited in Humphrey Carpenter, *A Serious Character: The Life of Ezra Pound* (London: Faber, 1988), p. 111.
2. Frank Kermode, *An Appetite for Poetry* (London: Collins, 1989), p. 6.
3. Christopher Norris, *Derrida* (London: Fontana, 1987), p. 177.
4. Steven Knapp and Walter Benn Michaels, 'Against Theory', *Critical Inquiry*, 8 (Summer 1982), 723–42; replies and responses, ibid., 9 (June 1983), 726–800; reprinted in W. J. T. Mitchell (ed.), *Against Theory: Literary Studies and the New Pragmatism* (Chicago: Chicago University Press, 1985).
5. Walter A. Davis, 'Offending the Profession (After Peter Handke)', *Critical Inquiry* 10 (June 1984), 706–18; p. 706; see also Walter A. Davis, 'The Fisher King: *Wille zur Macht* in Baltimore', ibid., 668–94; Stanley Fish, 'Fear of Fish: A Reply to Walter Davis', ibid., pp. 695–705.
6. Christopher Norris, 'Some Versions of Narrative', *London Review of Books*, 2 August 1984, 14–16; p. 14.
7. Stanley Fish, *Doing What Comes Naturally* (Durham and London: Duke University Press, 1989), p. 215. See, however, 'Consequences' (1985); ibid., pp. 315–41, in which Fish denies that anti-foundationalism 'cuts the ground out from other conviction' (p. 323); a characteristically Fishean retreat to the position that 'theory has no consequences' (p. 325).
8. J. Hillis Miller, 'The Function of Rhetorical Study at the Present Time', in James Engell and David Perkins (eds), *Teaching Literature*

(Cambridge, Mass., 1988); cited in Frank Kermode, *An Appetite for Poetry*, p. 225n.

9. Paul de Man, *Allegories of Reading* (New Haven, Conn.: Yale University Press, 1979), p. 19.

10. Richard Rorty, 'Philosophy Without Principles', *Critical Inquiry* 11 (March 1985), 459–65; p. 462.

11. Ibid., pp. 461–2.

12. Jacques Derrida, *Positions*, tr. Alan Bass (Chicago: University of Chicago Press, 1981), pp. 4–5. Cf. translator's preface to *Of Grammatology*, tr. Gayatri Chakravorty Spivak (Baltimore: Johns Hopkins University Press, 1974): 'If you have been reading Derrida, you will know that a plausible gesture would be to begin with a consideration of "the question of the preface"' (p. ix). Derrida's 'impossibilism' extends even to the 'question' of having his photograph taken:

The philosopher should start by meditating on photography, that's to say the writing of light, before setting out towards a reflection on an impossible self-portrait.

(Cited in editorial note, *London Review of Books*, 15 August 1991, p. 2.)

13. Franz Kafka, 'The Great Wall of China', in *Metamorphosis*, tr. Edwin and Willa Muir (Harmondsworth: Penguin, 1961), pp. 76–7.

14. Ibid., p. 79.

15. Cf. Derrida, *Memoires: For Paul de Man*, tr. Cecile Lindsay, *et al.* (New York: Columbia University Press, 1986): 'I have never known how to tell a story' (p. 3).

16. Jacques Derrida, 'Biodegradables: Seven Diary Fragments', *Critical Inquiry* 15 (Summer 1989), 812–73; p. 855.

17. Quoted by John Sutherland in 'Presidential Criticism', *London Review of Books*, 10 January 1991, 3–6; p. 5.

18. Franz Kafka, *The Trial*, tr. Edwin and Willa Muir (Harmondsworth: Penguin, 1953), pp. 238–9.

19. Barbara Johnson, 'Nothing Fails Like Success,' *SCE Reports* 8 (Fall 1980), p. 9; cited in John Ellis, *Against Deconstruction* (Princeton: Princeton University Press, 1989), p. 6.

20. *The Trial*, pp. 239–40.

21. Ibid., p. 241.

22. Robert Scholes, 'Deconstruction and Communication', *Critical Inquiry* 14 (Winter 1988), 278–95; p. 284.

23. W. Wolfgang Holdheim, 'Jacques Derrida's Apologia', *Critical Inquiry* 15 (Summer 1989), 784–96; p. 786.

24. Derrida, 'Biodegradables', pp. 859–60.

25. Cf. Scholes's comment on Derrida's 'obvious pain and outrage at being misread' by two of his critics ('Deconstruction and Communication', p. 282).

26. *The Trial*, p. 233.

27. Ibid., p. 243.

28. Frank Kermode, 'Paul de Man's Abyss', *London Review of Books*, 16 March 1989, 3–7; p. 7.

29. Sutherland, 'Presidential Criticism', p. 5.
30. Cf. de Man, *Allegories of Reading*:

> Any question about the rhetorical mode of a literary text is always
> a rhetorical question which does not even know whether it is
> really questioning. The resulting pathos is an anxiety (or bliss,
> depending on one's momentary mood or individual temperament)
> of ignorance ... (p. 19).

31. W. B. Yeats, 'Anima Hominis', *Mythologies* (London: Macmillan, 1959),
    p. 332.
32. Christopher Norris, *Derrida* (London: Fontana, 1987), p. 12.
33. Cf. Richard Stern:

> There are writers who cannot bear the thought of not writing
> about every subject on earth, every person they've met, every
> thought they've had. The four thousand sarcophogal pages of
> Sartre's unfinished book on Flaubert exhibit the almost heroic
> vanity/insanity of this inability to stop.

('Derridiary', *London Review of Books*, 15 August 1991, 20–1.
34. Norris, *Derrida*, pp. 15–16.
35. Ibid., p. 187.
36. Ellis, *Against Deconstruction*, p. 41.
37. In *On Deconstruction* (Ithaca: Cornell University Press, 1982), pp.
    149–50.
38. Richard Rorty, 'Deconstruction and Circumvention', *Critical Inquiry*
    11 (September 1984), 1–23; pp. 2–3.
39. Ibid., pp. 2–3.
40. Ibid., p. 16.
41. Ibid., p. 23.
42. Salinsky, *Criticism in Society*, pp. 238–9.
43. John Sutherland, 'Presidential Criticism', p. 3.
44. John Sturrock, 'Sabotage', *London Review of Books*, 31 March 1988,
    18–19.
45. Norris, *Derrida*, pp. 14–15.
46. Ibid., p. 27.
47. Ibid., p. 20.
48. Ibid., p. 20.
49. Ibid., p. 16.
50. Jacques Derrida, *Memoires: For Paul de Man*, p. 18.
51. Russell Hoban, *Riddley Walker* (1980; London: Picador, 1982), pp.
    123–4.
52. Louis Menand, 'The Politics of Deconstruction', *New York Review of
    Books*, 21 November 1991, 39–44; p. 40.
53. John Ellis, 'Radical Literary Theory', *London Review of Books*
    8 February 1990, 7–8; p. 8.
54. Terry Eagleton, *Criticism and Ideology: A Study in Marxist Literary
    Theory* (London: New Left Books, 1976), p. 43.
55. 'The phrase "George Eliot"', he later informs us,

signifies nothing more than the insertion of certain specific ideological determinations – Evangelical Christianity, rural organicism, incipient feminism, petty-bourgeois moralism – into a hegemonic ideological formation which is partly supported, partly embarrassed by their presence. (p. 113)

For an incisive analysis of Eagleton's Hegelian style ('full of empty and contentless verbs'), see Roger Poole, 'Generating believable entities: post-Marxism as a theological enterprise', *Comparative Criticism* 7 (1985), 49–71; pp. 54–9.

56. See, for example, Terry Eagleton, *The Significance of Theory* (Oxford: Basil Blackwell, 1990), pp. 79–80.
57. Louis Menand, 'What are Universities For?', *Harper's* (December 1991), 47–56; p. 56.

7. The Law and the Prophets

1. Jonathan Culler, *Framing the Sign* (Oxford: Basil Blackwell, 1988), p. 22.
2. Frederick Crews, 'The Grand Academy of Theory', *Skeptical Engagements* (NY: Oxford University Press, 1986), p. 172.
3. Culler, *Framing the Sign*, pp. 24–5.
4. Jonathan Culler, 'Humanities Centres and the Reconfiguration of Knowledge', conference paper, 1988, cited by Juliet MacCannell, letter to *London Review of Books*, 15 September 1988, p. 4.
5. Quoted in Fred Siegel, 'The Cult of Multiculturalism', *The New Republic*, 18 February 1991, 34–40; p. 40.
6. See Walter A. Davis. 'The Fisher King: *Wille zur Macht* in Baltimore', *Critical Inquiry* 10 (June 1984), pp. 668–94; Stanley Fish, 'Fear of Fish: A Reply to Walter Davis', ibid., pp. 695–705.
7. See Fish, 'Profession Despise Thyself: Fear and Self-Loathing in Literary Studies' 1983); reprinted in *Doing What Comes Naturally* (Durham and London: Duke University Press, 1989), 197–214; citation p. 209.
8. Ibid., p. 214.
9. Stanley Fish, 'The Young and the Restless', in H. Aram Veeser (ed.), *The New Historicism* (New York and London: Routledge, 1989), p. 315.
10. W. J. T. Mitchell, 'The Golden Age of Criticism: Seven Theses and a Commentary', *London Review of Books*, 25 June 1987, 16–18; p. 18.
11. J. Hillis Miller, 'Presidential Address 1986. The Triumph of Theory, the Resistance to Reading, and the Question of the Material Base', *PMLA* 102 (1987), 281–91; p. 287.
12. Kermode, *An Appetite for Poetry*, p. 21.
13. John Ellis, *Against Deconstruction* (Princeton: Princeton University Press, 1989), pp. 150–1.
14. See Gerald Graff: *Literature Against Itself* (Chicago: Chicago University Press, 1979); 'The Pseudo-Politics of Interpretation', *Critical Inquiry* 9 (March 1983), 597–610; 'Co-optation', in Veeser (ed.), *The New Historicism*, 168–81; also Robert Scholes, 'Deconstruction and

Communication', *Critical Inquiry* 14 (Winter 1988), 278–95; Peter Washington, *Fraud: Literary Theory and the End of English* (London: Fontana, 1989), pp. 41–50; John Ellis, 'Radical Literary Theory', *London Review of Books*, 8 February 1990, 7–8. Cf. Tzvetan Todorov ('N.B.' on Heidegger, *TLS*, 17–23 June 1988, pp. 676, 684);

> The apparently modest position of Hartman and other deconstructionists – 'One can never be sure of anything' – actually betrays an extraordinary contempt for all those who aspire to achieve a little more justice and a little more truth.

15. Robert Weimann, 'Text, Author-function and Society', in Peter Collier and Helga Geyer-Ryan (eds), *Literary Theory Today* (Ithaca: Cornell University Press, 1990), p. 103.
16. John Sutherland, 'Presidential Criticism', p. 3.
17. See, for example, W. T. J. Mitchell's attack on Graff in 'The Golden Age of Criticism: Seven Theses and a Commentary', *London Review of Books*, 25 June 1987, 16–18; p. 18; Graff's reply, 3 September 1987, p. 4; Mitchell's response, 17 September 1987, p. 5.
18. Culler, *Framing the Sign*, p. 38.
19. Mas'd Zavarzadeh, review of Culler, *The Pursuit of Signs* (1981), *Journal of Aesthetics and Art Criticism* 40 (1982), 329–33.
20. See Allan Bloom, *The Closing of the American Mind* (1987; Harmondsworth: Penguin, 1988); Charles Sykes, *ProfScam: Professors and the Demise of Higher Education* (New York; St. Martin's Press, 1989); Roger Kimball, *Tenured Radicals: How politics has corrupted our Higher Education* (New York; HarperCollins, 1991). For an ascerbic commentary on this phenomenon, see John Sutherland, 'Down with DWEMS', *London Review of Books*, 15 August 1991, pp. 17–18; also Robert Hughes, *Culture of Complaint* (New York: Oxford University Press, 1993), passim.
21. Roger Kimball, 'Multiculturalism and the American University', *Quadrant* (July–August 1991), 22–31; p. 29.
22. John Sturrock, 'Sabotage', *London Review of Books* (31 March 1988), 18–19, p. 18.
23. Jacques Derrida, 'Biodegradables: Seven Diary Fragments', *Critical Inquiry* 15 (Summer 1989), 812–73, p. 860.
24. Paul de Man, *Blindness and Insight: Essays in the Rhetoric of Contemporary Criticism*, 2nd edn (London: Methuen, 1983), p. 282.
25. Ellis, *Against Deconstruction*, pp. vii–viii.
26. Peter Collier and Helga Geyer-Ryan (eds), introduction to *Literary Theory Today* (Ithaca: Cornell University Press, 1990), p. 1.
27. Thomas Sheehan, 'A Normal Nazi', *New York Review of Books*, 14 January 1993, 30–35; p. 30.
28. For a full account of the episode, see David Lehman, *Signs of the Times: Deconstruction and the Fall of Paul de Man* (London: André Deutsch, 1991). Lehman's coverage of the ensuing dispute is thorough, but he aggrandises deconstruction by presenting it as dangerous and threatening. Louis Menand's 'The Politics of Deconstruction'

(*New York Review of Books*, 21 November 1991, 39–44) is the best critique of Lehman to date.

29. Collier and Geyer-Ryan, *Literary Theory Today*, introduction, pp. 2–3.
30. Barbara Johnson, 'The Surprise of Otherness: A Note on the Wartime Writings of Paul de Man', in *Literary Theory Today*, p. 13.
31. Howard Felperin, *Beyond Deconstruction* (Oxford: Clarendon Press, 1985), p. 43 (emphasis Felperin's).
32. See, for example, the introduction to Luc Herman, Kris Humbeeck and Geert Lernout (eds), *(Dis)continuities: Essays on Paul de Man* (Amsterdam: Rodopi, 1989), p. 11.
33. Jonathan Culler, '"Paul de Man's War" and the Aesthetic Ideology', *Critical Inquiry* 15 (Summer 1989), 777–83; p. 783; see also Culler, 'De Man's Rhetoric', *Framing the Sign*, 107–35; Christopher Norris, 'Paul de Man's Past', *London Review of Books*, 4 February 1988, 7–11; Barbara Johnson, 'The Surprise of Otherness', J. Hillis Miller, 'NB', *TLS*, 17–23 June 1988, pp. 676, 685; Jacques Derrida, 'Like the Sound of the Sea Deep within a Shell: Paul de Man's War', tr. Peggy Kamuf, *Critical Inquiry* 14 (Spring 1988), 590–652.
34. Paul de Man, *The Resistance to Theory* (Manchester: Manchester University Press, 1986), p. 11.
35. Miller, 'NB', pp. 676, 685.
36. Miller, in Lindsay Waters and Wlad Godzich (eds), *Reading de Man Reading* (Minnesota: University of Minnesota Press, 1989), cited in Frank Kermode, 'Paul de Man's Abyss', *London Review of Books*, 16 March 1989, 3–7; p. 7.
37. Paul de Man in *Het Vlaamche Land*, 7–8 June 1942; cited by Stanley Corngold, 'Paul de Man', *TLS*, 26 August – 1 September 1988, p. 931.
38. Paul de Man, 'Les Juifs dans la littérature actuelle', *Le Soir*, 4 March 1941, quoted in Jacques Derrida, 'Like the Sound of the Sea Deep within a Shell: Paul de Man's War', p. 623.
39. Miller, 'NB', p. 685.
40. See Stanley Corngold, 'Paul de Man on the Contingency of Intention', in Luc Herman, Kris Humbeeck and Geert Lernout (eds), *(Dis)continuities: Essays on Paul de Man* (Amsterdam: Rodopi, 1989), 27–42; pp. 31–2.
41. Kermode, 'Paul de Man's Abyss', p. 3.
42. See Kermode, 'Paul de Man's Abyss', for an incisive overview of this argument.
43. Corngold, 'Paul de Man on the Contingency of Intention', loc. cit.
44. Paul de Man, *The Resistance to Theory*, p. 11.
45. John Sutherland, 'Presidential Criticism', p. 5; see Miller, 'Presidential Address 1986. The Triumph of Theory, the Resistance to Reading, and the Question of the Material Base', *PMLA* 102 (1987), 281–291.
46. Derrida, 'Paul de Man's War', pp. 624–5.
47. Ibid., p. 269.
48. Ibid., p. 651. Derrida quotes Charles Dosogne:

    Is there not room to ask certain questions concerning a document that does not figure among 'Le Soir's' own collection, and, on the

copy to be found at the Bibliotheque Albertine, is marked by three
asterisks. Why?? (p. 651n)

The special anti-Semitic number of *Le Soir* (under Nazi control and
known to locals as *Le Soir Volé*) in which de Man's 'Les Juifs dans
la littérature actuelle' appeared was hardly the paper's finest hour;
the postwar management would have been justifiably concerned to
destroy, rather than preserve it. Nor is the content of de Man's
article in any way consistent with the hypothesis of forgery – though
its stress on 'the organic relation between language, culture, and
national destiny', in Christopher Norris's phrase, is consistent with
the rest of his output for the paper.

49. Ibid., p. 651.
50. See the essays by Jean-Marie Apostolides, Marjorie Perloff, Jonathan
    Culler, W. Wolfgang Holdheim, John Weiner, John Brenkman and
    Jules David Law in *Critical Inquiry* 15 (Summer 1989), 755–811; Derrida
    'Biodegradables', pp. 812–73.
51. Derrida, 'Biodegradables', p. 820. Derrida's 'calendar' identifies
    Edmund Husserl's 'Origin of Geometry': An Introduction (first pub.
    1962) as the beginning of deconstruction. Yet in 'Paul de Man's War'
    he attacks Jon Wiener's 'dogmatic summary' which

    > attributes to me, for example, the foundation of deconstruction
    > even as he also describes me as attributing its paternity to the
    > 'progenitor' Heidegger ... (p. 647n).

52. Derrida, 'Paul de Man's War', p. 647.
53. Ibid., pp. 646–7.
54. Claude Rawson, 'Old Literature and its Enemies', *London Review of
    Books*, 25 April 1991, 11–15; p. 14.
55. See Thomas Sheehan, 'A Normal Nazi', *New York Review of Books*,
    14 January 1993, 30–5, and the ensuing correspondence between
    Derrida, Sheehan and others through to 22 April 1993.
56. Humphrey Carpenter, *A Serious Character*, p. 506.
57. See, for example, William French, 'On E. Fuller Torrey, The Baiting
    of Dead Giants', *Paideuma* (1984), 131–7.
58. Tzvetan Todorov, 'N.B.' (on Heidegger), *TLS*, 17–23 June 1988, pp.
    676, 684.
59. Ellis, *Against Deconstruction*, p. 84.
60. Claude Rawson, 'Old Literature and its Enemies', p. 13.
61. Frank Kermode, *Essays on Fiction 1971–82* (London: Routledge &
    Kegan Paul, 1983), p. 7.
62. Richard Ohmann, *Literature in America* (New York: Oxford Univer-
    sity Press, 1976), p. 5. From 1959 to 1966, attendance at the MLA's
    annual convention increased from around 5000 to 12 300. See John
    Sutherland, 'The Annual MLA Disaster', *London Review of Books* (16
    December 1993), 11–12.
63. Graff, *Professing Literature*, p. 206.
64. Paul de Man, 'Semiology and Rhetoric', in Josué Harari (ed.), *Textual*

Strategies: Perspectives in Post-Structuralist Criticism (Ithaca: Cornell University Press, 1979), p. 138; cited in Graff, *Professing Literature*, 241.

65. Having plucked 'seventeen' out of the air, I find that Jeremy Hawthorn, in his *Concise Glossary of Contemporary Literary Theory* (London: Edward Arnold, 1992), identifies seventeen current schools and approaches. See pp. x–xiii.

66. Edward Said, 'Opponents, Audiences, Constituencies and Community' (1982) repr. in Neil Foster (ed.), *Postmodern Culture* (New York: Pluto Press, 1985), pp. 135–59; p. 142.

67. Thomas Docherty, *After Theory: Postmodernism/postmarxism* (London: Routledge, 1990), p. 1.

68. Ibid., p. 219.

69. A. D. Nuttall, 'Return of the Real', *London Review of Books*, 23 April 1992, 5–6.

70. Robert Hughes, *Culture of Complaint* (New York: Oxford University Press, 1993), p. 72.

71. See Frank Kermode, *An Appetite for Poetry* (pp. 40–2) on Vincent B. Leitch's attempt at a systematic survey along these lines:

> Another independent critical performer . . . namely Richard Poirier, is, by a taxonomy as weird as Borges' famous Chinese dog system, affiliated to 'The New York Intellectuals' because he has lived in New York and was once an editor of *Partisan Review*, standards by which I too am a New York intellectual. Poirier is simply bundled into the handiest category; no reader will take away the slightest notion of the character of his work, of the penetration of his reading, or of his importance in the present crisis of the subject.

72. Randall Jarrell, 'The Age of Criticism', in *Poetry and The Age* (London: Faber, 1955), p. 86 (emphasis Jarrell's).

Index